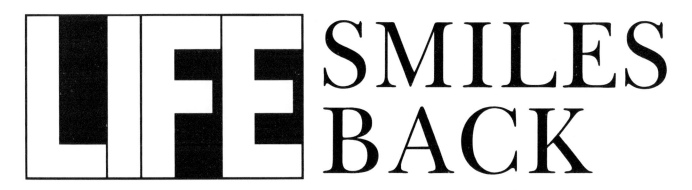

LIFE SMILES BACK

by
Philip B. Kunhardt, Jr.

A FIRESIDE BOOK
Published by Simon & Schuster Inc.
New York London Toronto Sydney Tokyo Singapore

Fireside

Rockefeller Center
1230 Avenue of the Americas
New York, New York 10020

First Fireside Edition, 1988

LIFE is a registered trademark of Time Inc. Used with permission.
FIRESIDE and colophon are registered trademarks
of Simon & Schuster Inc.

Designed by Irving Perkins Associates
Manufactured in the United States of America

10 9 8 7 6 5 4 3
20 19 18 17   Pbk.

Library of Congress Cataloging in Publication Data
LIFE smiles back.

1. Photography, Humorous.   I. Kunhardt, Philip B.
II. Life (Chicago, Ill.)
TR679.5.L54   1987   779'.09'04   87-12876

ISBN 0-671-64399-1
ISBN 0-671-67222-3 Pbk.

Gedeon 'de Margitay was picture coordinator for
this book. Gretchen Wessels was in charge of
picture research.

CONTENTS

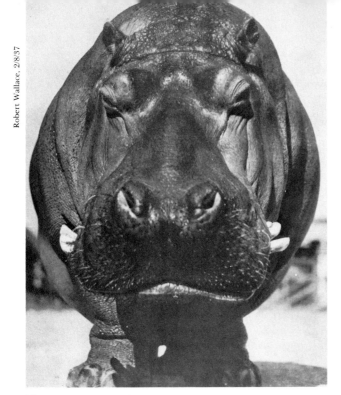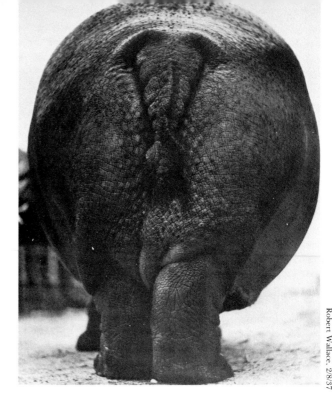

These two views of a hippo named Lotus ran on back-to-back pages in 1937 and began LIFE's love affair with animal humor.

INTRODUCTION

FOR many years LIFE magazine signed off each week's issue with a final page designed to leave the reader smiling, or at least feeling pretty good about the world. The title of the page was Miscellany. By definition, a miscellany is "a mixture of various things." In this case the "things" were children galore, often up to no good, or animals by the score—especially dogs, cats, monkeys, and elephants—or people in awkward or unusual or amazing positions, or sights that belied the truth, frequently pictorial puzzles that made you blink, look twice, and shake your smiling head. Most of the time it was a page of sheer delight, a single black-and-white picture with an immediate message that warmed the heart or tickled the funny bone—or both.

In a note from the editor in 1966 the magazine tried to define the page for its readers. "We consider humor the prime ingredient," the editor said. "The picture is usually a very simple one—an animal caught in a human predicament, a human trapped by the unexpected, a trick of the lens whereby a perfectly ordinary event recorded on film at just the right angle becomes ridiculous and thereby laughs out loud at all of us."

I was hired by LIFE in 1950. The staff of the fourteen-year-old magazine was rapidly expanding back then and the people at the helm usually wanted to have a few rookie reporters waiting in the wings so that if a job in one of the many departments suddenly opened up, there would be a body available to fill it at a moment's notice. Most often twenty-two-year-olds like me would do their waiting in the Production Department, run errands, go get prints across the street where the lab was, learn the names of the hundreds of people who worked in the New York office, keep the layouts in order, and drag "the packet" down to Penn Station each evening and make sure it got on the overnight express to Chicago where the magazine was printed. "The packet" was a huge, red canvas satchel with hooks and leather straps and a padlock, which contained all the pictures and layouts that had been selected for next week's issue. I wanted desperately to get into the thick of things and drag the packet, but no such luck. Instead I was assigned to the contributions editor.

Ruth Lester was (and still is) a charming, soft-spoken person who sat unperturbed in a loud bullpen filled with people doing things with pictures—logging them in, stamping their backs, checking their credits, paying their owners. Ruth made the decisions on the pictures submitted to the magazine by unknown outsiders. If one of these picture takers, either amateur or professional, was any good, he or she wasn't unknown to Ruth for very long. Ruth would send helpful critiques, urge the picture taker on, and build up a long-distance friendship.

Of course, the majority of the contributors were hopeless. So many camera owners assumed that all you had to do to get a picture published in LIFE was to make your baby grin or put a funny hat on your pet. On each of the envelopes submitted by these contributors Ruth wrote "Reject" with a brief comment telling why. My job was to write her rejection letters.

It wasn't a matter of merely smacking the rejected picture into a new envelope and sticking in a form letter. In those days form letters were

considered cold and hostile and there were plenty of people like me around to write personalized replies. So I would study each picture carefully and then type out a note that showed that the submission had been appreciated and given serious thought and, in fact, had almost made the grade. The note could not be overly nice or the same picture would come right back in the next mail with a new letter pleading the picture's case all over again and demanding a new trial.

Even though LIFE was, and still is, best known for its picture stories in which a number of intertwining photographs illustrate the people, the places, and the events of the times, single pictures that stand on their own have always been important too, especially funny ones. The grim ones—the news pictures of disasters, accidents, wars—always seemed easy to find. They arrived in droves over the wire-service machine or they were carried to the magazine daily by the New York representatives of the world's photo agencies. Because of the literal nature of photography, the funny ones were much harder to find. Whenever Ruth turned one up, it was usually published in a Pictures to the Editors section. Sometimes it made Speaking of Pictures. Or if it was really special, it could even get picked as Picture of the Week, which ran each issue in the place of honor opposite the editorial page.

LIFE published funny pictures right from its start in 1936. A courtroom photo in its third issue marked the beginning. It showed a man without pants standing before a judge. The judge can't see that the man is pantless, but we can. We laugh at the man's predicament, we laugh at what the judge doesn't seem to know, and we laugh with relief that it isn't one of us standing cross-legged and pantless before the bar.

In a February 1937 issue LIFE had its first real fun with animals. Filling a full right-hand page was a head-on view of a massive hippopotamus named Lotus. On the backing page in exactly the same position was Lotus's rear end. "Lotus fore . . . and Lotus aft" read the wicked headline. Two

Bettmann/UPI, 12/7/36

This was LIFE's very first humorous picture. It ran in the magazine's third issue, back in December of 1936.

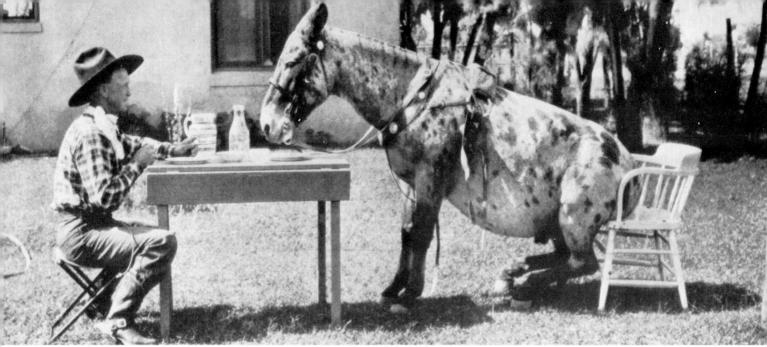

Slapstick snapshots of people and animals together helped give the magazine its early reputation for being something less than serious.

months later, with the publication of a snapshot of a mule sitting down to lunch with a cowboy, LIFE had joined man and beast in one silly picture and had sown the seed for hundreds more to come.

If one picture can be singled out as the inspiration behind the Miscellany page, it is a shot of a dog climbing a fence. Edward K. Thompson (Ed to us), who would soon become LIFE's managing editor (and its greatest one), was traveling through Minnesota when he spotted the picture in the Sunday rotogravure section of the *Minneapolis Tribune*. An Elaine Wilsey had read that the paper would pay $5 for whatever "highly unusual picture of any upper Midwest subject" it deemed worth publishing. Elaine Wilsey's offering of a pointer scaling a wire fence in a most human manner struck Ed and many others as being a remarkable and mirthful sight. He ordered the picture up and ran it in LIFE as a Picture of the Week along with these words:

"Some people might not find it unusual—the dog looks rather bored; he is merely climbing the fence, not jumping it. Furthermore he is not carrying a suitcase and has forgotten his hat. . . ." Mrs. Wilsey received $200 for the use of her picture and when Miscellany got going awhile later, it was said around the magazine that the page rate for it was the best money LIFE spent each week.

The creation of the Miscellany page by Thompson gave the magazine a lighthearted, always expected, yet completely unpredictable way to end each week. The Speaking of Pictures section, also breezy in character, had always started off each issue. Now there were two bright bookends to surround the week's news and give the reader a sense of continuity and familiarity. Speaking of Pictures and Life Goes to a Party had long been the readers' favorite sections but now Miscellany surpassed them. It was not long before a hoard of humor addicts, particularly teenagers, began starting each issue from the back.

Surprisingly, there were skeptics on the LIFE staff who believed that photographs could not be funny, and that if occasionally they were it was by mistake, and that there certainly weren't fifty-two mistakes around each year. These faithless souls had not reckoned on Ruth Lester and how,

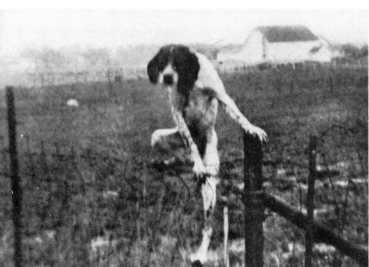

The picture that inspired the editors to invent the Miscellany page.

over the years, she had been cultivating so many of the very best amateur shooters. Having been in the Contributions Department since the very first issue of LIFE, my first boss came to receive ten thousand submitted pictures each year, twenty-five hundred of which were specifically earmarked for Miscellany. George Hunt, managing editor of the magazine throughout the sixties, had this to say about Ruth: "She has built up a long list of Lester fans who send her notes and Christmas cards and drop in to see her when they're in town. One, a Mr. Jack B. Guss, then of Denver, who had sent in forty-three different candidates and got them all back, cheerfully sent Ruth his forty-fourth try—a picture of her forty-three letters of rejection." Over the seventeen years of Miscellany's existence Ruth's department provided at least ninety percent of the pictures.

The very first was Jimmy, a white horse with coloration on his front in the shape of a baseball chest protector. His markings weren't the point; Jimmy was roller skating in the picture (he periodically worked out at a rink with real people). The trouble was, you could hardly see the skates. The headline—"Merrily he rolls along"—helped a bit, as so many headlines were to do. Thank goodness LIFE had an army of ingenious caption and headline writers. They were always at the managing editor's beck and call but never more ready and waiting than on closing day.

And it wasn't until the closing day of each week's issue that the managing editor would finally call for the current stack of Miscellany candidates. He would sort through all the layouts, chucking them about until a picture caught his fancy, and then the copy editor would assign a writer to it. If you were a writer, you'd try not to be around your phone in the afternoon of closing day. Somebody would find you, though, and even with two or three other stories to juggle, you'd meekly accept another. Of course there'd be no information to write from. Frantic calls were put through to whoever had done the submitting but that person always was out. So you'd struggle away, creating humorous things about what was going on in the picture, trying desperately to fill twenty lines of sixty-eight letters apiece. Your copy finally arrived on the copy editor's desk and by and by you were summoned. You'd usually get a baleful look, a dissatisfied smacking of lips, and a couple of grunts, and your copy would be handed back to you. "Be funnier," you were told.

The genesis of *LIFE Smiles Back* was in work I had been doing on another book, a fiftieth anniversary pictorial history of LIFE. For two years I slowly rummaged through a thousand back issues. I could not read all the millions of words that had gone into LIFE, but I did look at every single picture it had ever published and I copied more than five thousand of them, keeping files of my favorite photographs and stories for each of the fifty years. Finally, as I waded through these files to make my selections for the anniversary book, time and time again I was struck by how many Miscellanies I had copied and how very good they were.

Pulling them all out of their files one night on a whim, I threw them down on the carpet, entirely encircling myself with comical images. Sud-

Joe Scherschel, LIFE, 5/19/52

A picture of a horse on roller skates marked the inauspicious beginning of the Miscellany page in 1952. For the next 17 years, each regular issue of LIFE ended with this single-page feature, until it was decided to expand the section and rename it Parting Shots. Some pictures from Parting Shots are included in this book.

9

Amusing pictures of cute kids sometimes found their way onto the cover. Fifteen years later this 1937 cover boy concentrating on his game of marbles would have been a more likely candidate for the newly invented Miscellany page.

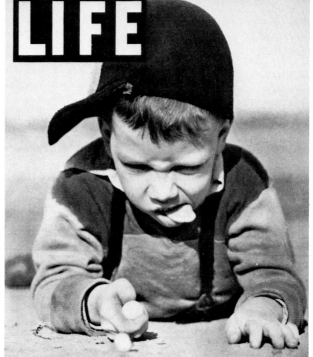

LIFE, 5/10/37

denly I was transported to a different world, a world of pranks and preposterous sights where silly kittens were being spooned out of spaghetti pots and kids were painting the wash, where bodies assumed impossible positions, heads rolled, limbs disappeared, where postmen mailed themselves and signs told roosters where to walk, where skunks sniffed daffodils and frogs wouldn't fit into pockets, a world where seals and dogs winked knowingly and apes baked themselves with sunlamps. It was the apes that did it. Right there and then I knew this book had to be made.

How to do it, though? How to make some kind of sense out of so much nonsense? I threw the whole mess into a warm drawer for six months to

let it gestate, and when I took all those pictures out again, somehow they had sorted themselves out. Categories seemed to have invented themselves, chapters slid into place. Certain pictures cried to be opposite certain others, and who was I to stop them? Two independent but facing pictures often sent off sparks. A few pictures wanted to spread themselves over two pages and be opposite nothing. Others wanted to be in a crowd.

Every picture, no matter how quiet, had something to say about its headline and caption. A few of the bolder ones were not only suggesting—they were insisting. If there was a trick involved or a special explanation needed, most of the pictures voted to keep mum, to let the reader wonder. They wanted, they said, to keep the reader guessing as well as laughing.

In the writing, many of the pictures opted for puns or at least expressions with double meanings. Others felt they'd rather be described in a straightforward manner, with names and places clearly identified. All agreed that the book be written in the present tense, even though some of the children shown are parents now, with chil-

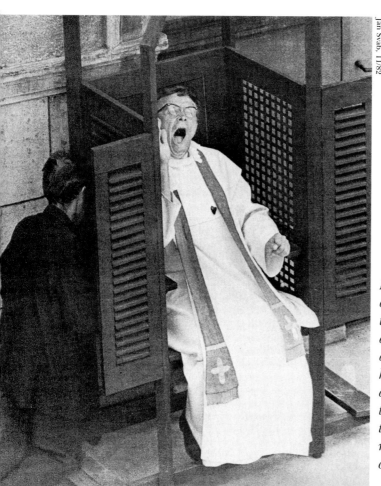

Jan Svab, 11/82

LIFE has been a monthly for almost a decade now and its final page is entitled Just One More. The pictures that appear there are usually in color and are often chosen for reasons other than humor. Occasionally an old-time black-and-white belly laugh like this one has turned up. There will be a lot more in the future, says the new editor, who is returning to the original miscellany concept.

Not all the Miscellany pictures LIFE ran were necessarily funny. A few were odd-looking news pictures in disguise, like this batch of 3-D movie watchers, a picture that became one of the magazine's most famous.

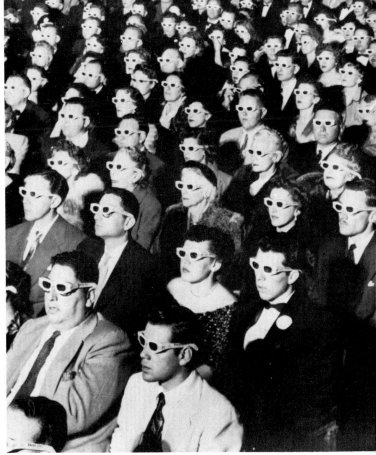

J. R. Eyerman, LIFE, 12/15/52

Bill Young, *San Francisco Chronicle*, 11/17/47

dren of their own, maybe even grandchildren. After all, they philosophized, the scenes and action they portray remain alive as long as we keep looking at them.

And finally, all the pictures agreed—it was unanimous—that the source of each picture be identified right next to it.

After all, they reasoned, the photographers had something to do with it, too.

Picture of the Week was always positioned opposite the editorial page and was meant to be a news picture, usually of a serious nature. But by the late forties more and more pictures like this "mouth tackle" were sneaking into this prized position. "Halfback Joe Mocha of San Francisco U. puts the bite on a Santa Clara tackler" read the caption for this hand-to-mouth sports picture which ran side by side with a deadly serious editorial on the Marshall Plan and the Soviet menace. A few photographs that originally ran as Pictures of the Week are included in this book.

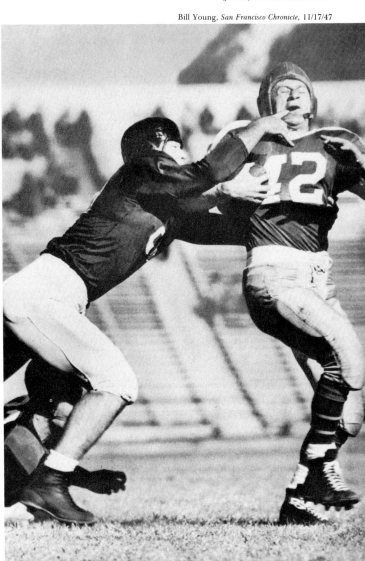

CHAPTER 1

John J. Horey, 8/8/60

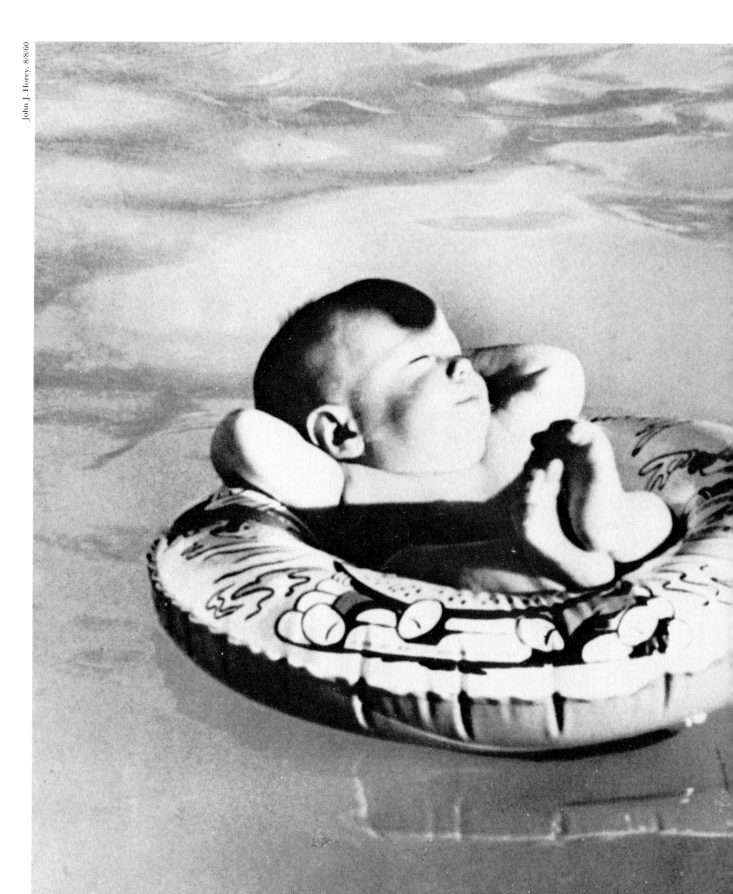

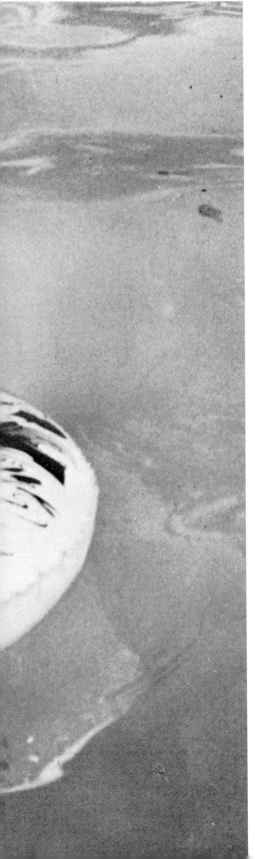

is all about
TAKING IT EASY

Cool Babe

In Big Spring, Texas, eight-month-old Liam Sean Horey spends his first summer in buoyant bliss.

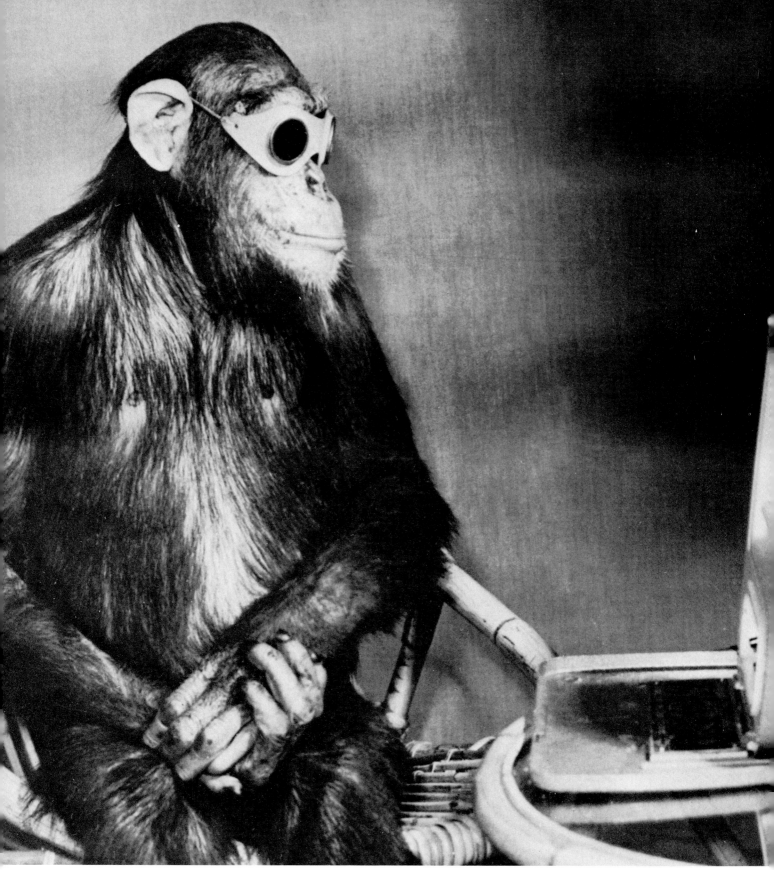

Hi Tech

To ward off chills and sneezes in the Usti Zoo, Czechoslovakian chimps get a daily bake from a sunlamp.

14

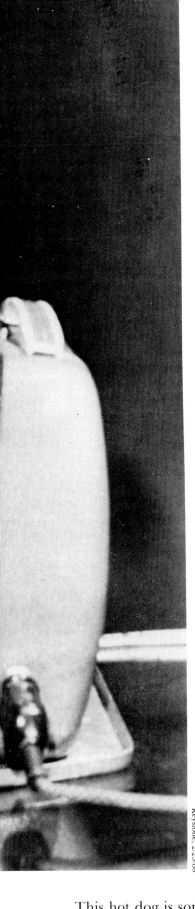

Jack Tinney, 8/25/60

Keystone, 2/23/68

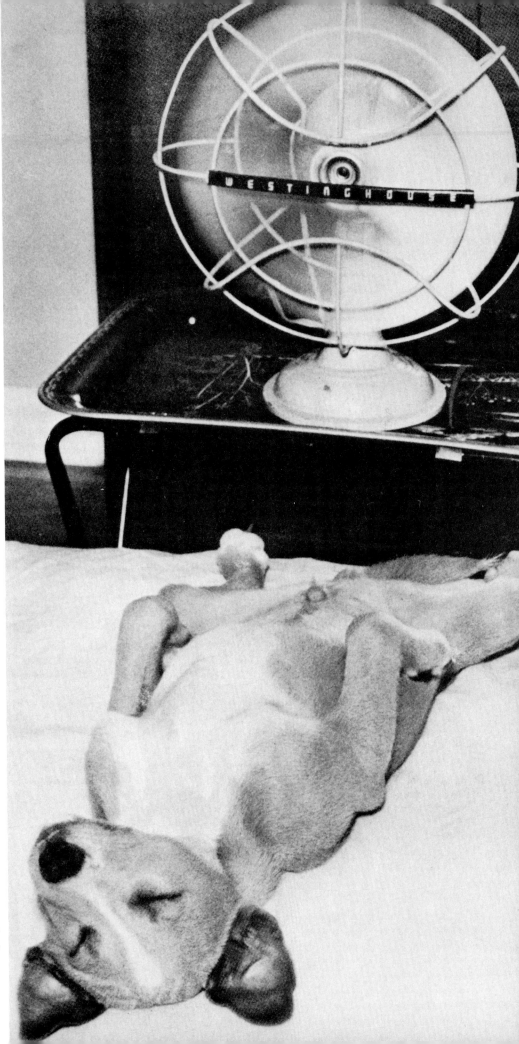

This hot dog is some cool
cat as he beats the heat in
Philadelphia.

Pack Animals Packed

In Algeria, a donkey gets a piggyback.

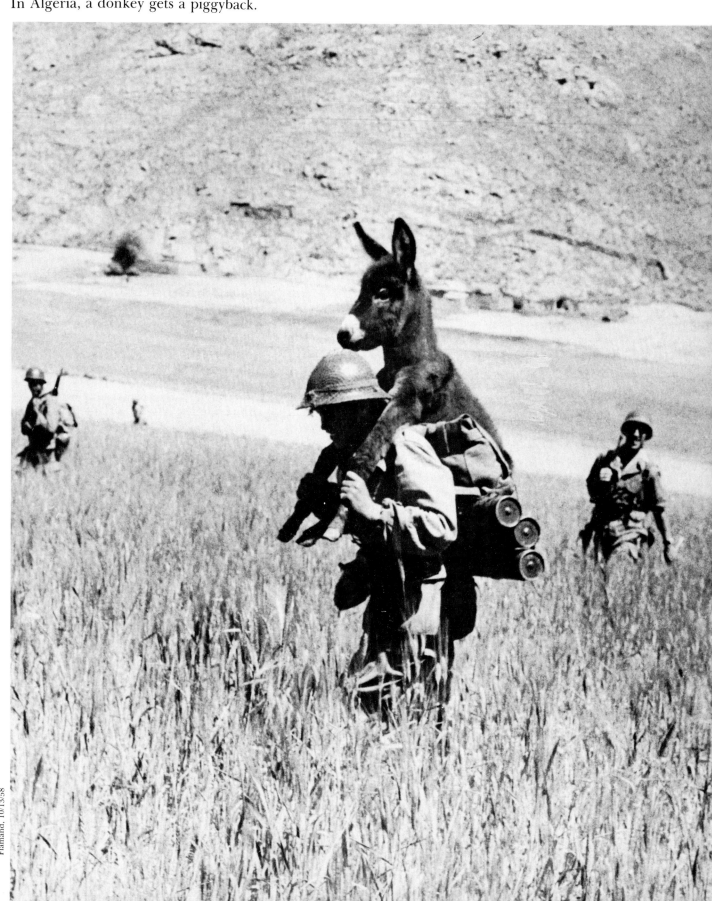

In England, a dwarf donkey travels in a satchel.

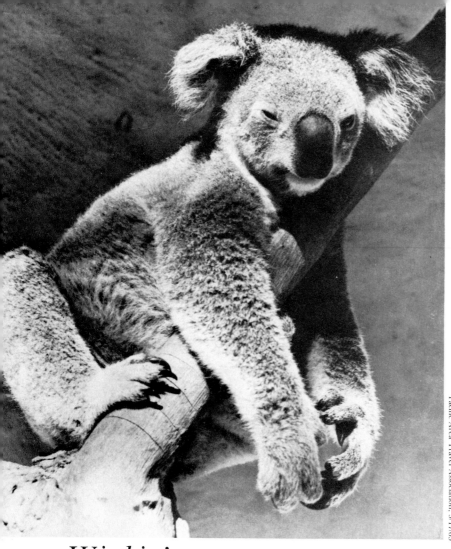

Pacific Area Travel Association, 5/17/63

Winkin',

In Australia, a koala bear demonstrates what sloth is all about.

Blinkin',

Meanwhile, in French Guiana, a sloth displays the real thing.

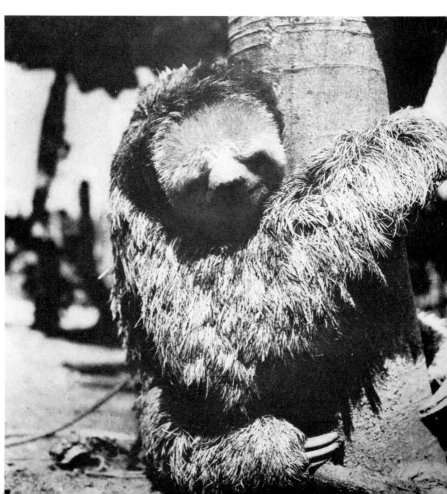

10/27/57

Camera Press, 9/14/59

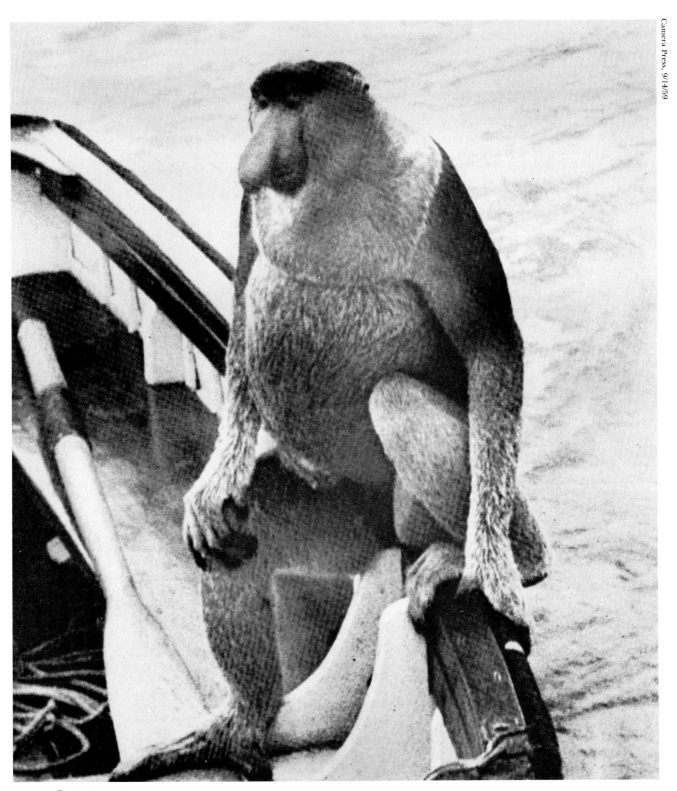

and Nod

A proboscis monkey takes his ease after a swim
in the South China Sea.

Getting Away from It All

An ingenious postman in Idaho takes refuge
from the rain in a mail storage box.

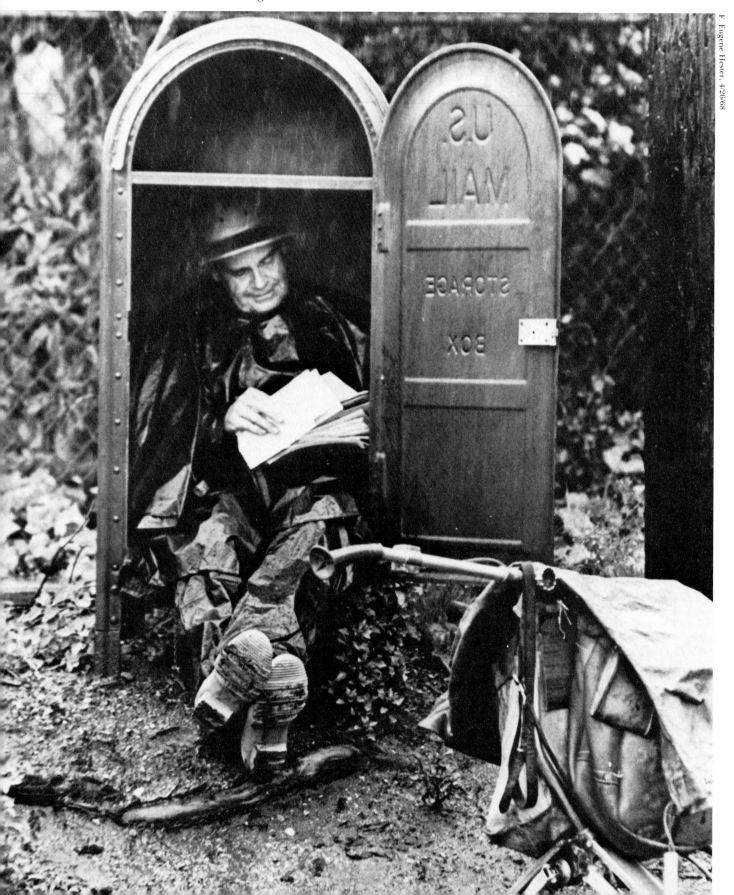

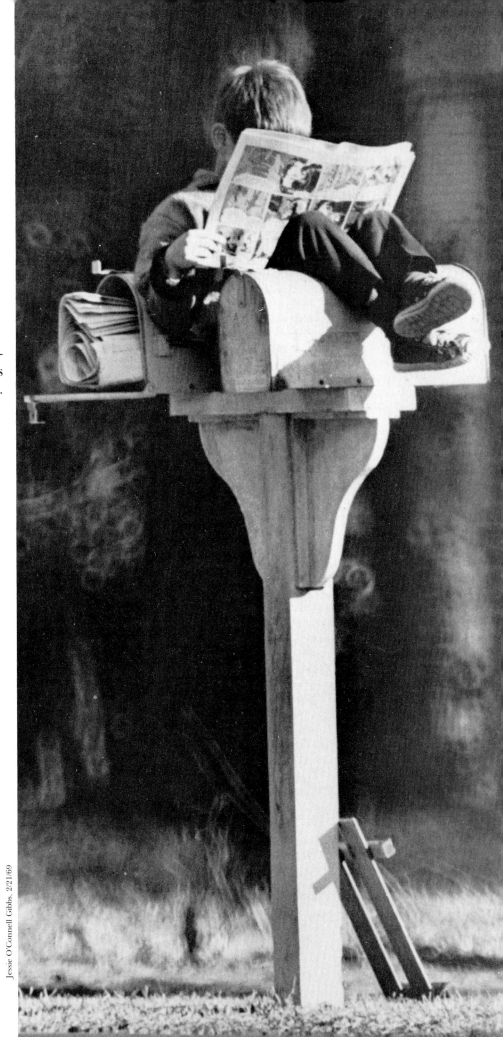

Gordon Breland of Charleston, South Carolina, perches atop his favorite getaway.

Playing It Cool

Wide World Photos, 4/12/68

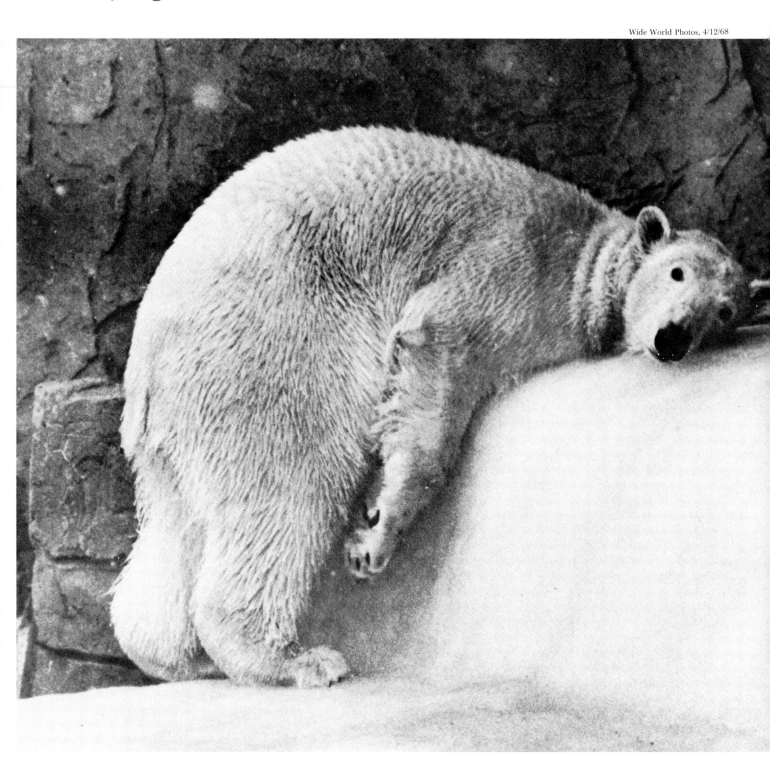

In Chicago, a polar bear drapes himself over a frozen snowbank.

Willis B. Foote, 3/24/67

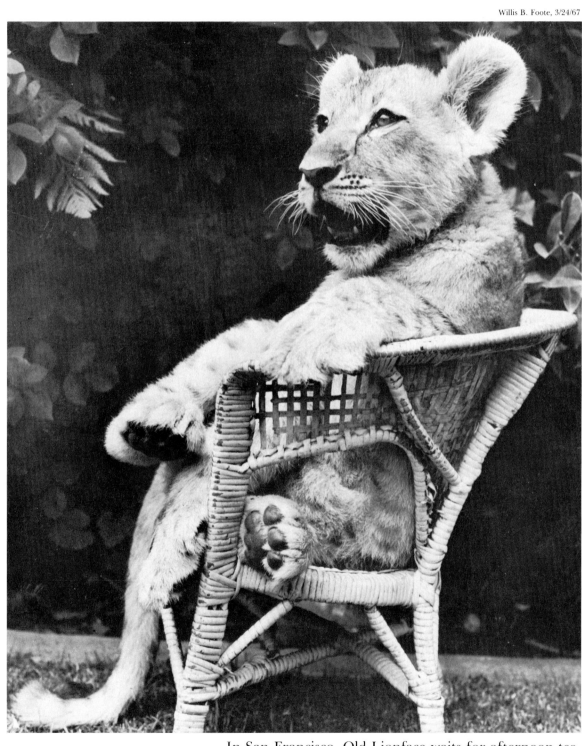

In San Francisco, Old Lionface waits for afternoon tea.

Bathing Beauties

Carolyn Parrish, 3/23/56

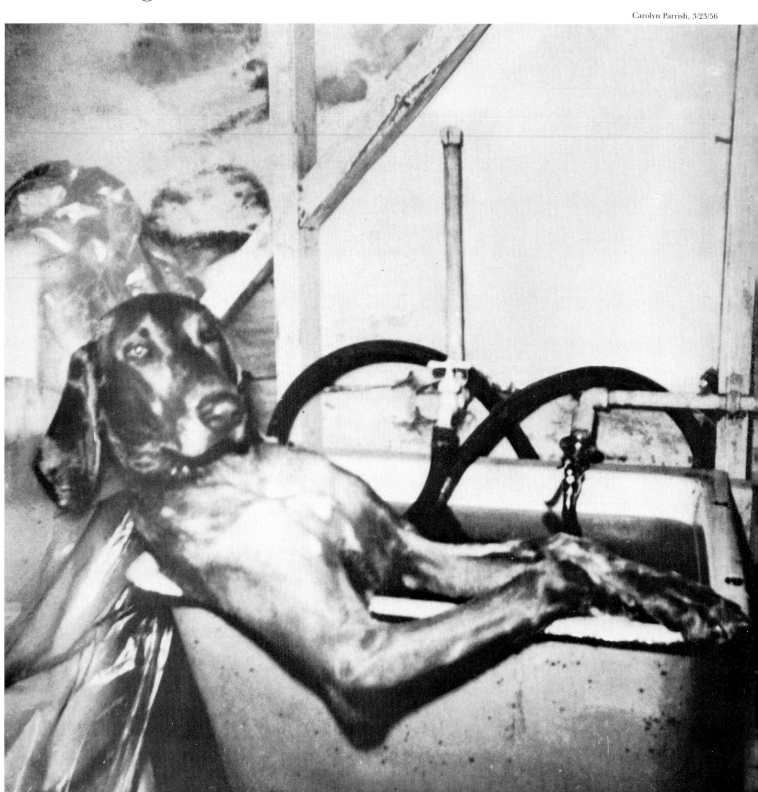

Frieda's bath has been drawn, a warm towel awaits her, and now she can lean back and relax in her kitchen sink turned hot tub.

P. E. Boisvert, 9/5/69

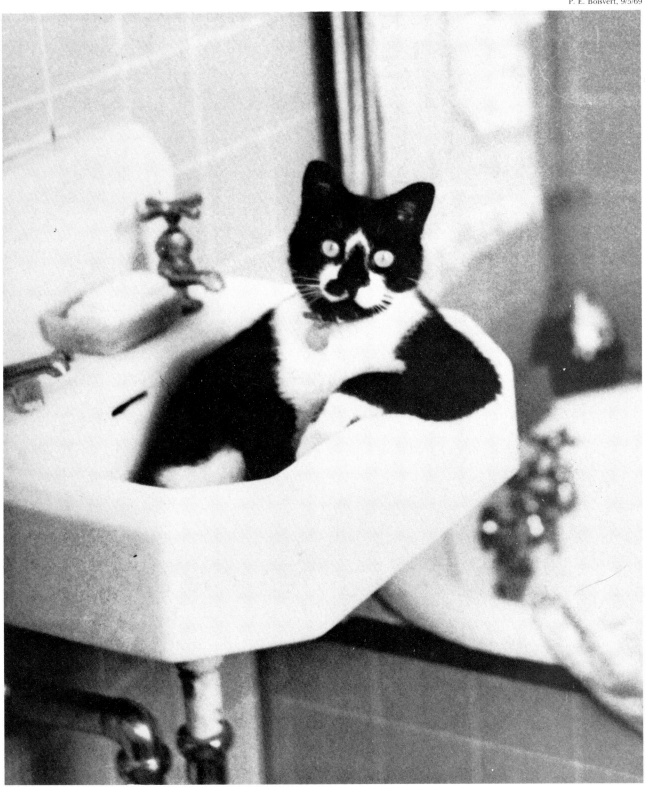

What smoother, cooler pool for a puss to curl up in?

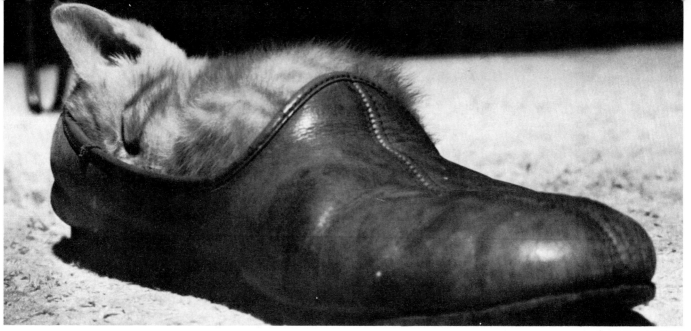

Kitten comfort in a Massachusetts slipper.

Fred I. Rose, Jr., 10/1/65

Robert Williams, *Memphis Commercial Appeal*, 10/3/60

Sweet Dreams

Guess who won the shoving match in Mississippi.

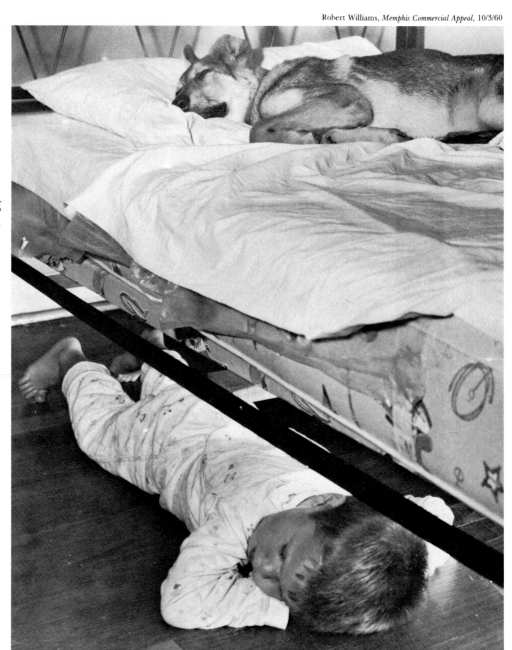

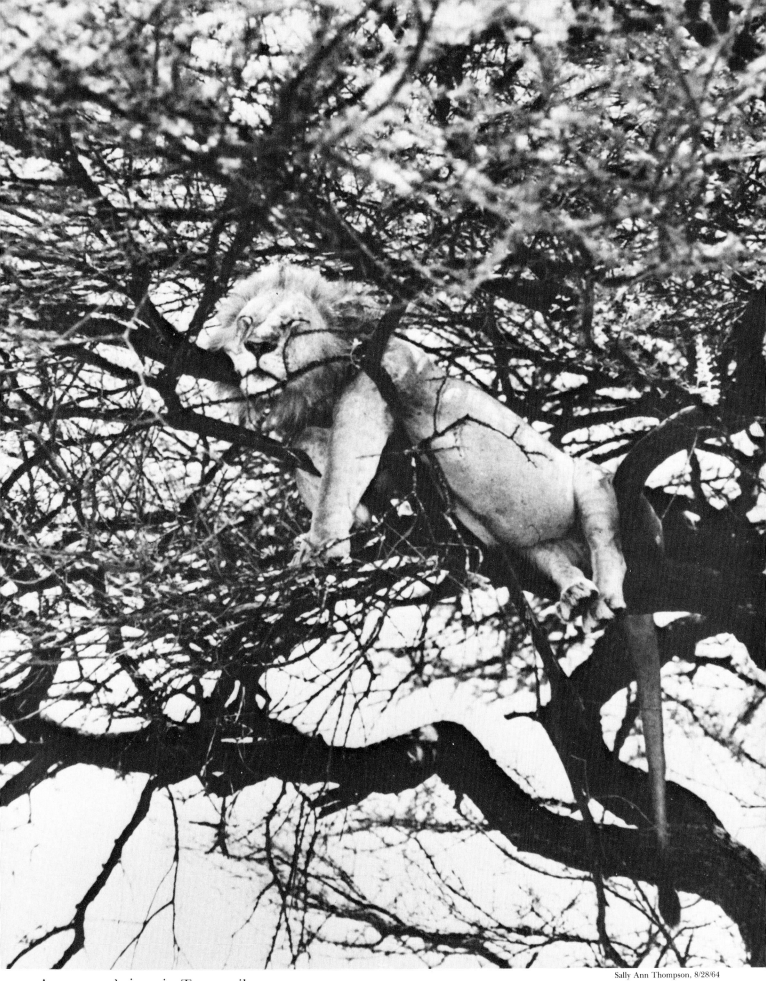

A contented siesta in Tanganyika.

Sally Ann Thompson, 8/28/64

CHAPTER 2
concerns
CLOSE ENCOUNTERS

After You, Alphonse

Mitten and Tosen are wondering who will go first. Even though she appears to be served up, Kim is really a friend and all three are pets of the Lyng family in Denmark.

Jytte Bjerregaard, 8/15/55

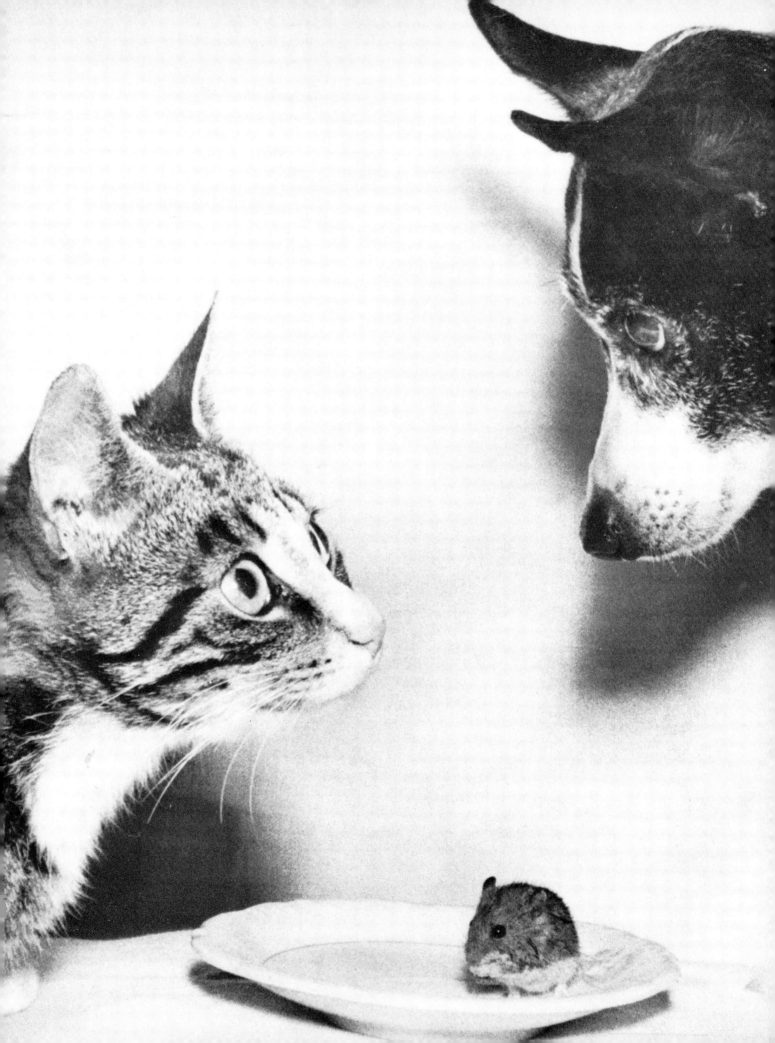

Ronald Treadle, *Sydney Sunday Sun*, 6/22/53

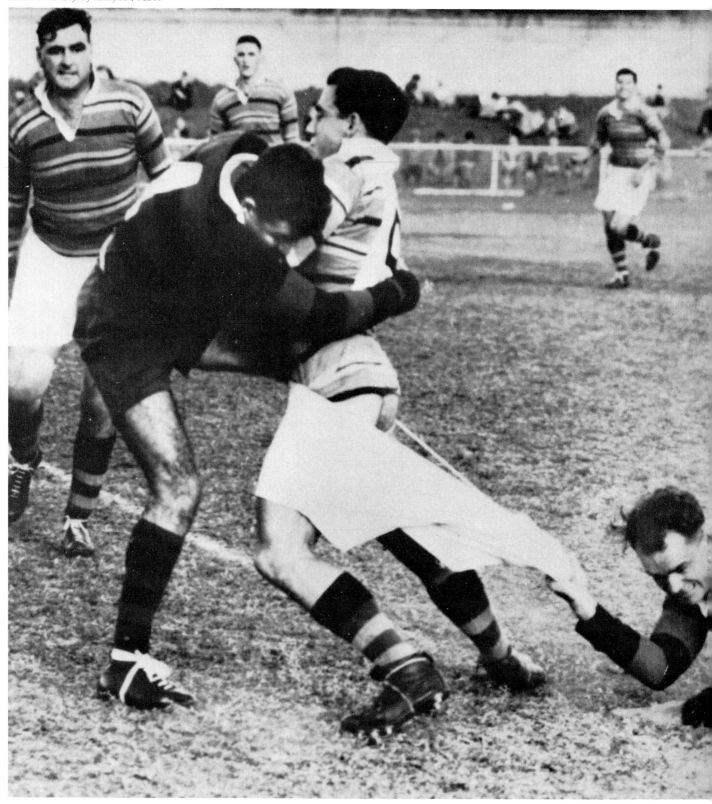

Panty Raids

Yes, they came off completely, but in Australia, where ruggers are gentlemen, Alf Hancock's teammates quickly formed a ring around him while a new pair was rushed out.

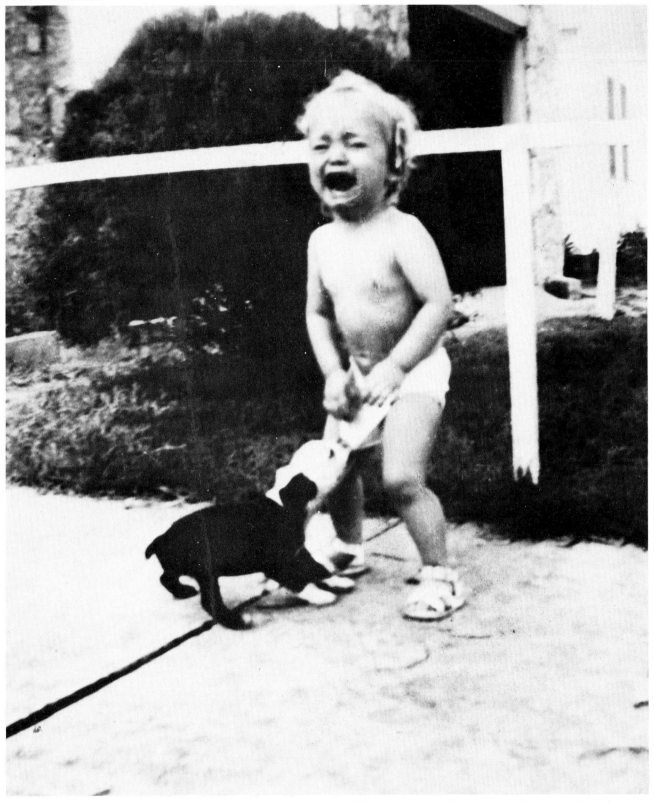

No, they stayed put, but still, Cynthia Caporal
didn't appreciate Stubby putting the bite on
her and had to call grandma to the rescue.

One in the Side Pocket

Crime is on the increase at the Baltimore Zoo.

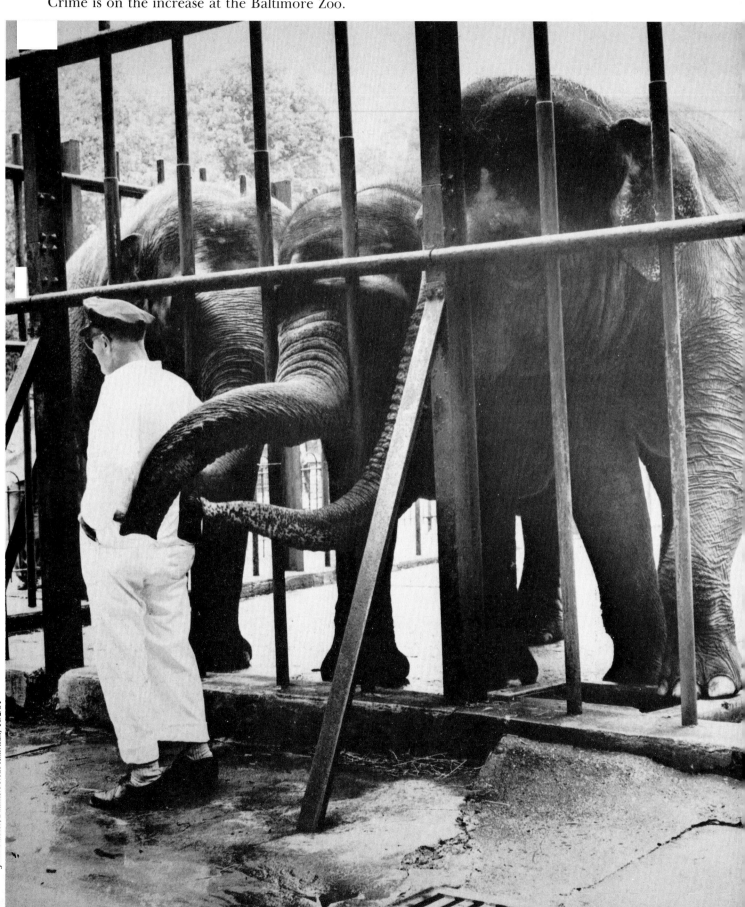

John Stadler, *Baltimore News-American*, 10/2/64

Five-year-old Thomas Robert Hester of
Raleigh, North Carolina, insists on stuffing,
even if his prize croaks.

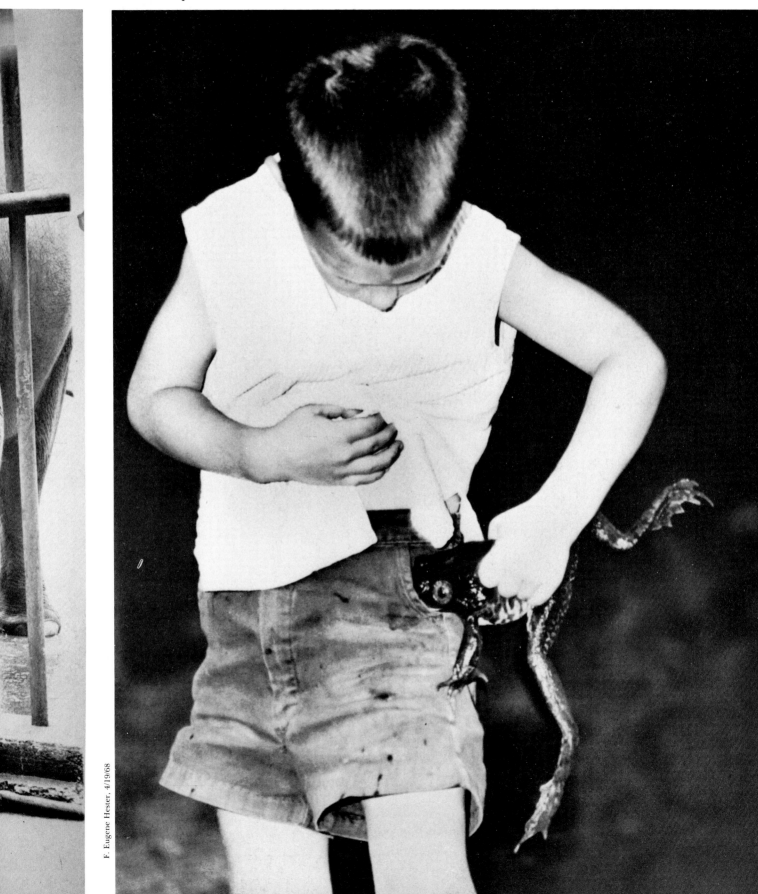

F. Eugene Hester, 4/19/68

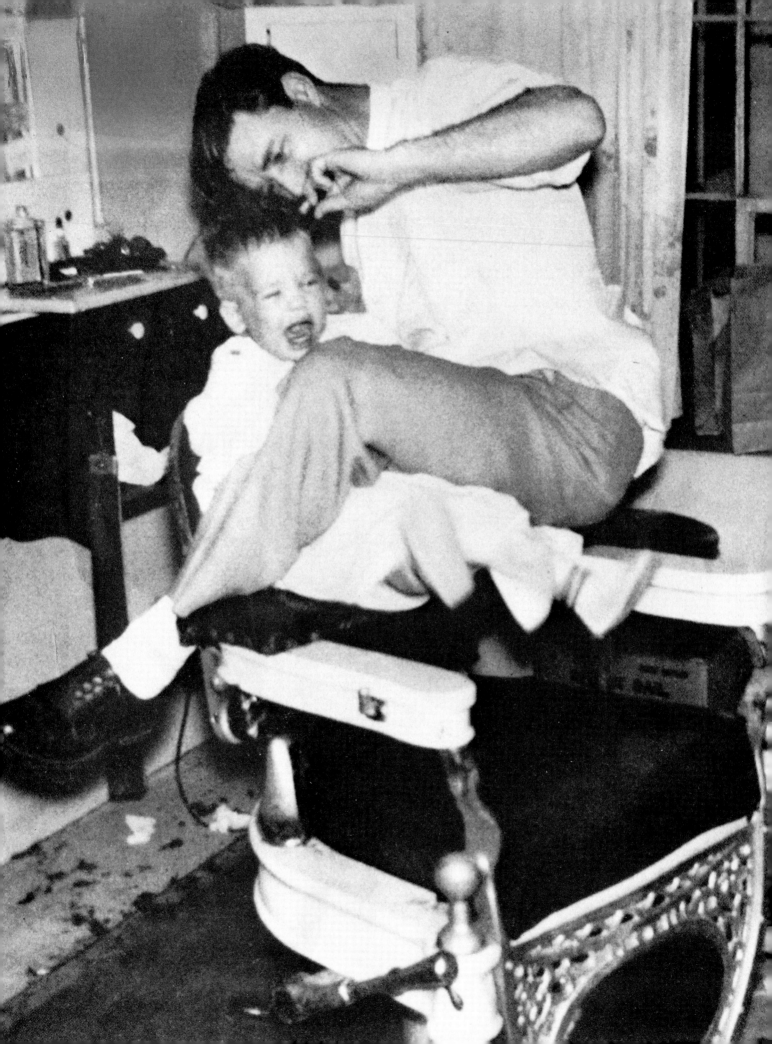

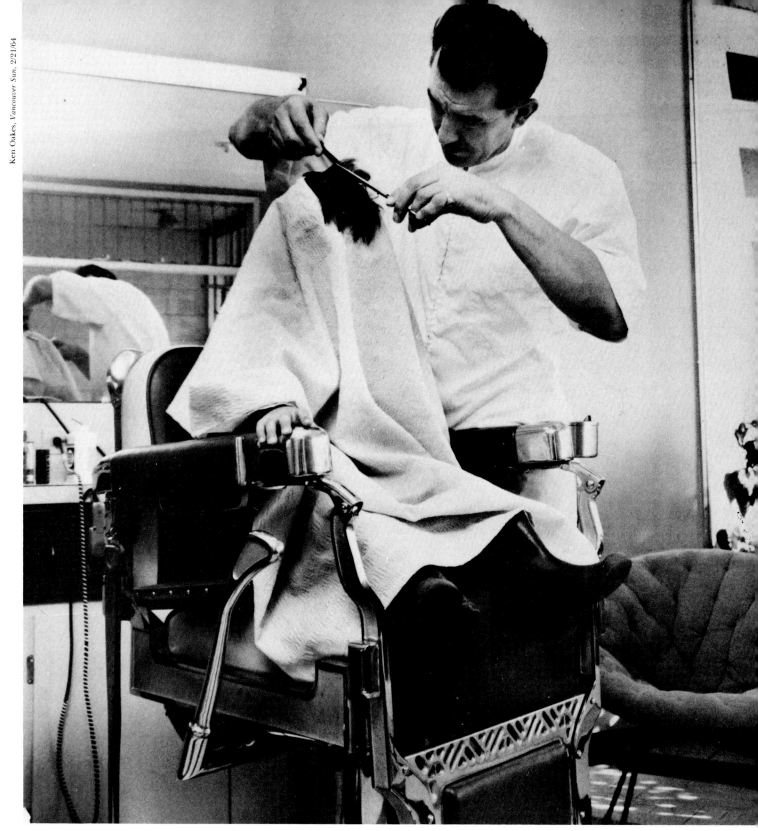

Ken Oakes, *Vancouver Sun*, 2/21/64

Hairy Dilemmas

George Romanoff of New Westminster, Canada, keeps tickling hair off faces and necks with this blanket solution.

When the small fry of Marquette Heights, Illinois, offers resistance, Harry Eubanks retaliates with a straitjacket made out of his leg.

Charles J. Hyde, 12/3/56

Run, Bobby, Run!

George Baker, *The Chattanooga Times*, 7/7/61

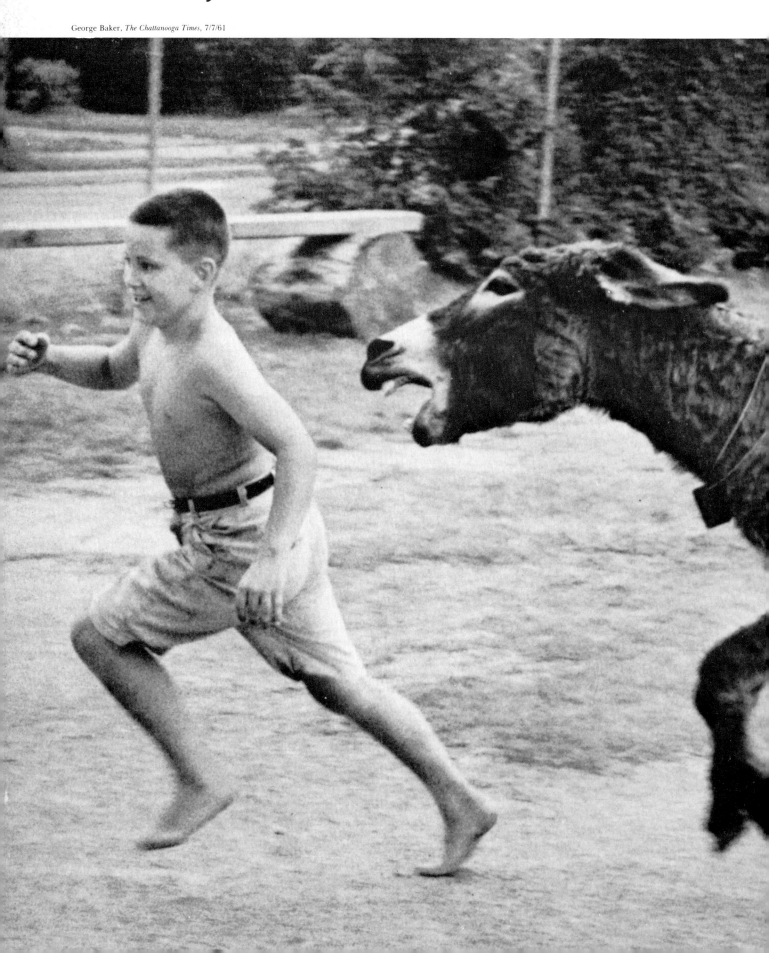

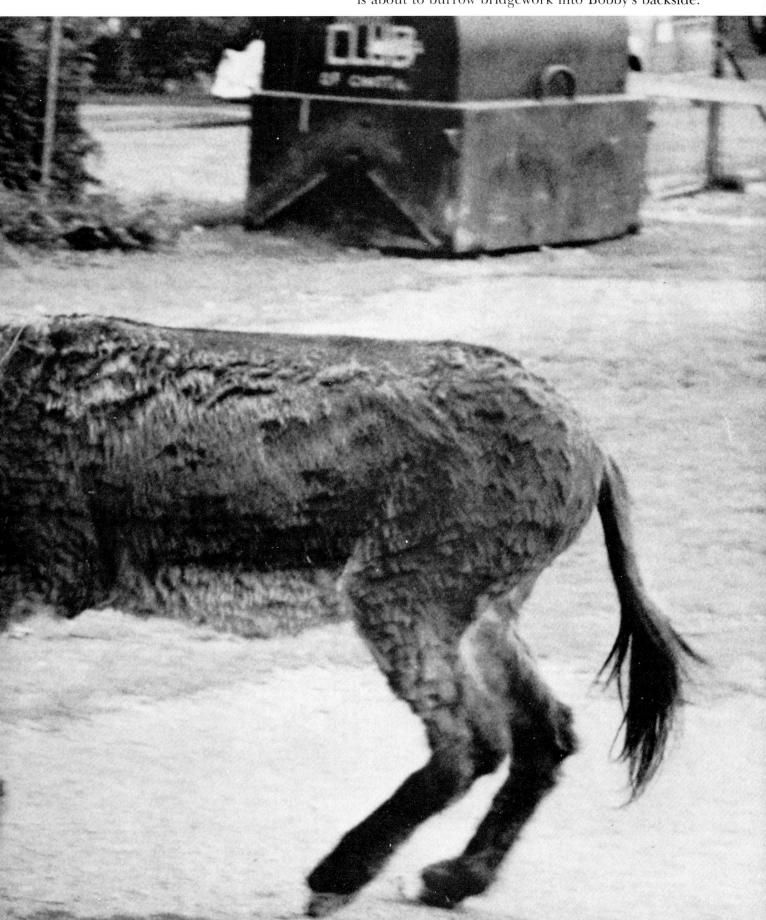

Bobby Burchfield better beat it fast, for Buster
is about to burrow bridgework into Bobby's backside.

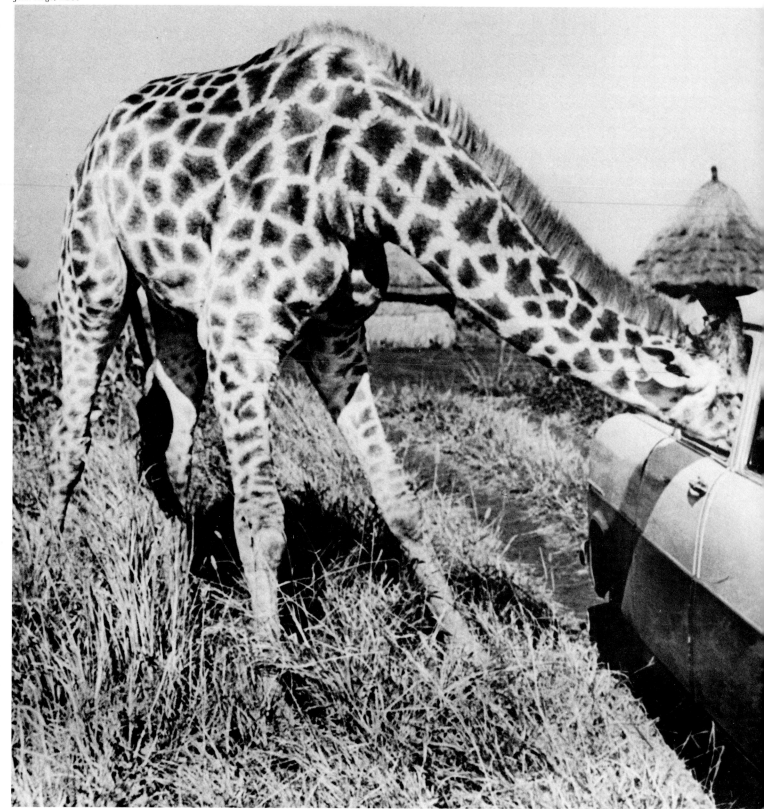

This South African giraffe knows his way around. Inside the car Cape Town's John Hugo is thanking his new friend with ripe plums.

Giving Directions

Bruce Roberts, 2/15/60

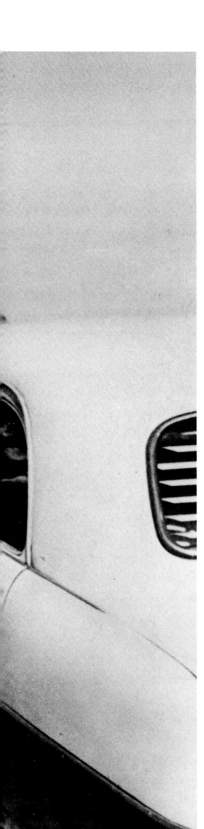
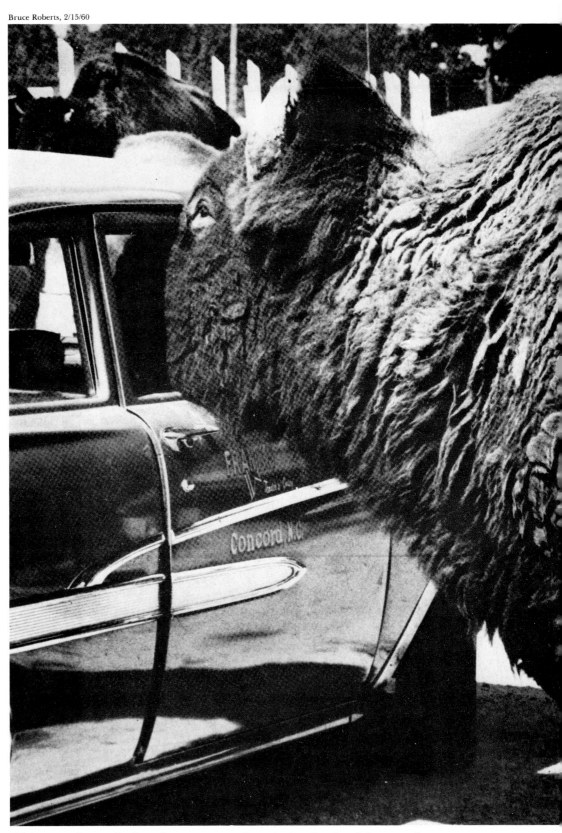

This nosy beast is showing meat packer A. B. Cook of Concord, North Carolina, almost too much affection. Shuffle off, buffalo!

Hounded Hounds

In Surrey, England, a three-month-old pup
tries to get his mother's ear.

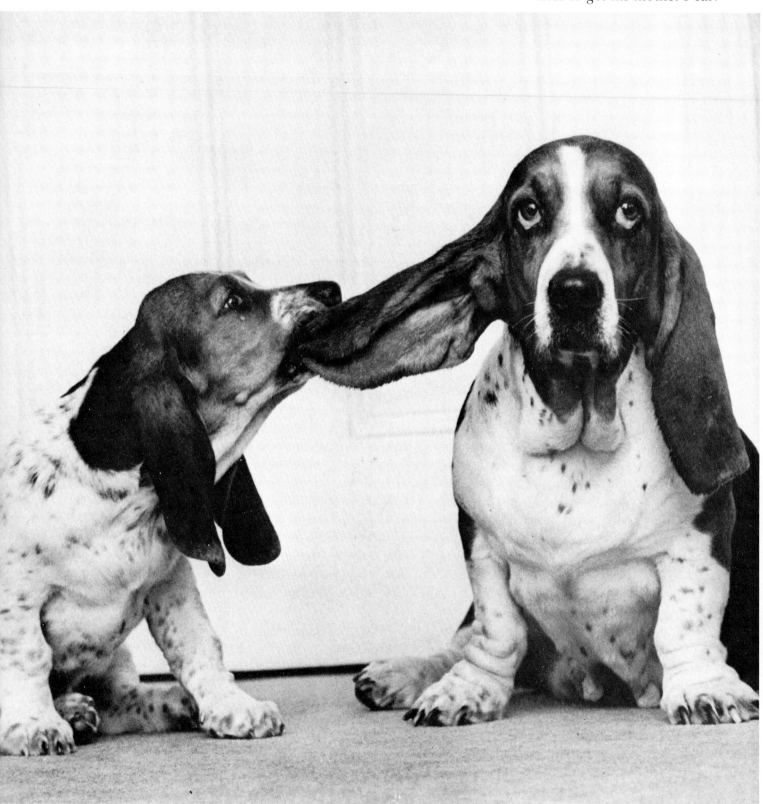

From his martyr's look you'd never know that
Lonesome Sam is only being kissed good night
by his friend, Joe.

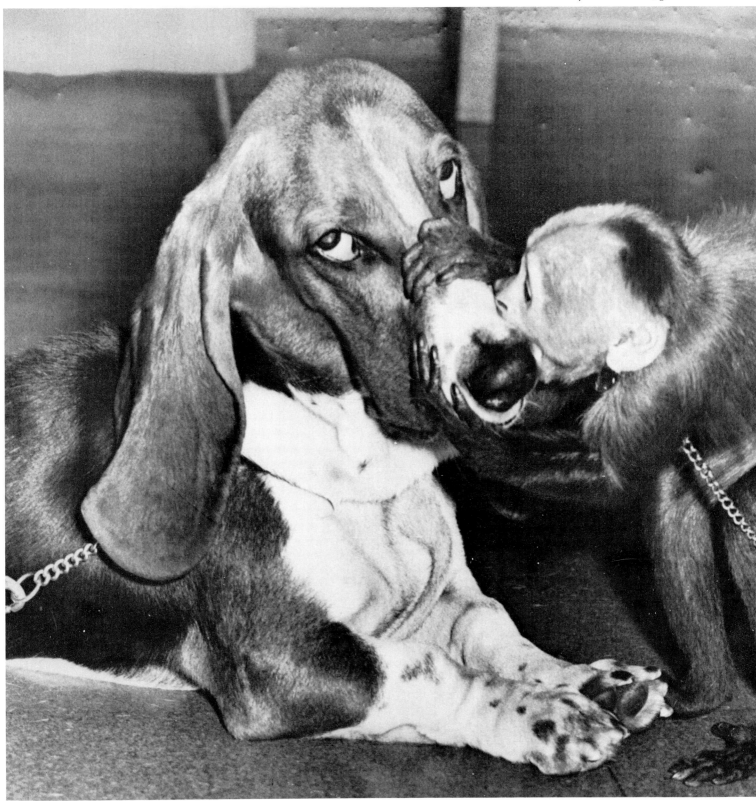

Alice H. Elmer, 1/19/59

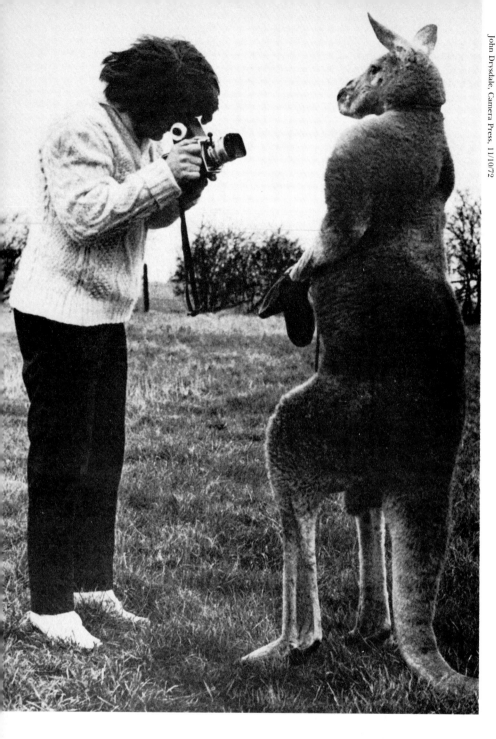

John Drysdale, Camera Press, 11/10/72

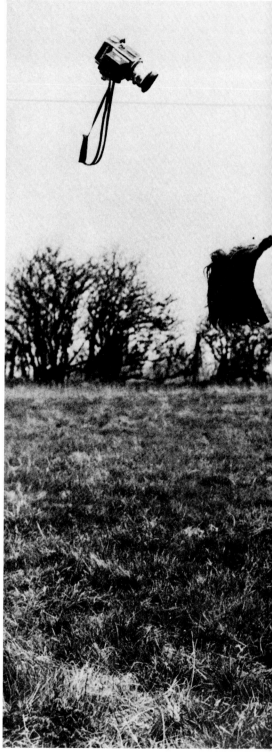

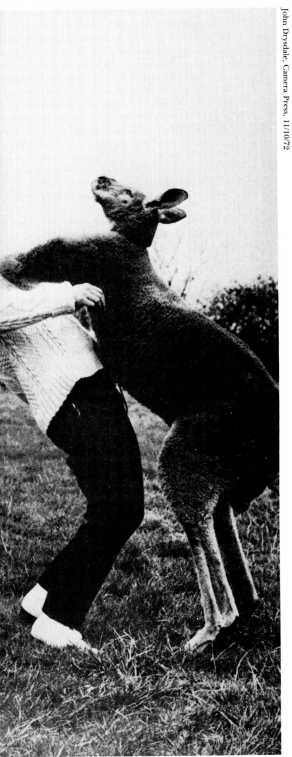

John Drysdale, Camera Press, 11/10/72

The Old One-Two

The guy with the camera is British circus owner Johnny Roberts. The guy with the boxing gloves is Sidney. Sidney works for Johnny as a pugilist. But his contract doesn't call for pictures. The sight of a camera pointed his way rang a bell. And it wasn't 'til afterward that he realized it was his boss he was licking.

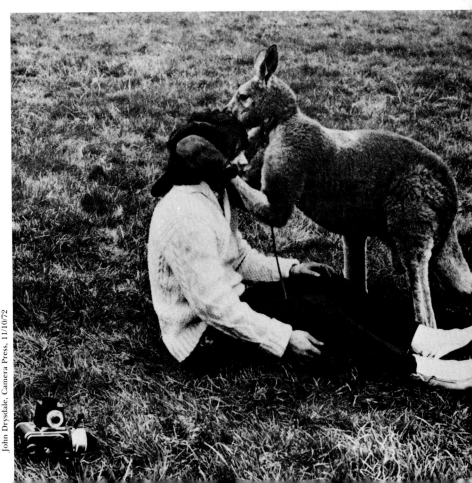

John Drysdale, Camera Press, 11/10/72

Watchit!!!

A puddle jumper in Sweden.

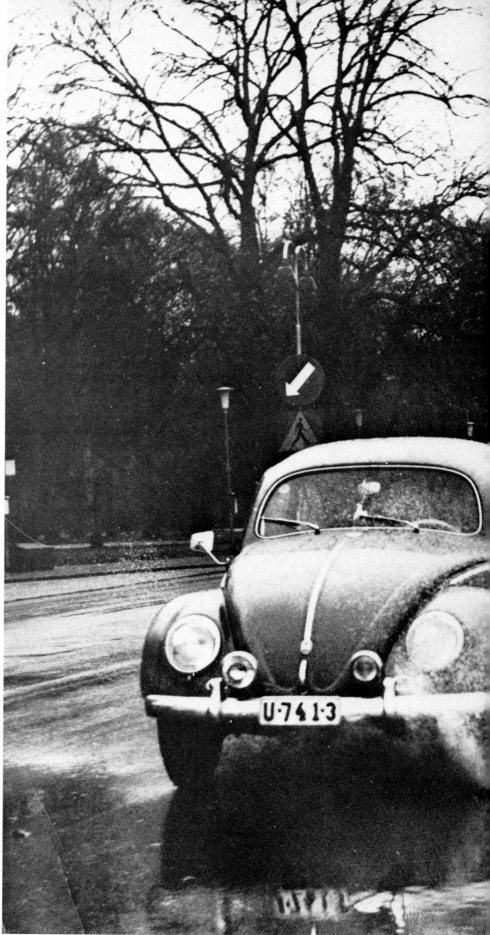

Bjorn Larsson, 12/15/61

44

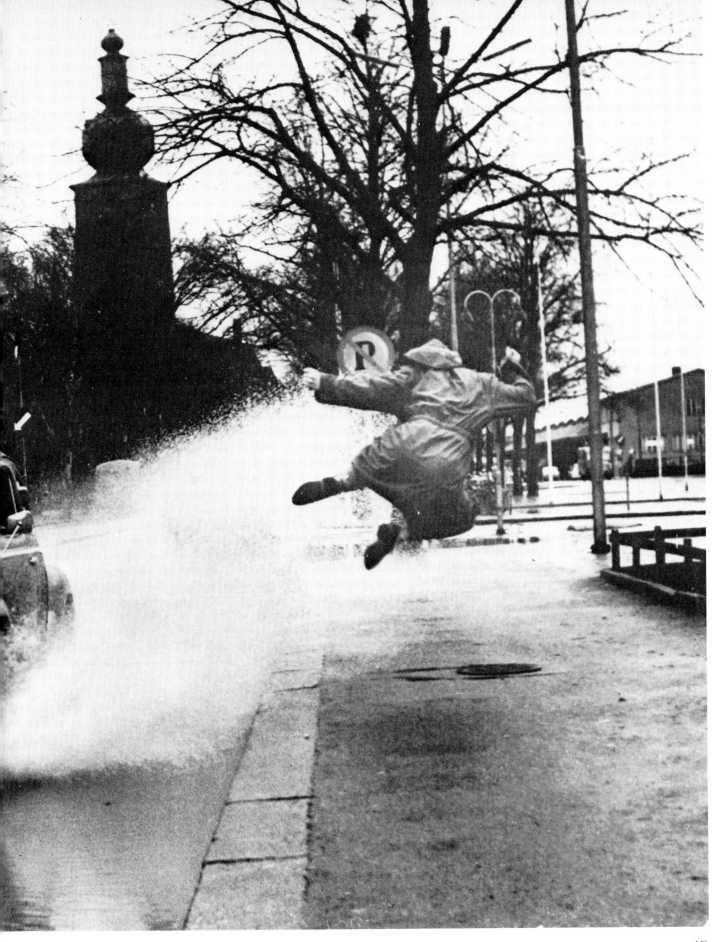

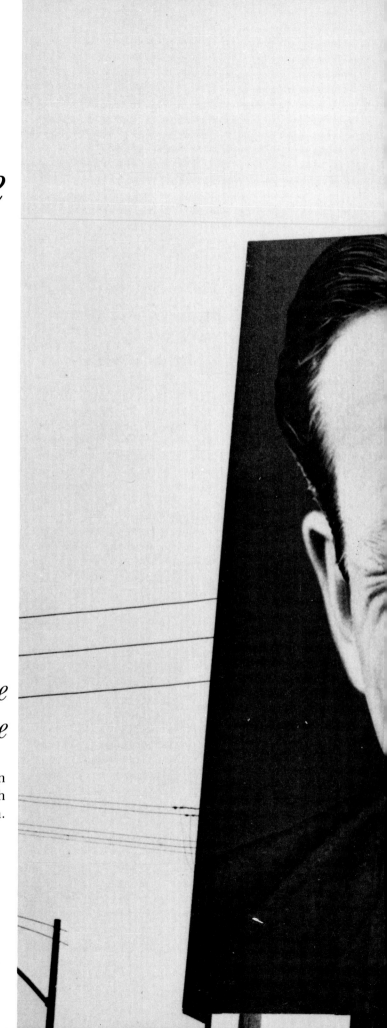

CHAPTER 3
displays some arresting SIGNS OF THE TIMES

A Little More to the Right, Please

After hosing down an oil-spattered billboard in Los Angeles, a workman tends to a ticklish situation with his long-handled brush.

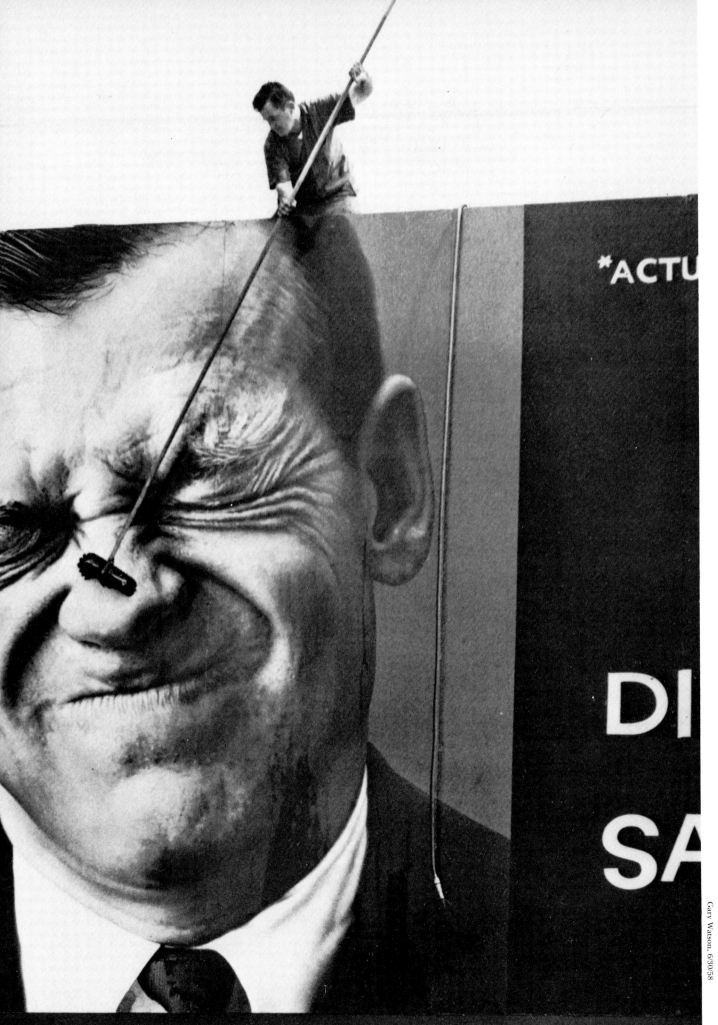

*ACTU

DI

SA

Gary Watson, 6/30/58

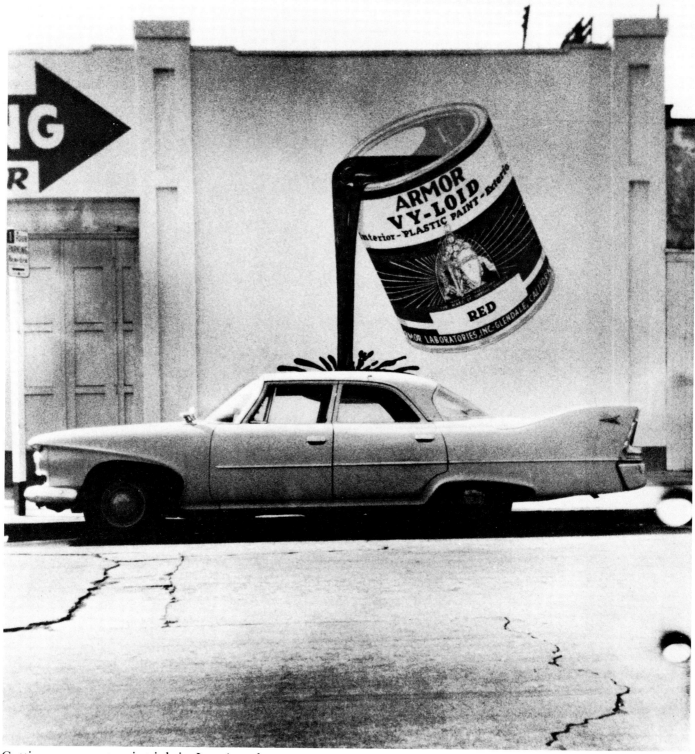

Getting a pop art paint job in Los Angeles.

Scenes That Fire the Imagination

C. B. Garrett, *Baltimore Evening Sun*, 8/19/66

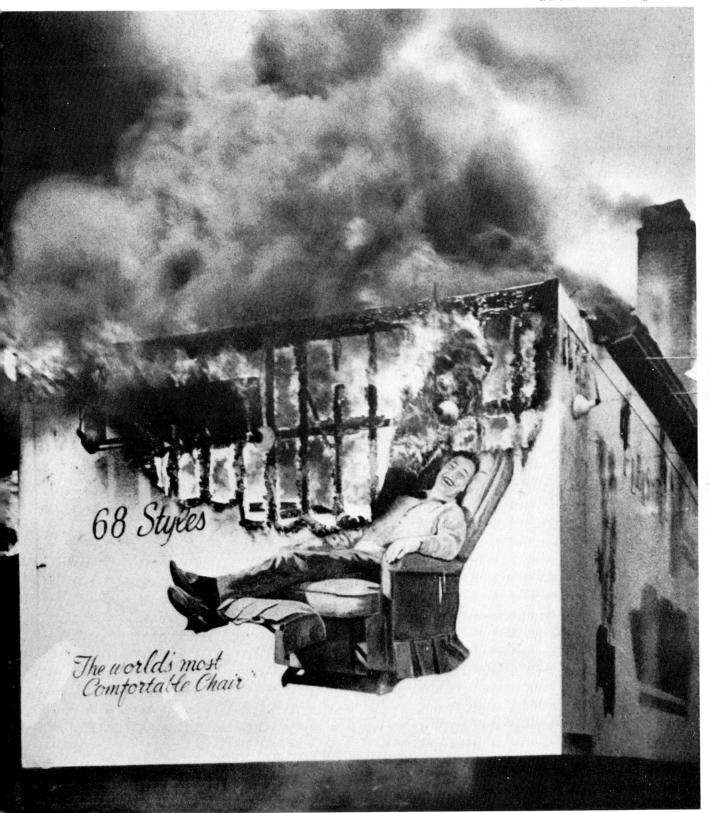

68 Styles

The world's most Comfortable Chair

Getting hot under the collar in Baltimore.

Really Spelling It Out

From the fortieth floor of the First National Bank Building in Seattle the good news is flashed for all the world to see, including the proud mother who can read it from her hospital window.

A California rancher sends a plowed plea to Navy pilots to knock off the sonic booms.

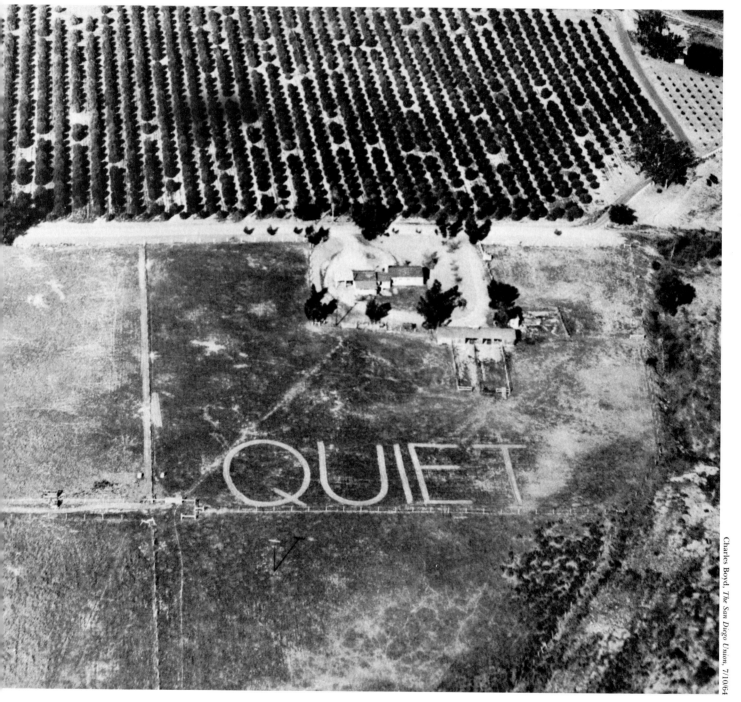

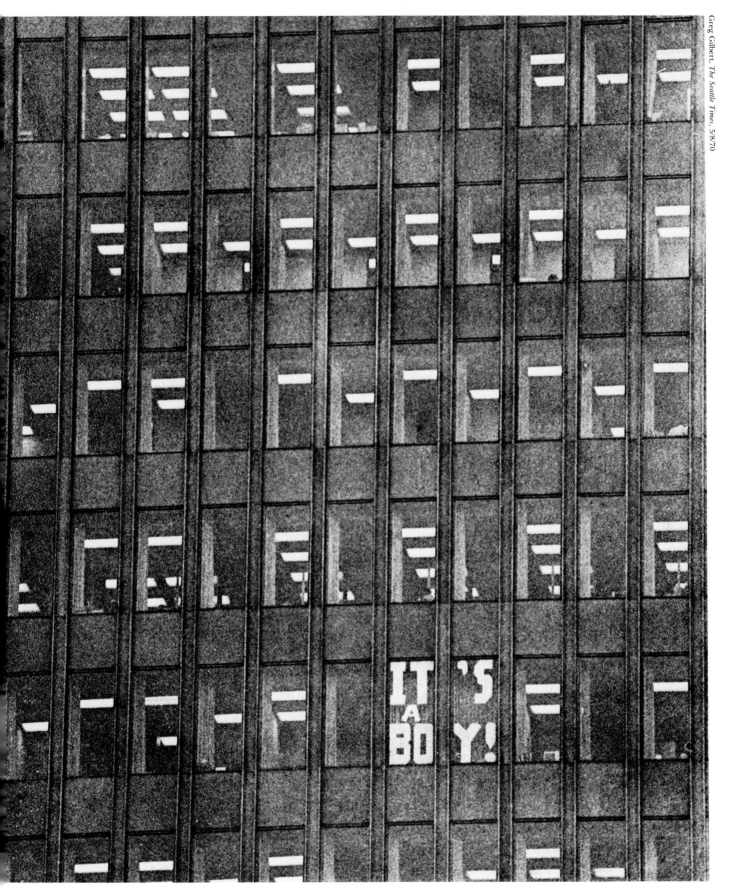

Greg Gilbert, *The Seattle Times*, 5/8/70

Dave McEnery, RDR Productions, 3/1/58

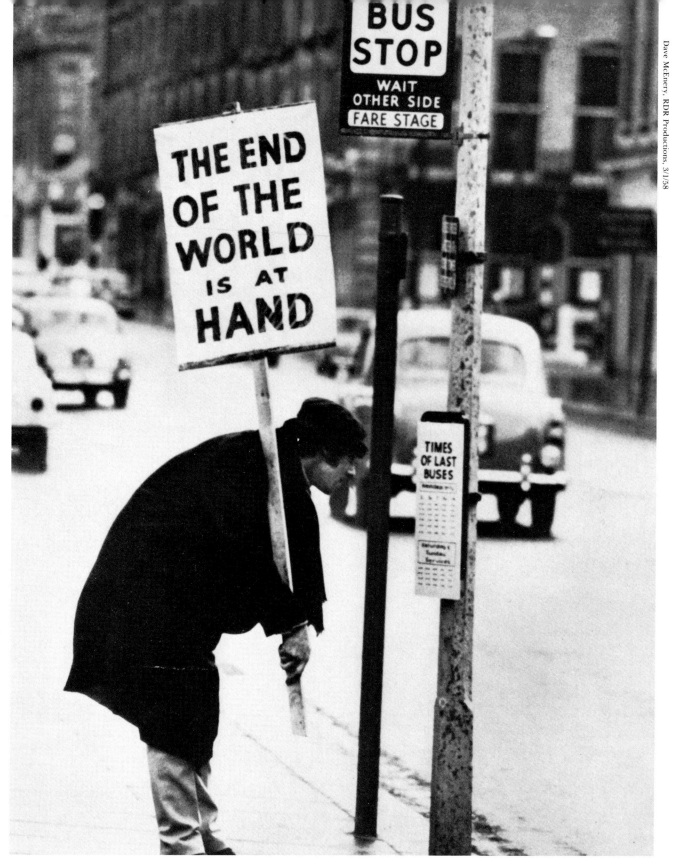

Dubious Forecasts

A pessimistic Londoner checks the schedule for the bus home after realizing the end of the day is at hand.

Marvin Kreisman, 6/7/68

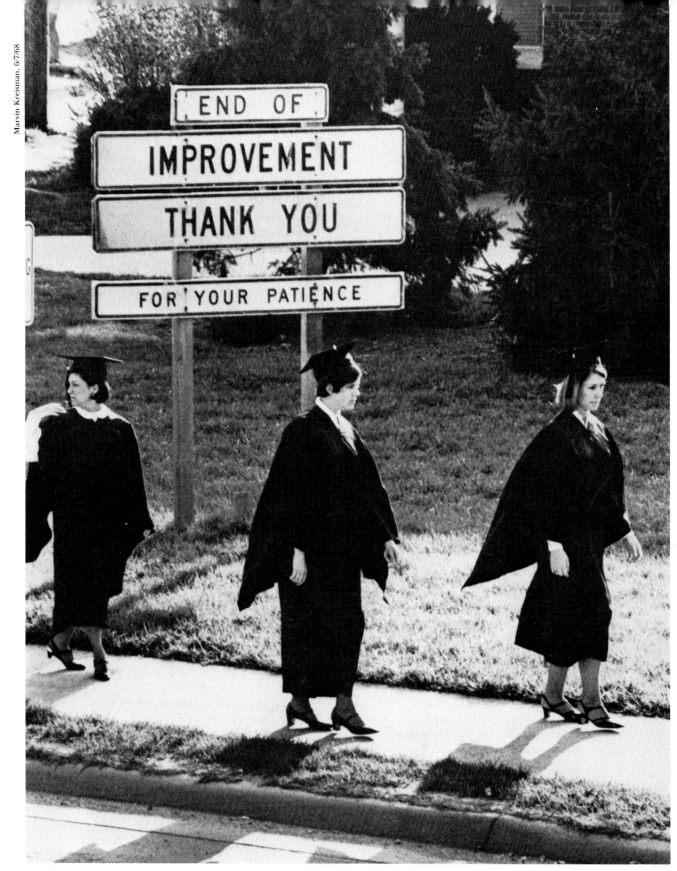

END OF
IMPROVEMENT
THANK YOU
FOR YOUR PATIENCE

Dead wrong! The end is just the beginning for these impatient
graduates.

Errors on the Road

Driving directions in this London suburb are slightly
CONFSUING.

London Daily Telegraph, 4/3/64

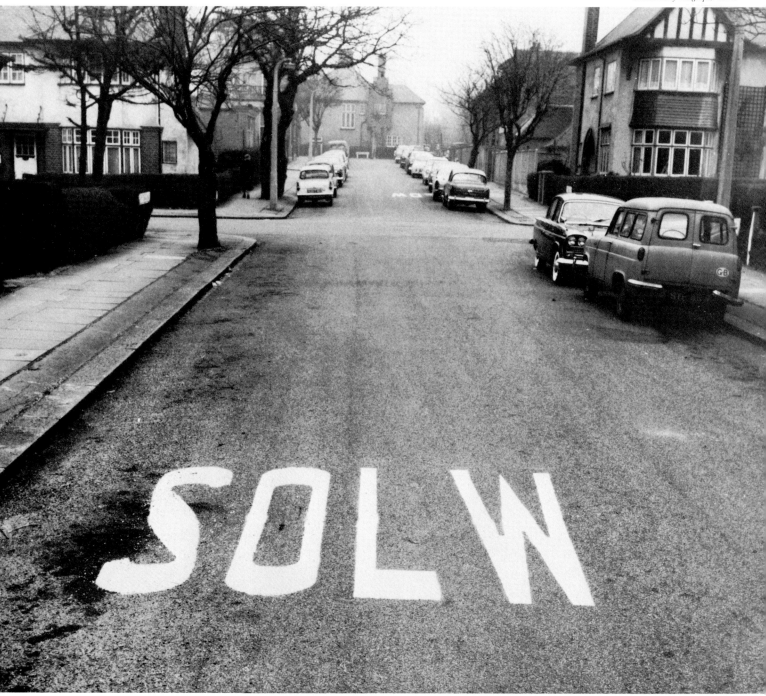

A twelve-and-one-half-foot-high truck spells out the upshot of its miscalculations. Earl W. McAnally. 11/11/66

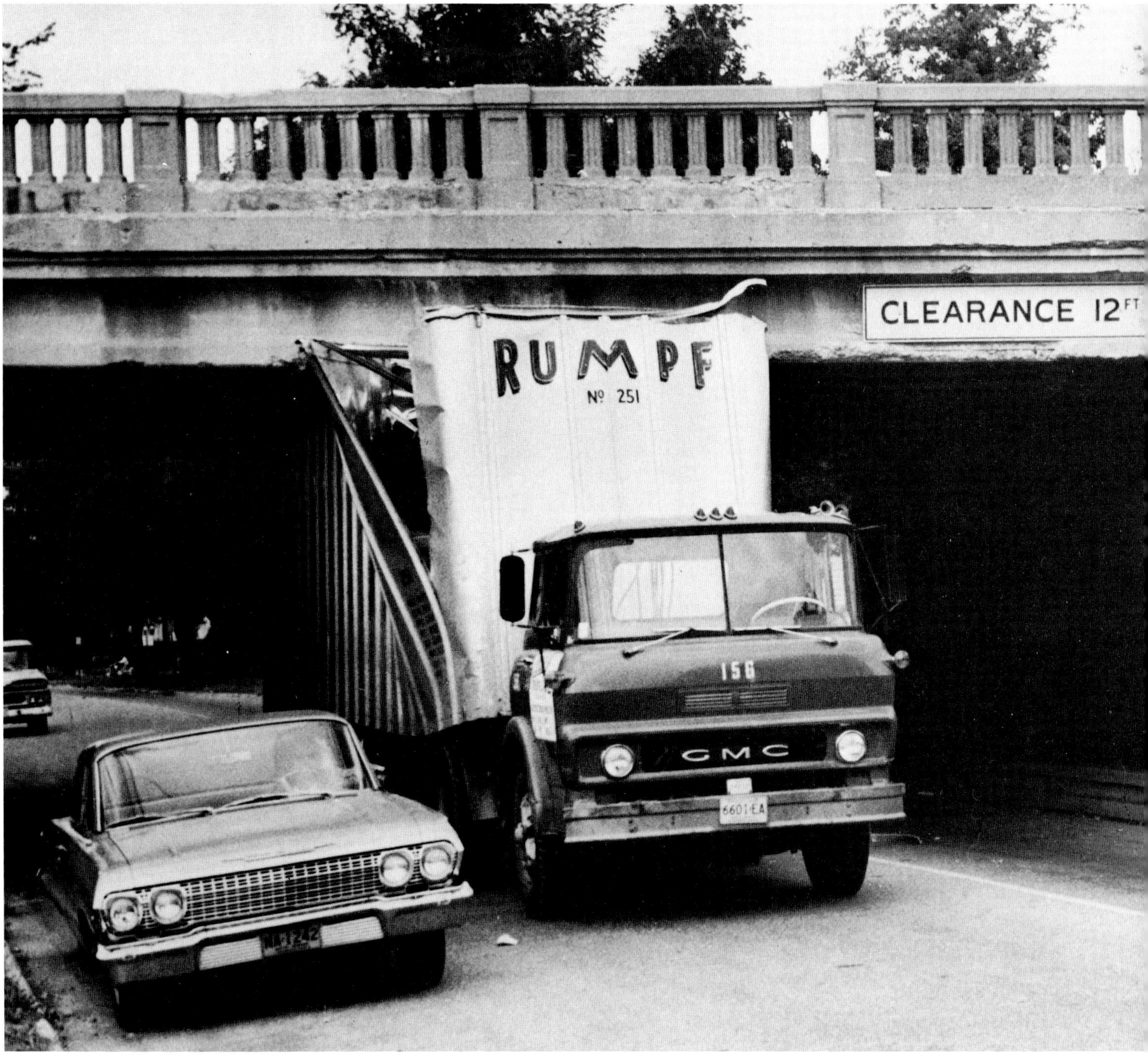

CLEARANCE 12 FT

RUMPF
No 251

GMC

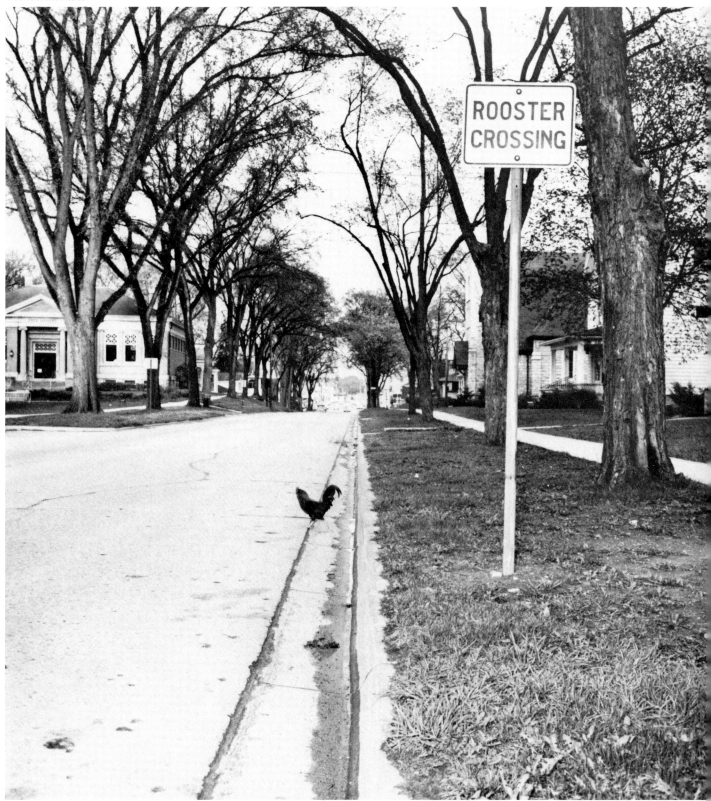

Traffic Warnings

In Whitewater, Wisconsin, even the roosters
must obey the rules.

Baron Wolman, 5/8/64

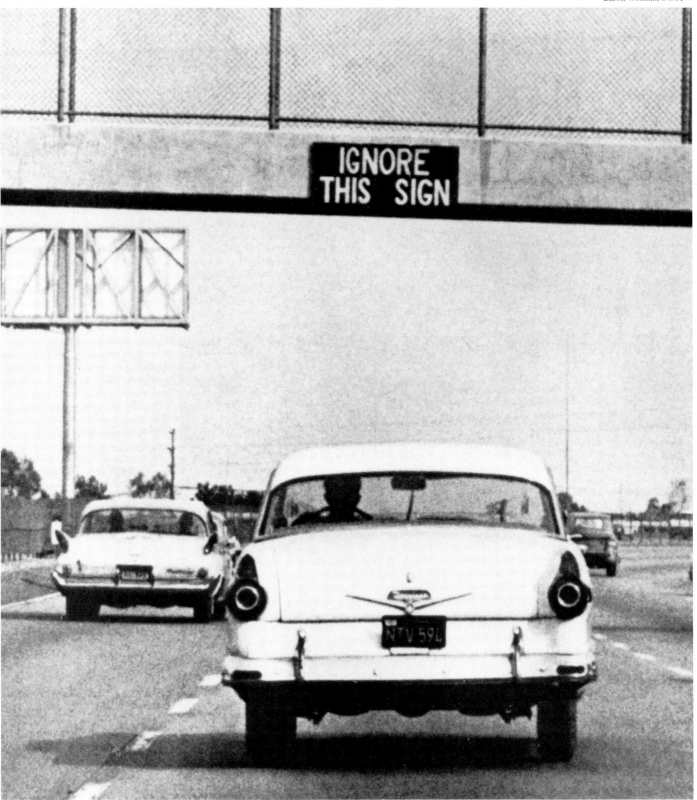

With all those directions to follow on the Los Angeles freeways, finally here's one to disregard. But how?

CHAPTER 4
offers some scenes
NOT FAR FROM HOME

Choking Up

T minus nine lives
and counting.

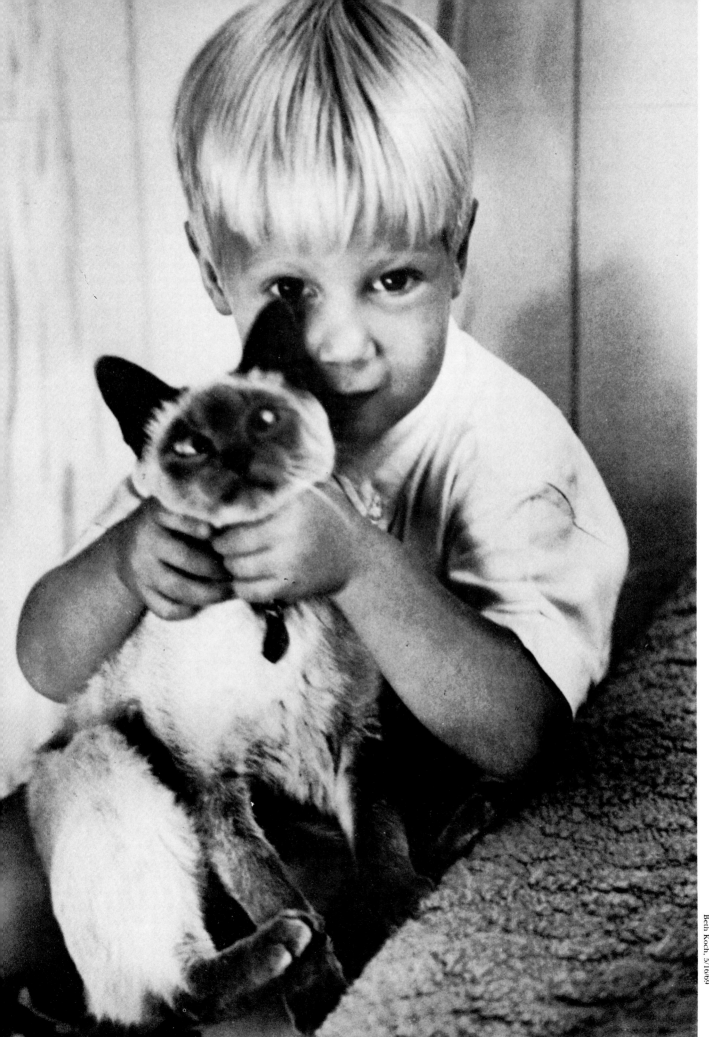

Beth Koch, 5/16/69

Do I Hear a Waltz?

Mona, the talking Afghan dog, can sing
as well as tickle the ivories.
Robert Gescheider, 1/10/49

In Schenectady, New
York, Blackie cuts in
on Herman
Lohmann who is
having a Christmas
dance with his
daughter Erika.

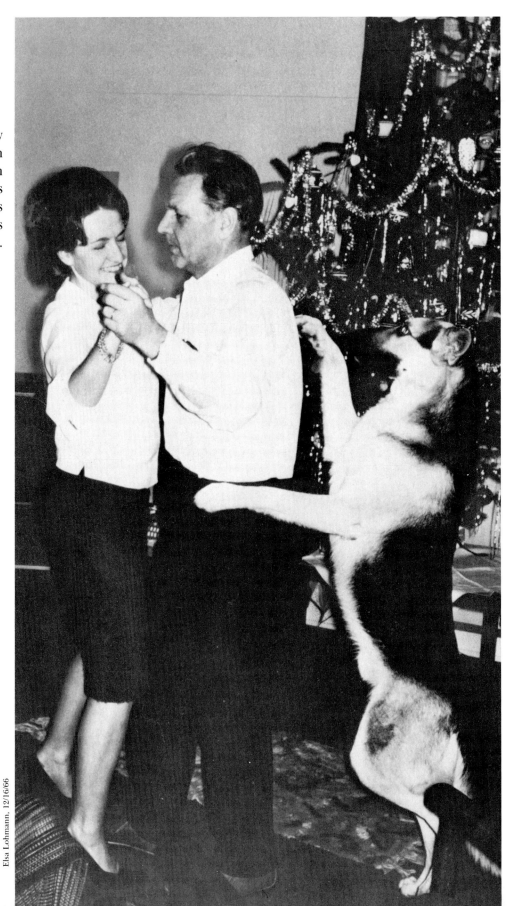

Elsa Lohmann, 12/16/66

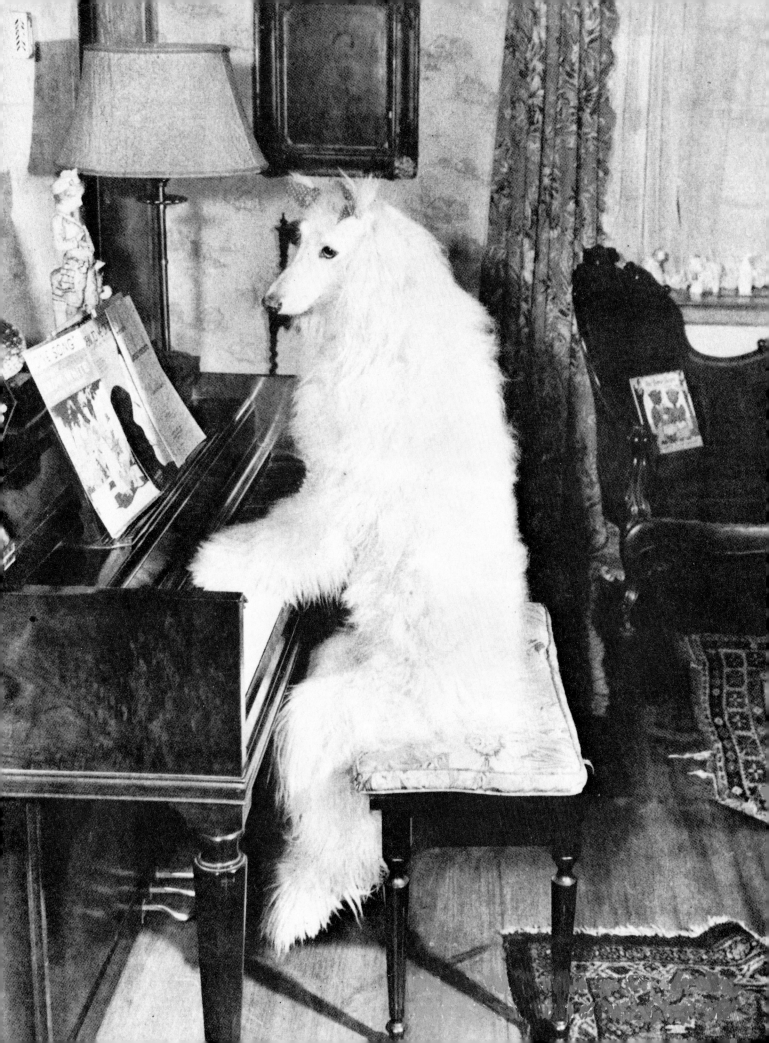

Making Faces

Watched pots do their own watching in a Dallas kitchen.

Jack Bonds, 2/20/56

Louis Stettner, 2/16/59

RDR Productions, 4/18/69

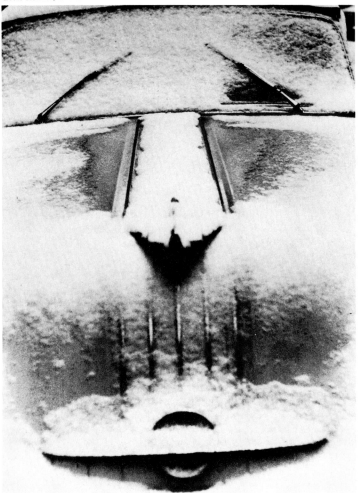

A wintry wink in New York City.

John Winter of Kentucky notices that his tire looks just like his old man—Old Man Winter, that is.

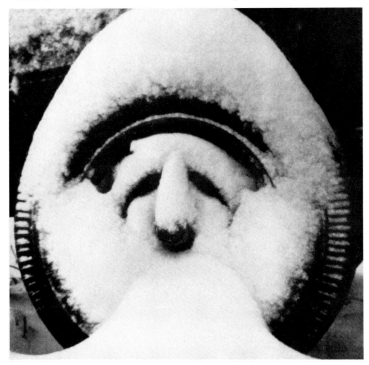

John C. Winter, 2/2/53

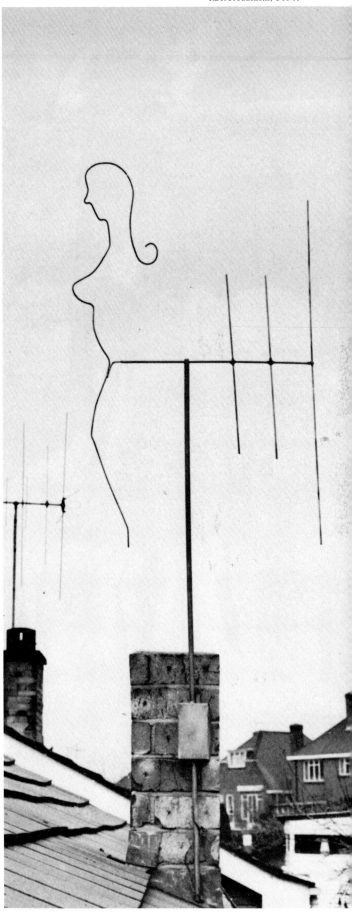

Ultrahigh receptionist.

Rex Features, 3/5/65

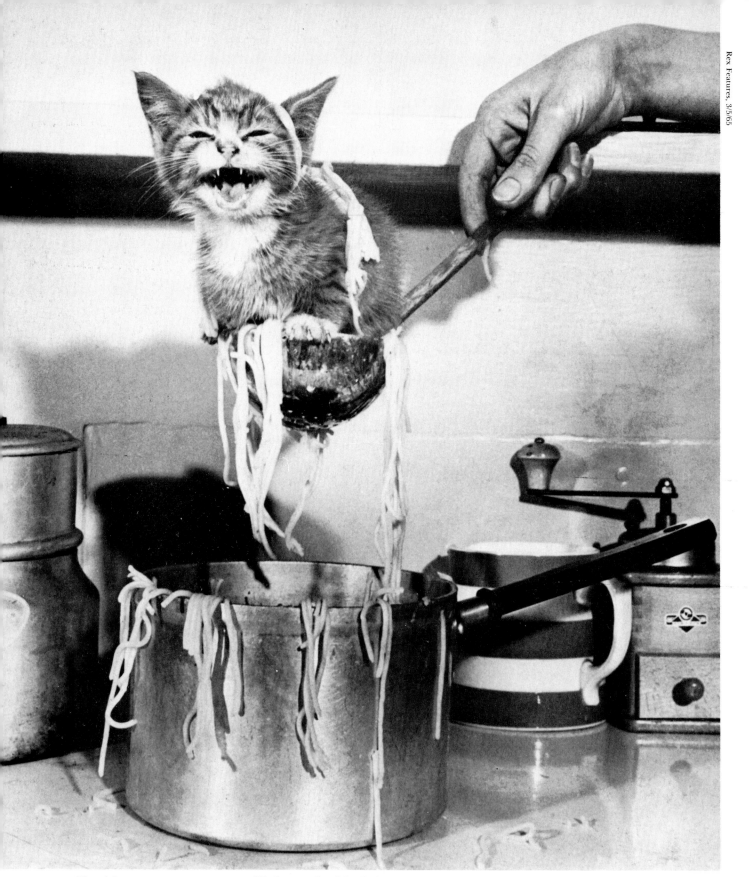

No, it's not pussycat sauce. Eight-week-old Fluff was noodling around and she fell in. Here she's being rescued.

Pasta Problems

George G. Trabant, *St. Petersburg Times*, 9/26/60

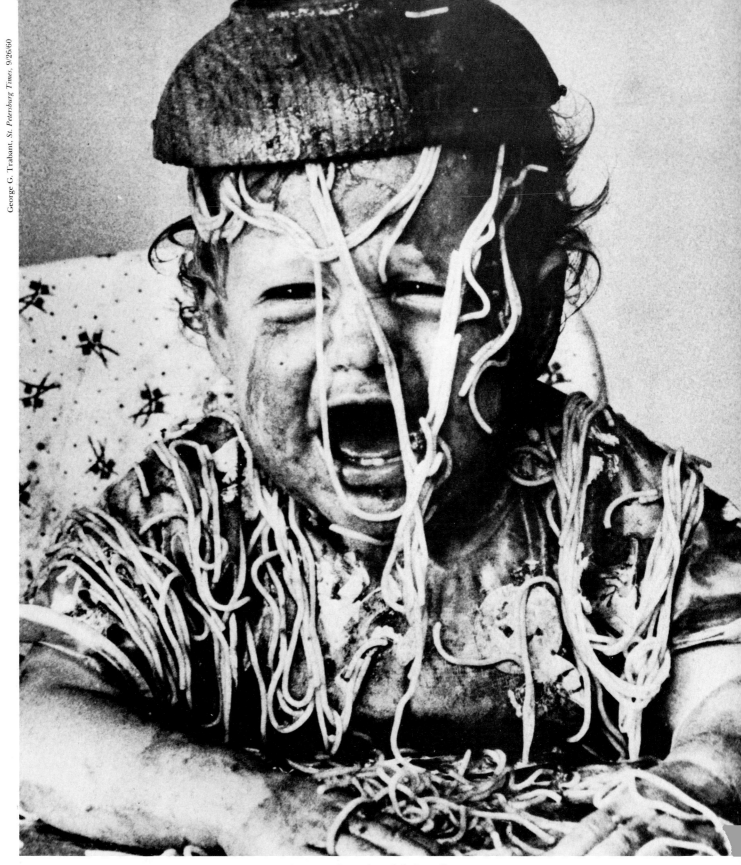

Wendy Rotes of St. Petersburg, Florida, shows what she thinks of supper.

Holy Smoke

David Miller of Denver is wide-eyed over his daddy's rings.

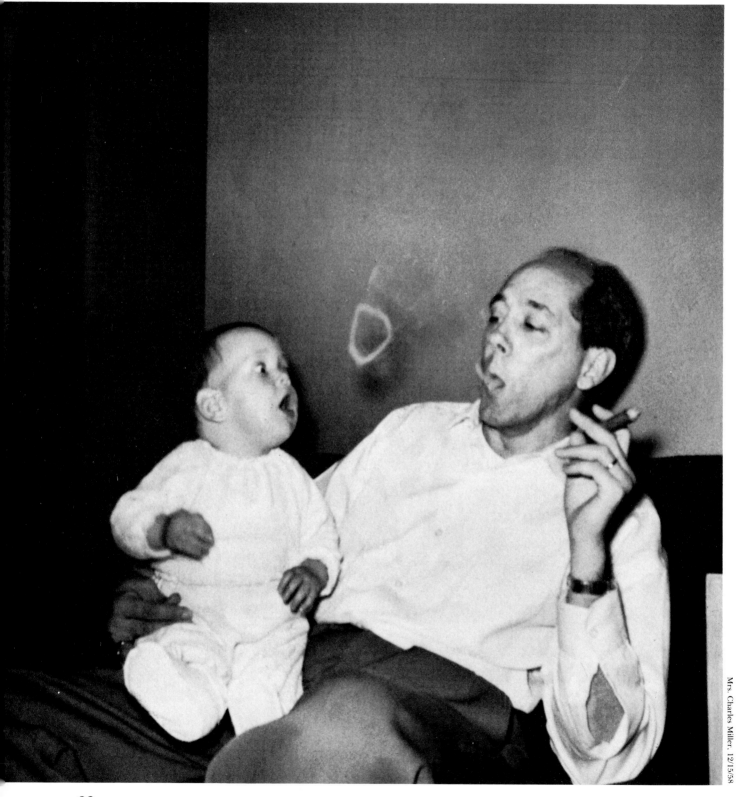

At the window of her second-floor apartment a New York pooch delicately taps her ash.

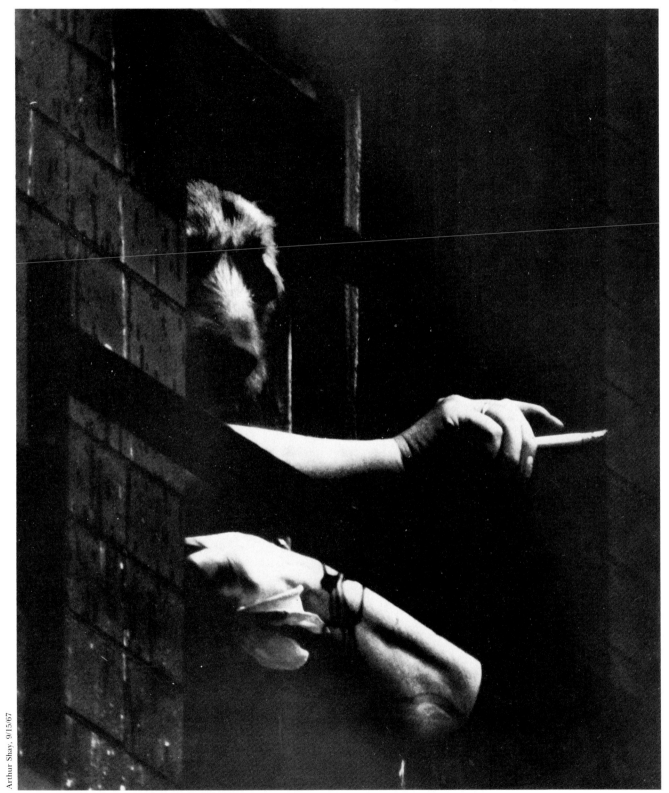

Feet That Come In Handy

Camille Kabbush of Oak Park, Michigan, has a well-balanced formula.

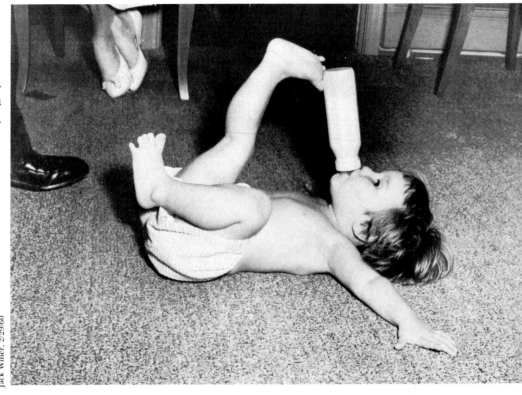

Jack Winer, 2/29/60

Eleven-year-old Elaine Scheer of Garberville, California, doesn't keep her homework at arm's length.

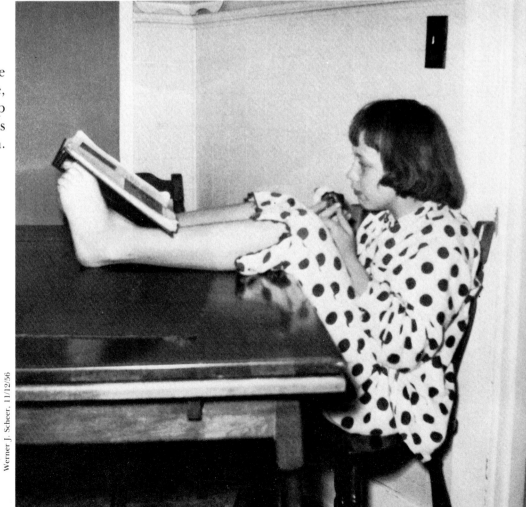

Werner J. Scheer, 11/12/56

Assuming the pretzel position, thirteen-year-old Diane Fuller of Minneapolis puts a new twist on homework.

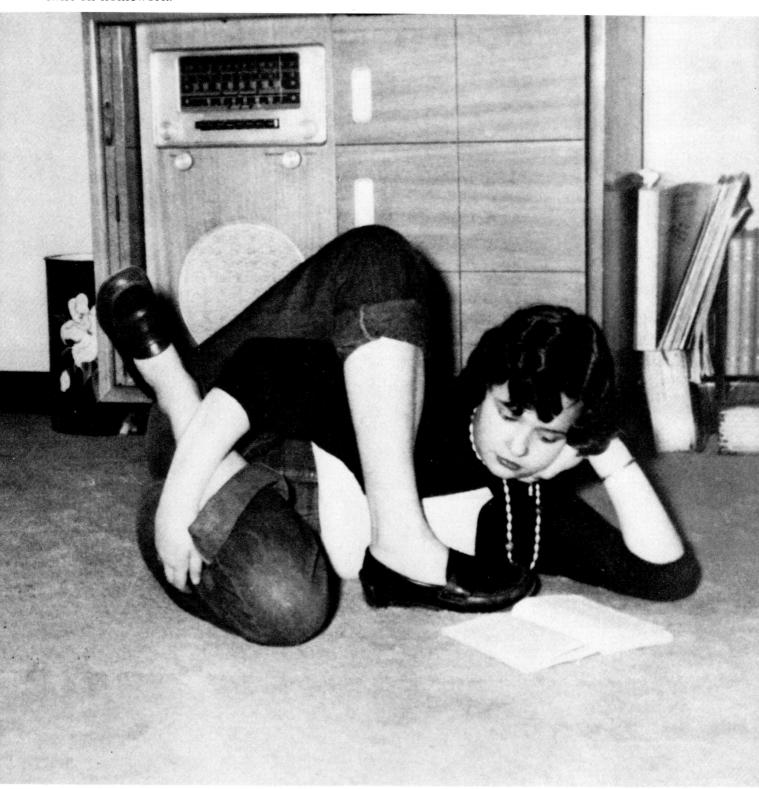

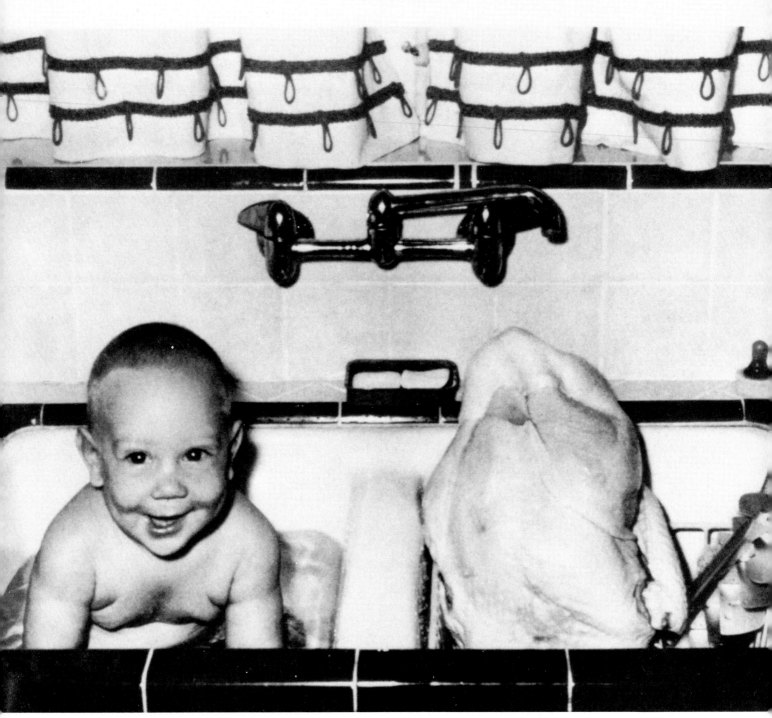

A Couple of Old Birds

Twenty-three-pound Danny Laszlo of Phoenix is drying off after a wash before being dressed for dinner. Next door fourteen-pound Tom is drying off, too, before—you guessed it—being dressed for dinner.

Charles Heckman, Bettmann/UPI, 4/20/53

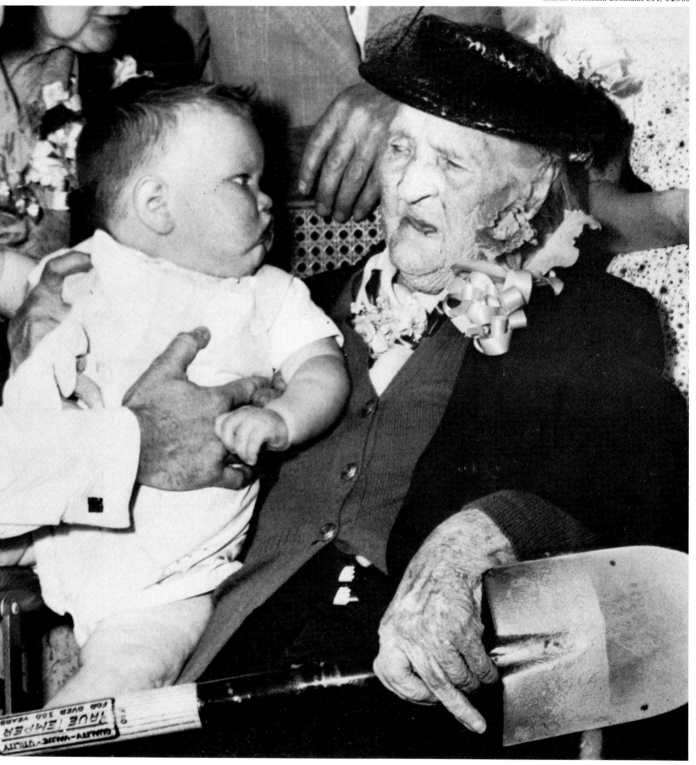

Here, 107-year-old Christine Nelson and her great-great-grandson, eight-month-old Richard Lynn Morris, eye each other with suspicion across a four-generation gap.

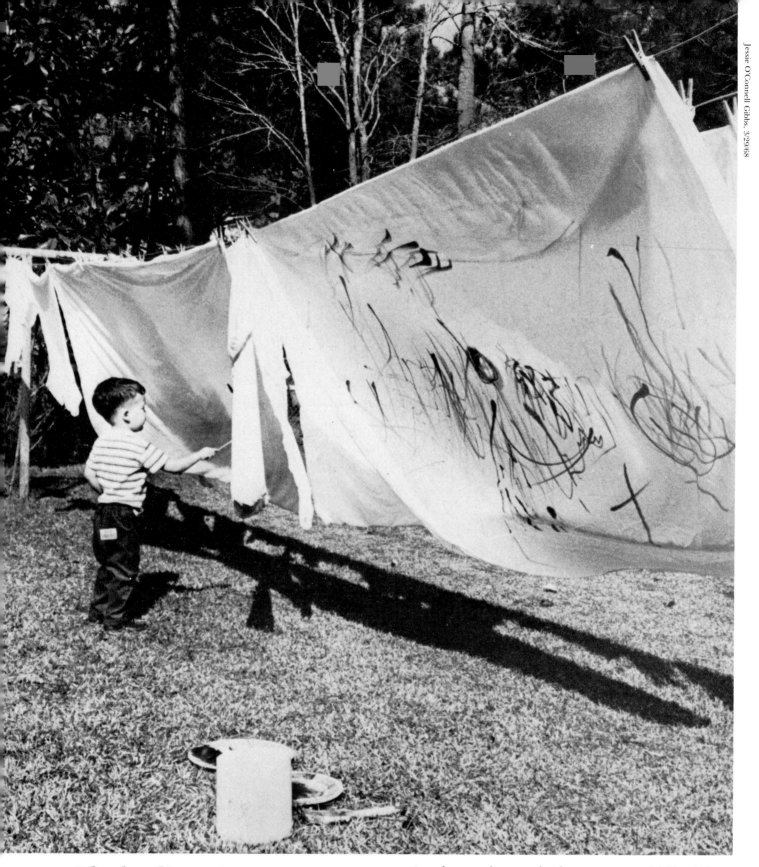

Jessie O'Connell Gibbs, 3/29/68

Clothesline Art

An abstract impressionist, two-year-old Patrick (Gene) Gibbs of Charleston, South Carolina, touches up his latest canvas.

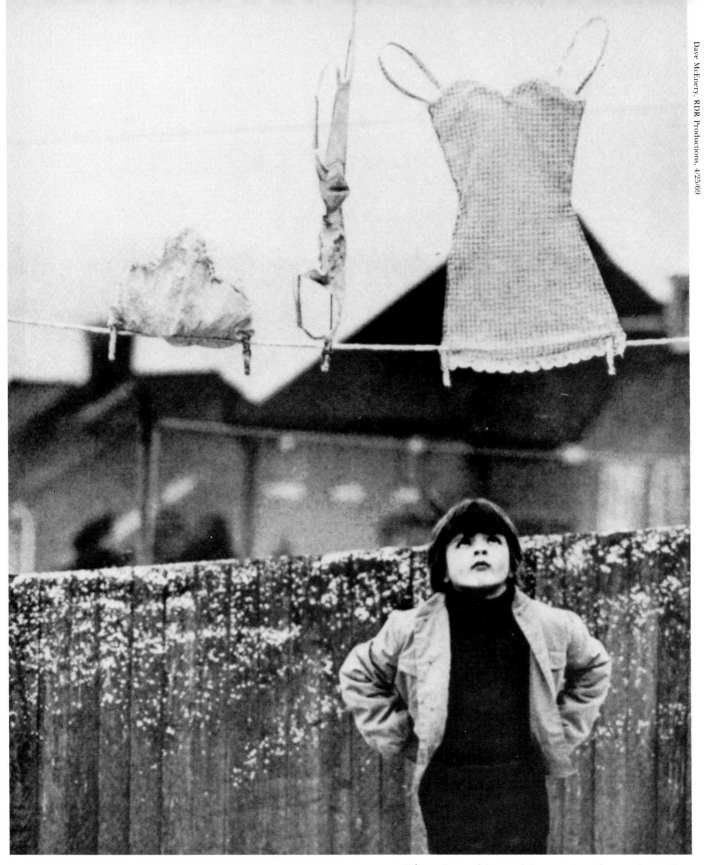

Dave McEnery, RDR Productions, 4/25/69

There's nothing wishy-washy about these frozen undergarments, is there, Sonny?

Horning In

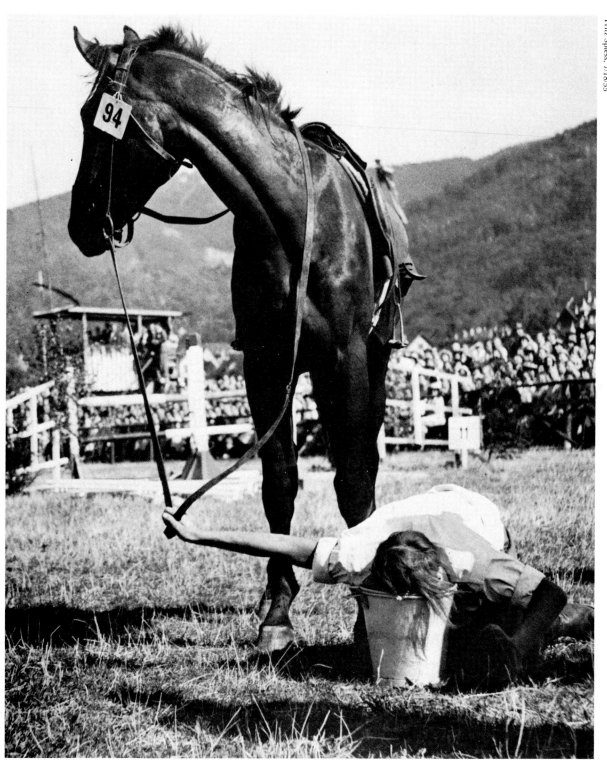

Fritz Spiess, 7/18/55

In Heidelberg, West Germany, rider beats horse to the water bucket.

Eighteen-month-old Chiara Chandoha gives food for thought to a visiting kitten.

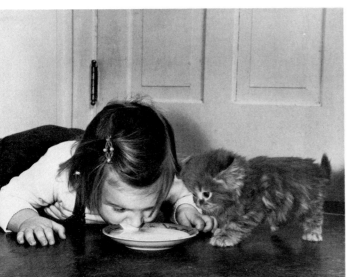

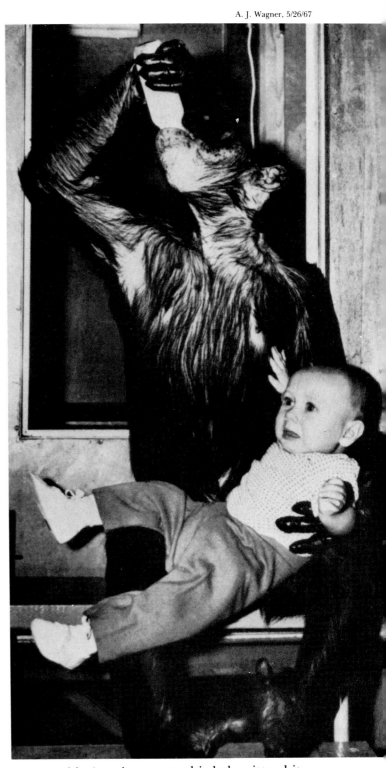

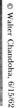

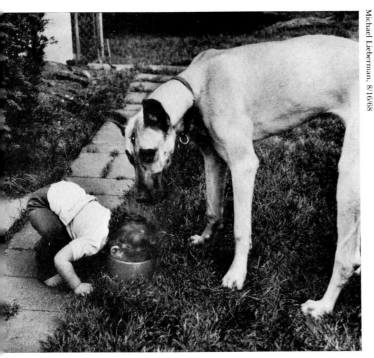

A hungry child checks out dinner under the gaze of a melancholy Dane.

Alan Kubler's going ape as his baby-sitter hits the bottle.

CHAPTER 5
plays a game of
HEADS
OR
TAILS

Man or Dog?

Here is a shepherd in keeper's clothes. He's German. Prince was dressed this way by his master Winfield Parks to protect some skin medicine the vet had applied.

Winfield Parks, Jr., 6/2/58

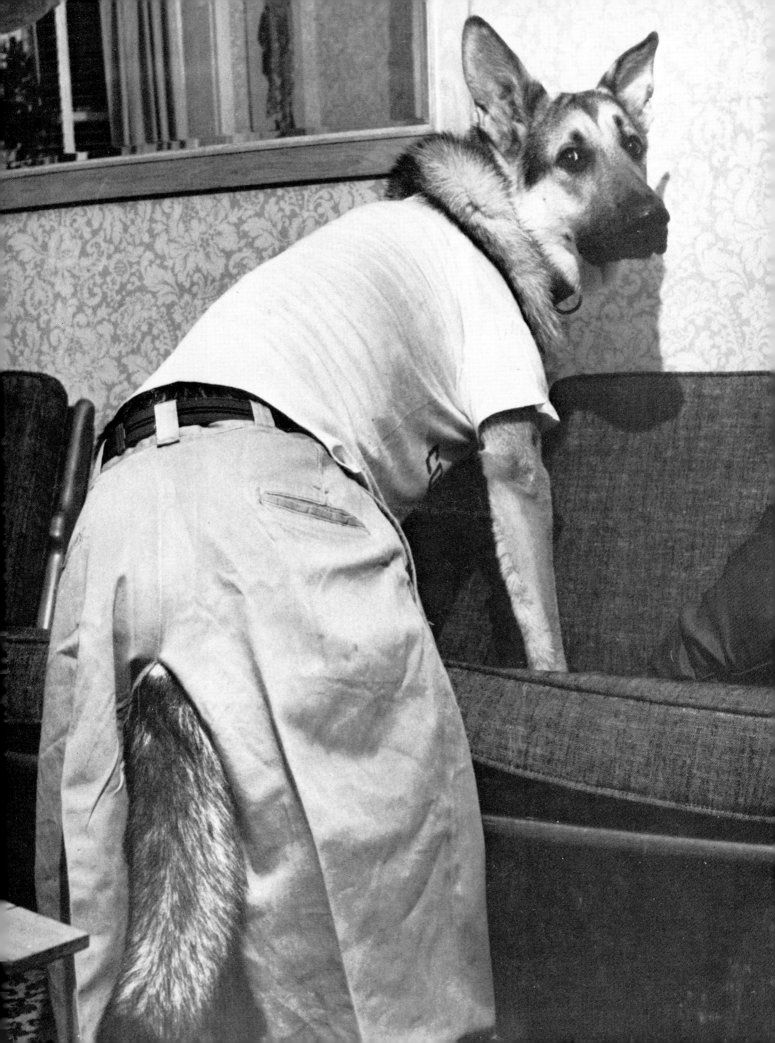

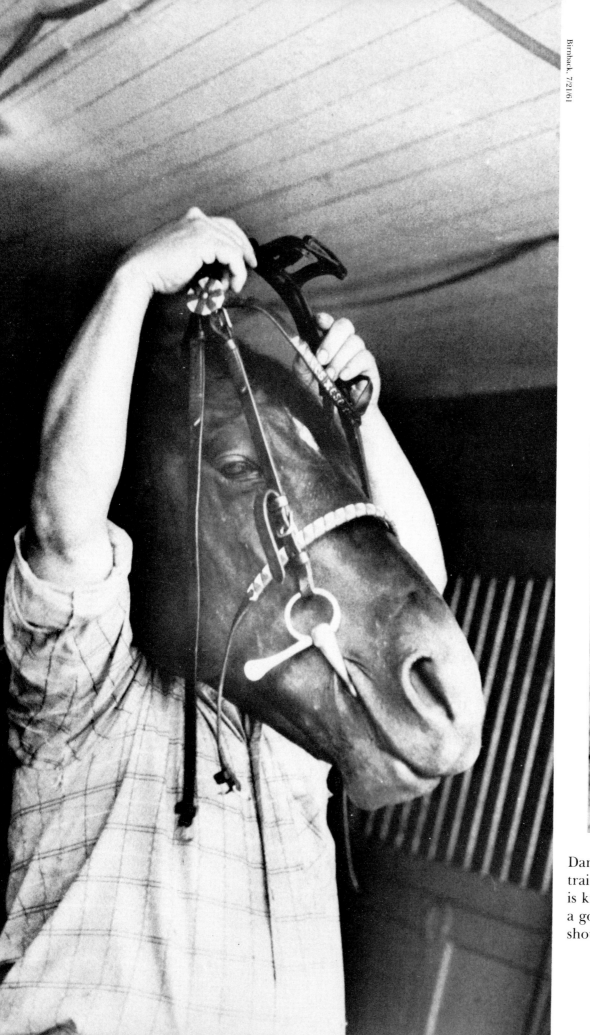

Danish racetrack
trainer Leif Neilson
is known for having
a good head on his
shoulders.

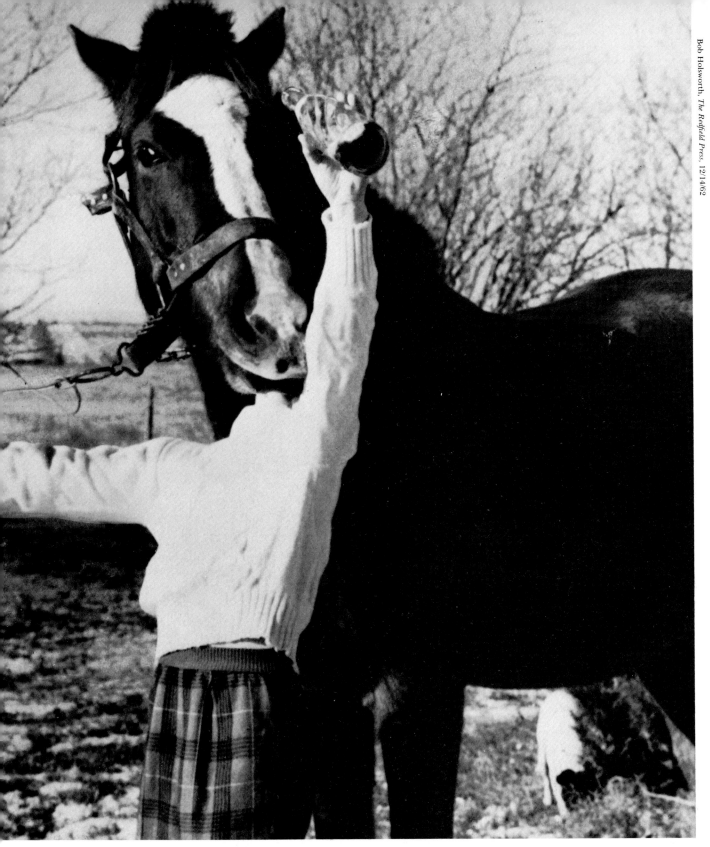

Bob Holsworth, *The Redfield Press*, 12/14/62

South Dakota's Mary Jo Sherman is known for her horse sense—which obviously has temporarily deserted her.

Just Horsing Around

Robert Landry, 6/29/59

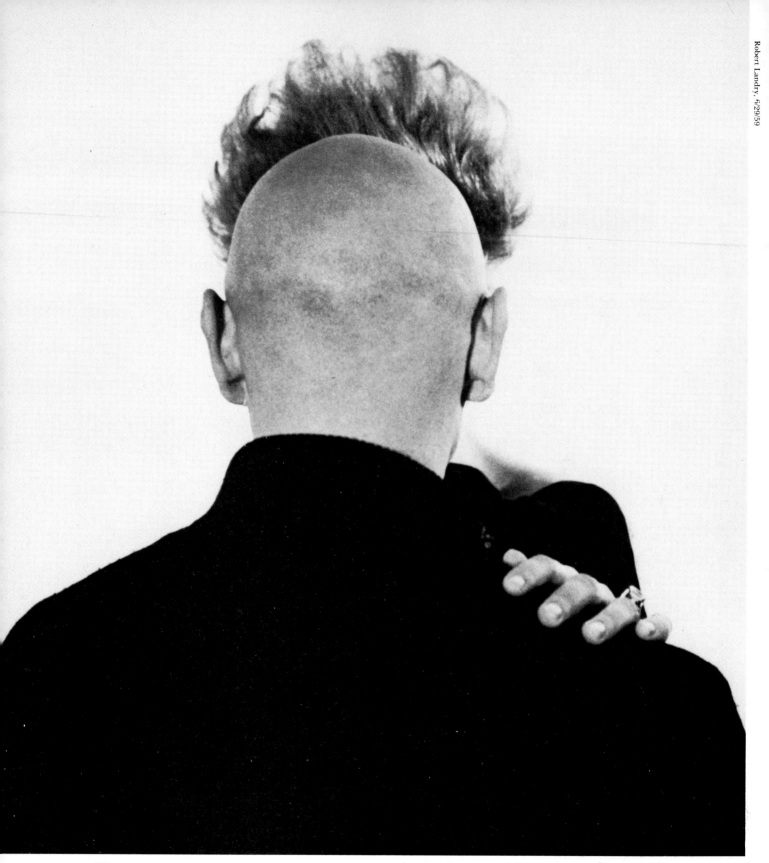

All Ears

Hairless actor Yul Brynner gets a fringe benefit during a movie kiss with actress Kay Kendall.

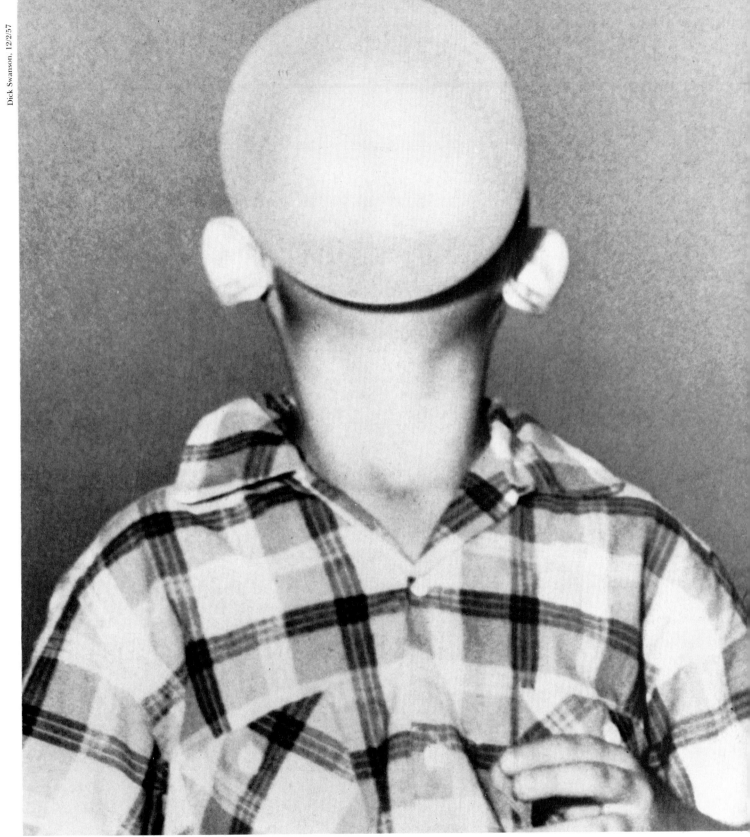

Every time seven-year-old Steve Wessels wins
a bubble-blowing contest he loses face.

Playing Peekaboo

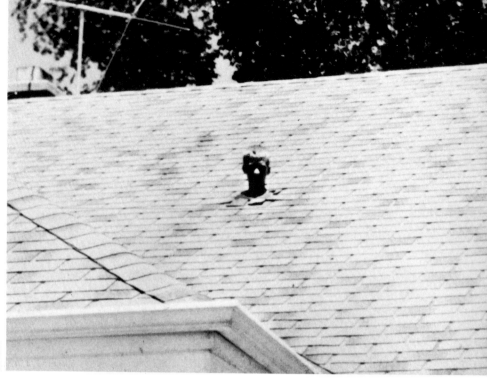

10/12/59

Twelve-year-old Mark Walsh pops through a hole in the roof of his house, proving that growing boys need head room.

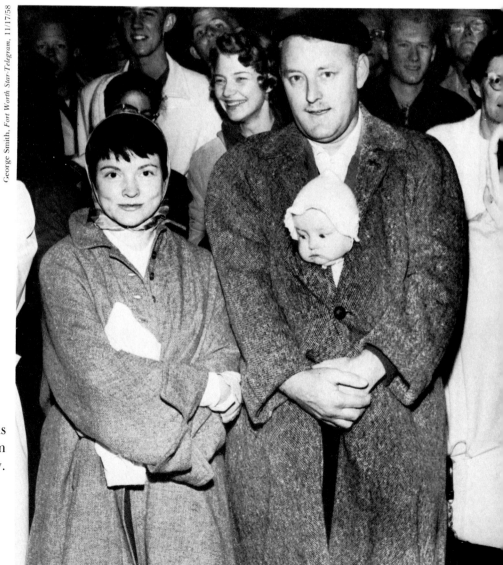

George Smith, *Fort Worth Star-Telegram*, 11/17/58

Six-month-old Olivia Duke peeks from her papa-pouch, a warm spot to watch the pep rally.

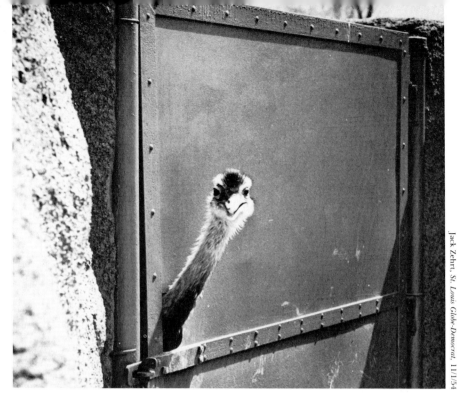

Jack Zehrt, *St. Louis Globe-Democrat*, 11/1/54

A happy rhea has found a latch hole in a door at the St. Louis Zoo, all the better to spy on the kangaroos.

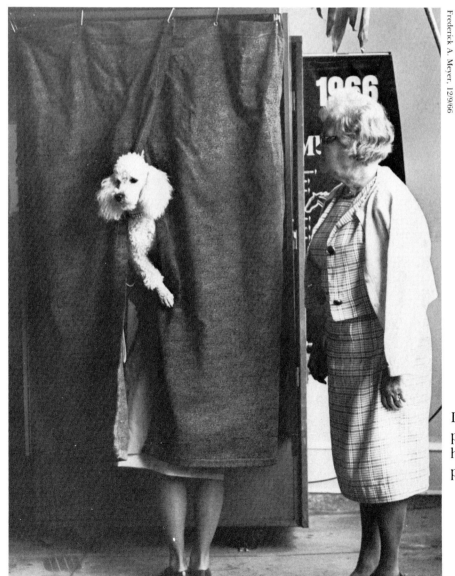

Frederick A. Meyer, 12/9/66

Is this an infraction? wonders a poll watcher as Pierre pokes his head out from the democratic process.

83

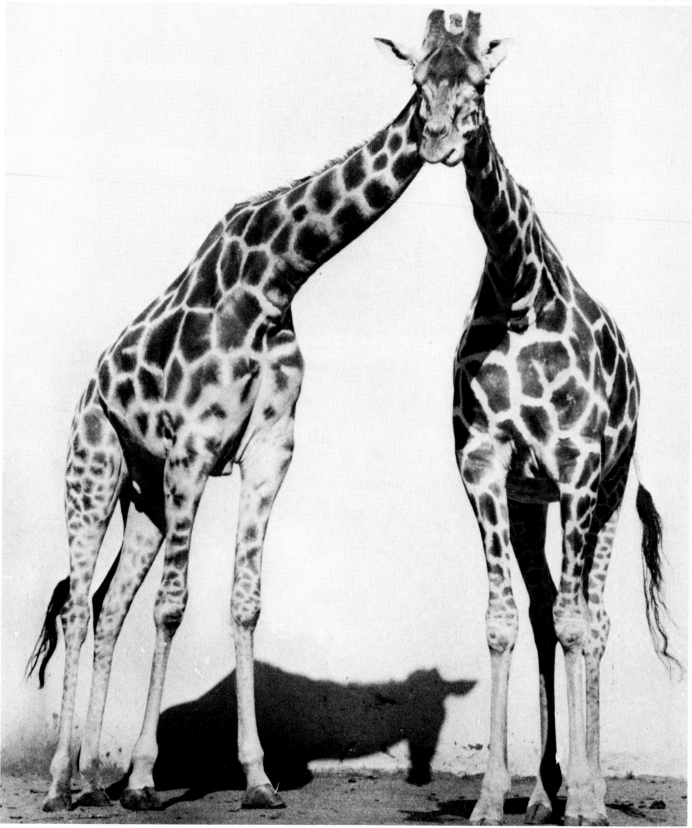

One Head Is Better Than None

Eight legs, two necks, one face. It all goes to prove that even in the lofty world of giraffes the shy male doesn't want to stick his neck out.

84

Joe Rudis, *Nashville Tennessean*, 10/13/61

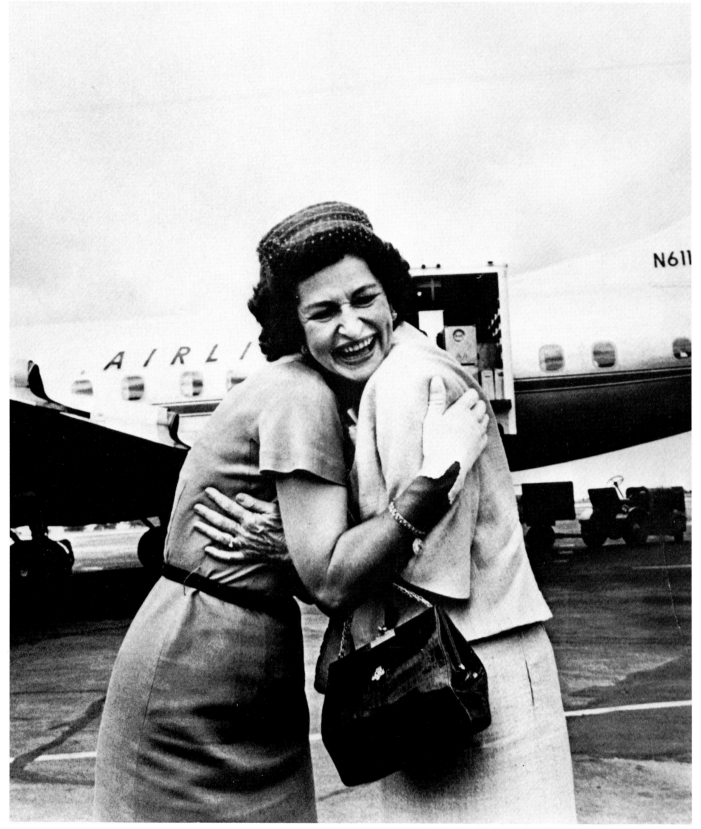

Sometimes "Lady Bird" Johnson has no trouble sticking her neck out. Here she presides over the decapitation of Mrs. Buford Ellington, wife of Tennessee's governor.

Seeing Double

When heads and tails are
interchangeable, the coin's rigged—
and so is the rhino.

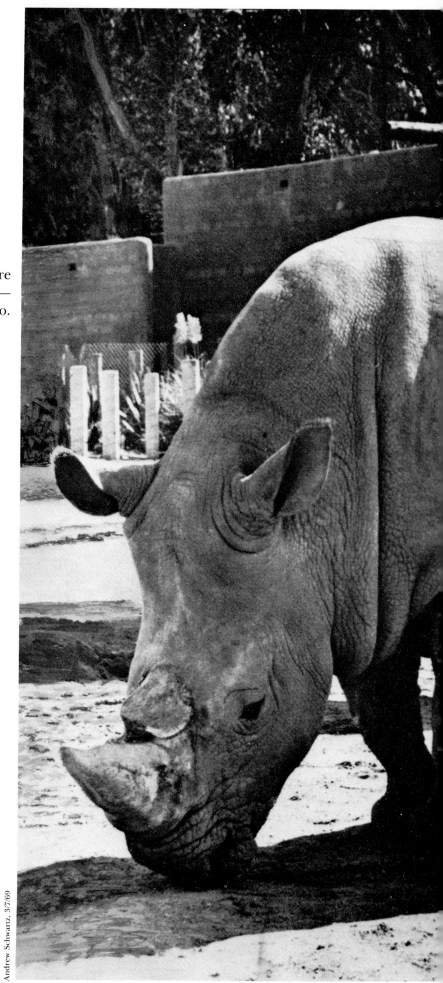

Andrew Schwartz, 3/7/69

86

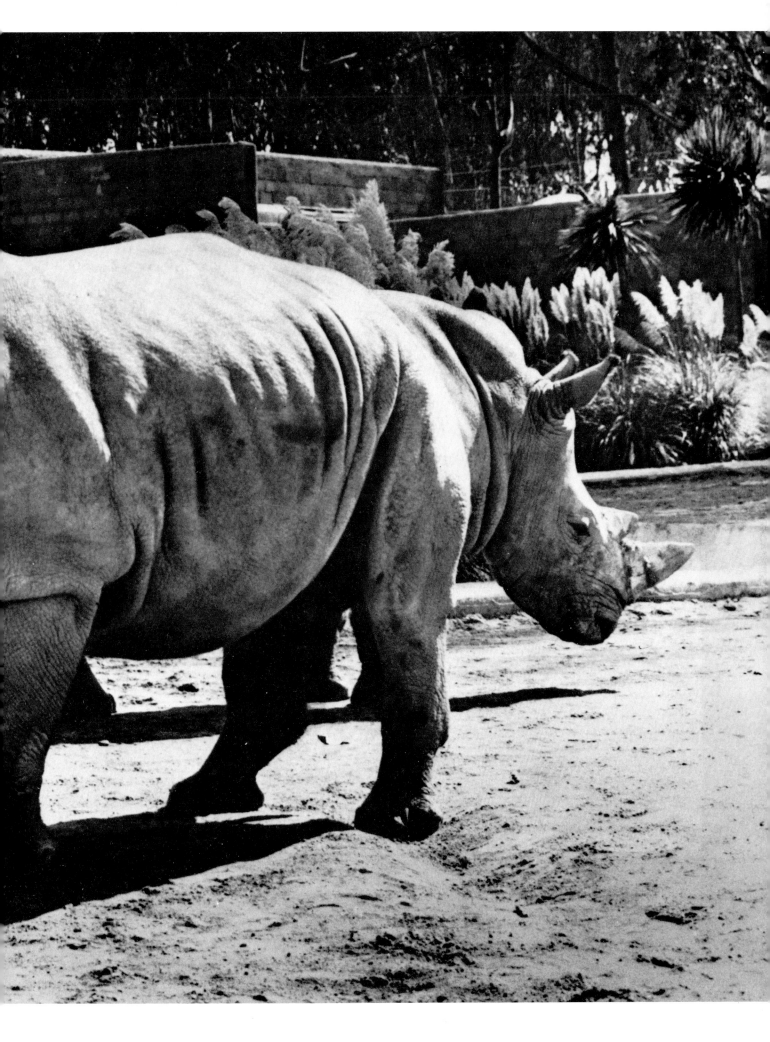

Larry Mulvehill, 5/3/63

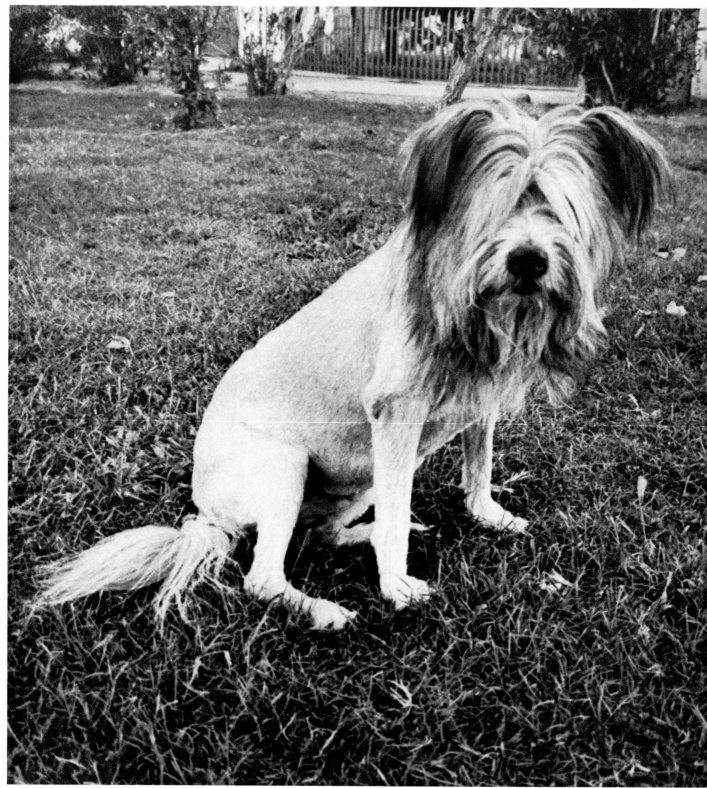

Questionable Coifs

This little fellow looks as if he needs a little less hair of the dog.

Cesco Ciapanna, 8/9/63

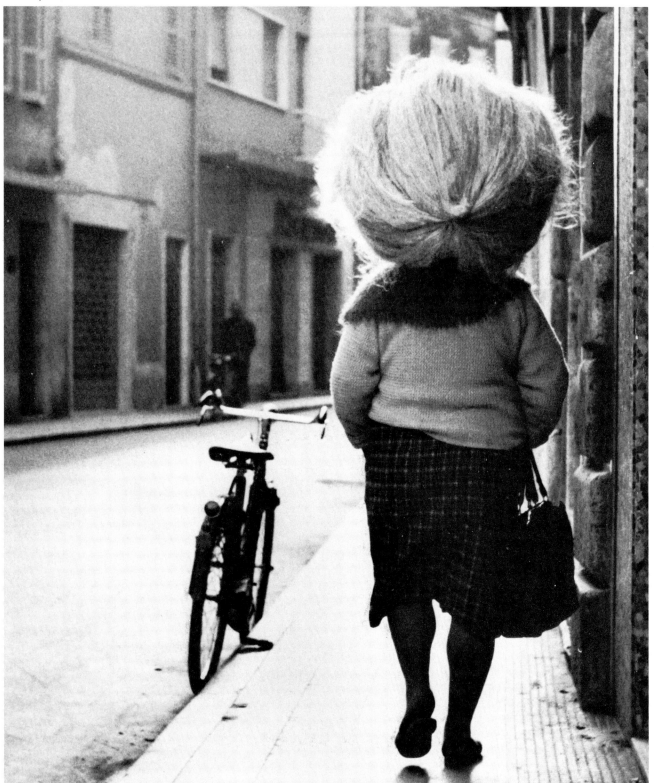

Teased hair is one thing, harassed hair another. Balancing a bundle of hemp gives you this stylish Italian look, too.

Losing Your Head

A soccer head shot in Montevideo exceeds all expectations.

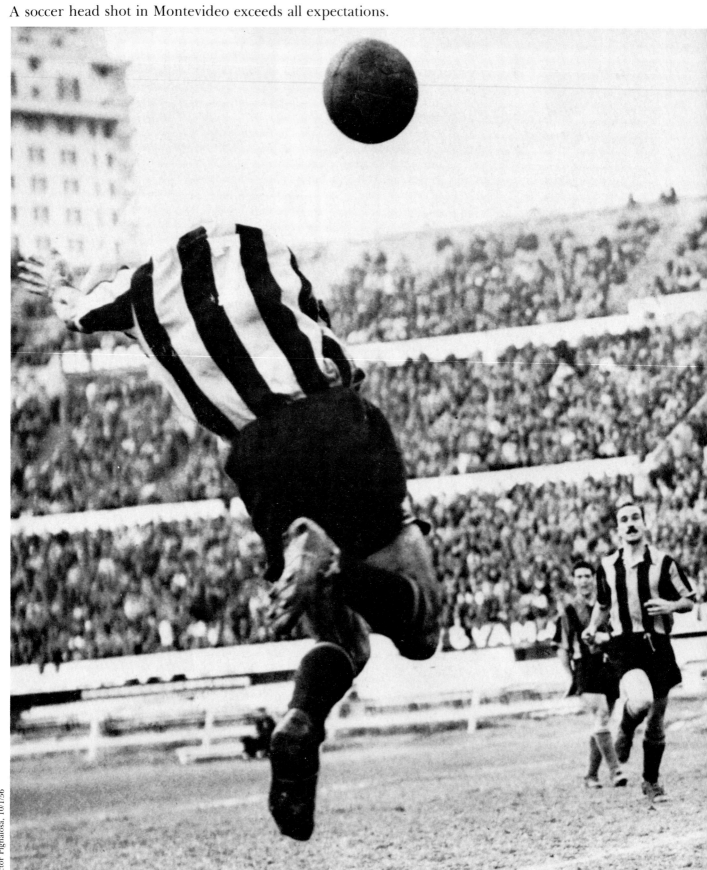

Hector Pignalosa, 10/1/56

A workman in Copenhagen creates the illusion that he is reaching for his fallen head, with the assistance of a cohort and the hole they are digging.

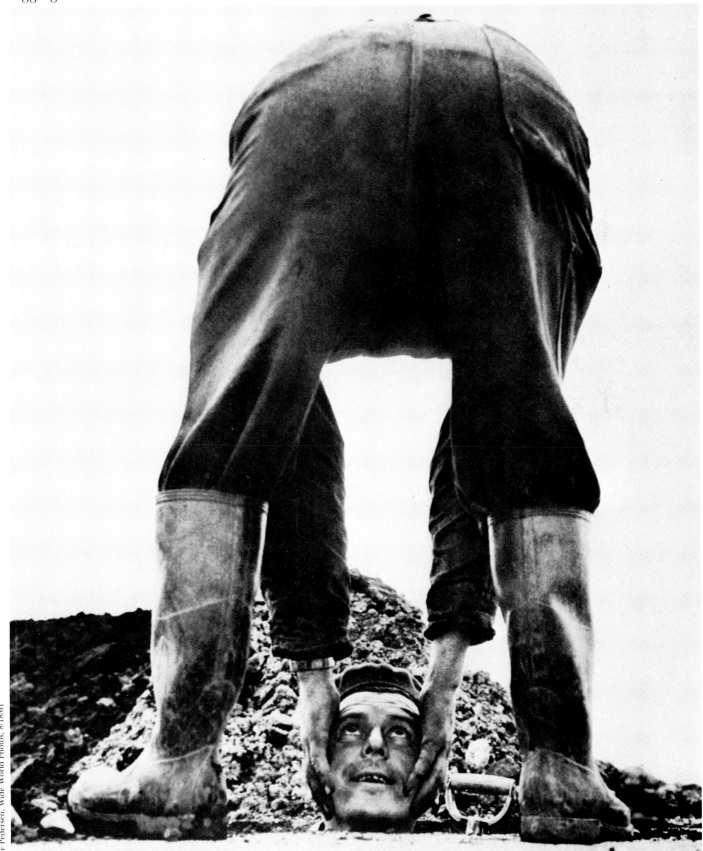

Peer Pedersen, Wide World Photos, 8/18/61

Tails in Trouble

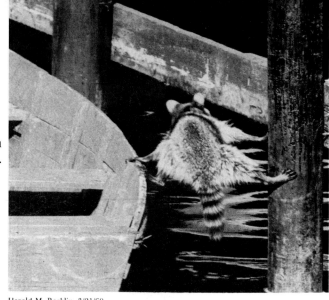

The moment of truth for a Florida raccoon.

Harold M. Becklin, 3/21/60

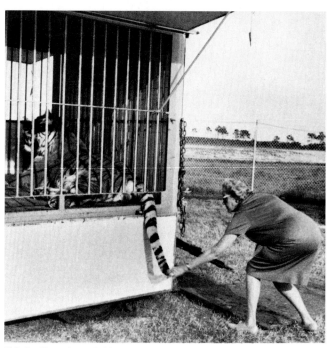

Sneaking up on a tiger cage in Sarasota, Ruth Singer assumes the pull position.

Dixie Cavalier Kudner, 4/21/67

John W. Ahlhauser, 7/29/66

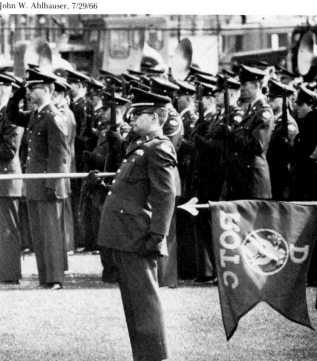

D Company of Marquette University's ROTC unit has a point.

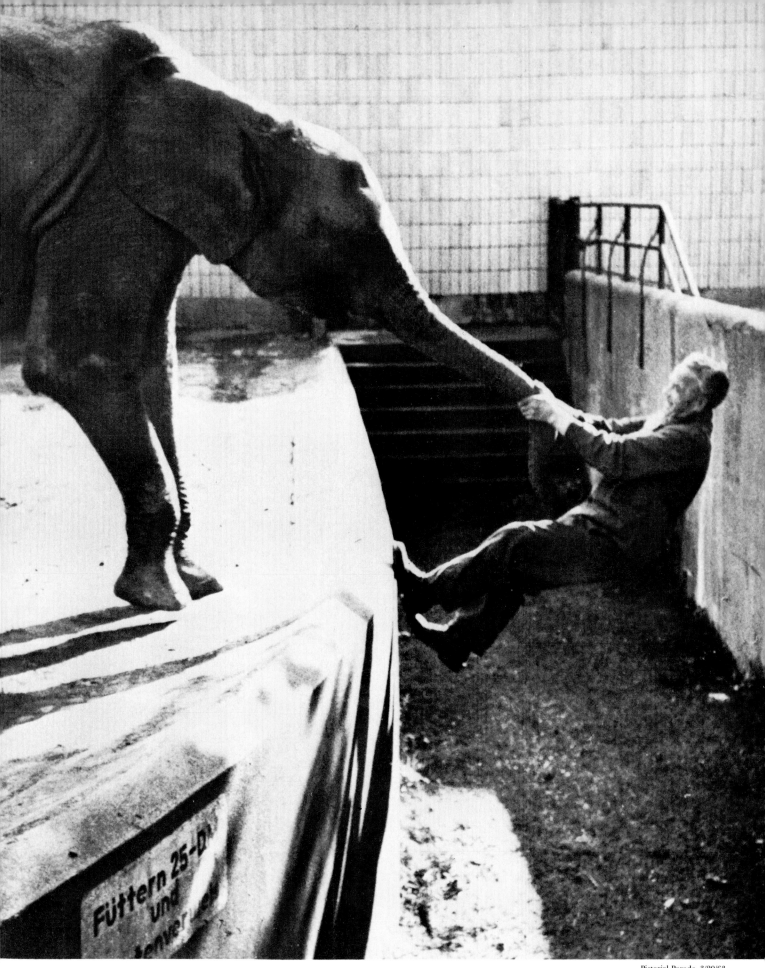

If the rescue line sneezes, Franz Eck will
be in for a one-point landing.

Pictorial Parade, 3/29/63

Weapon and Target

Beware of a soapy tail when shining up a cow for a fair.

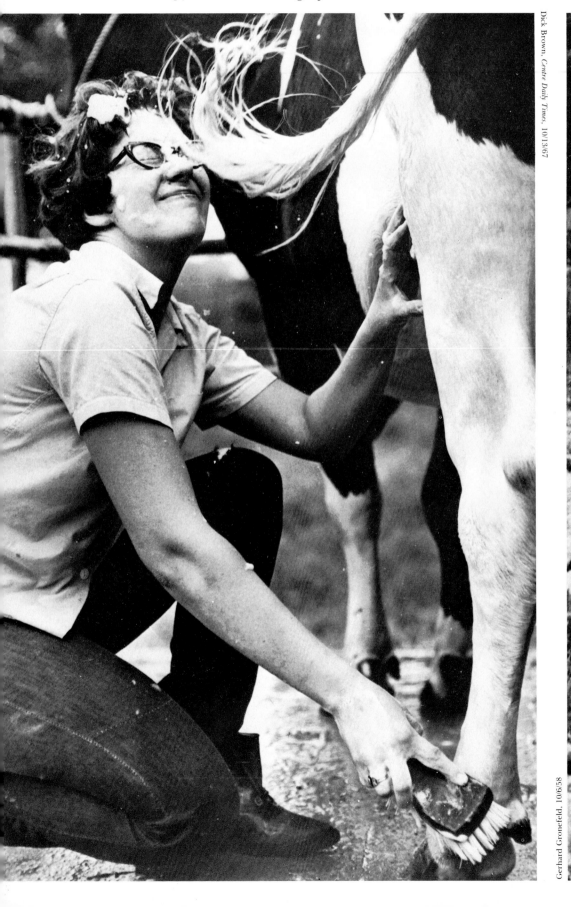

Dick Brown, *Centre Daily Times*, 10/13/67

Gerhard Gronefeld, 10/6/58

Hightail it out of there when bared molars approach.

Bettmann/UPI, 3/9/59

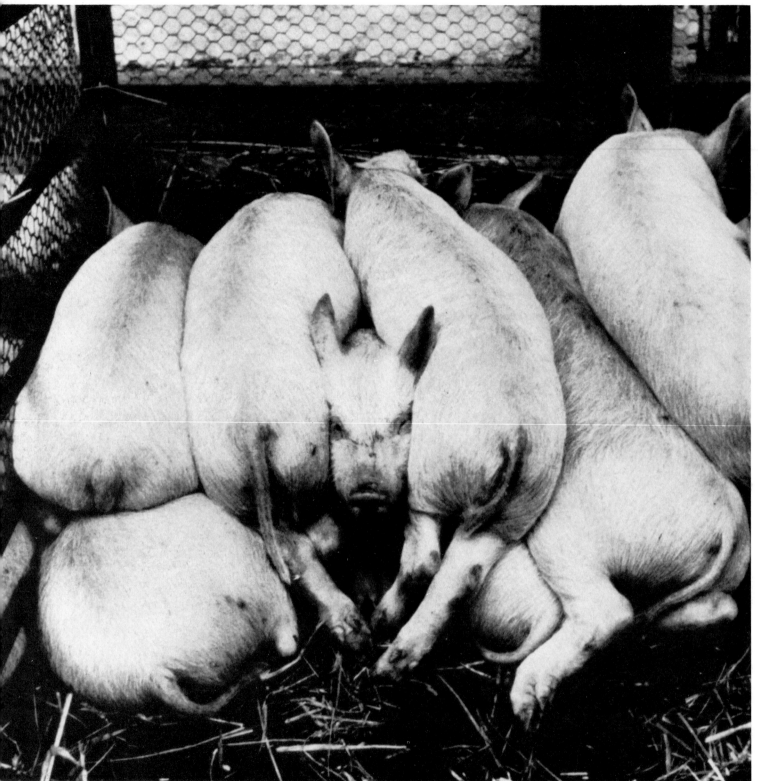

A Couple of Losers

Head-on portrait of a tight squeeze in Surrey, England.

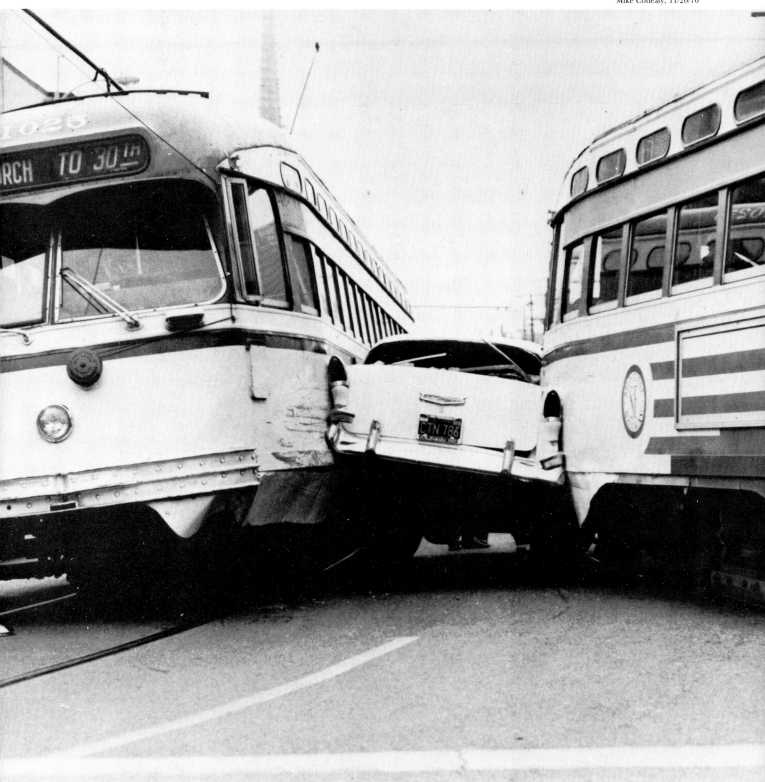

Tail-end portrait of a tighter squeeze in San Francisco.

CHAPTER 6

explores some themes found in

A DAY'S WORK

All Hands at Lunch

When he returns, the operator of this pneumatic drill can slip his pinkies right back into the hardened leather and hit the juice.

New York Herald Tribune, 9/27/54

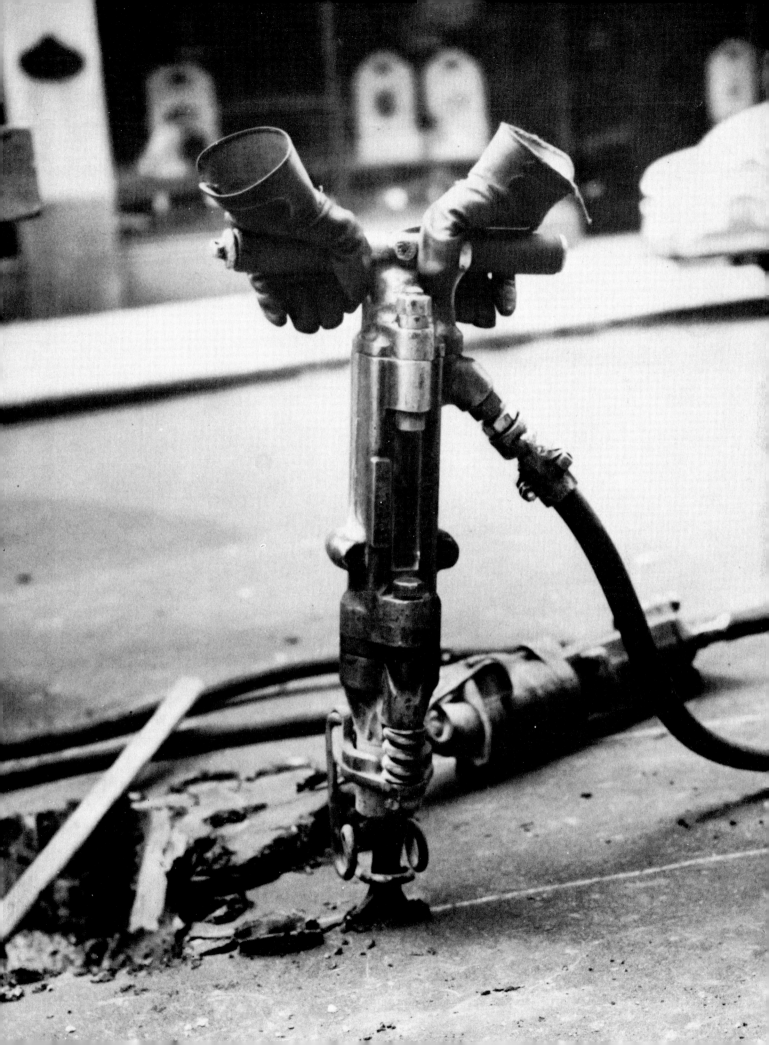

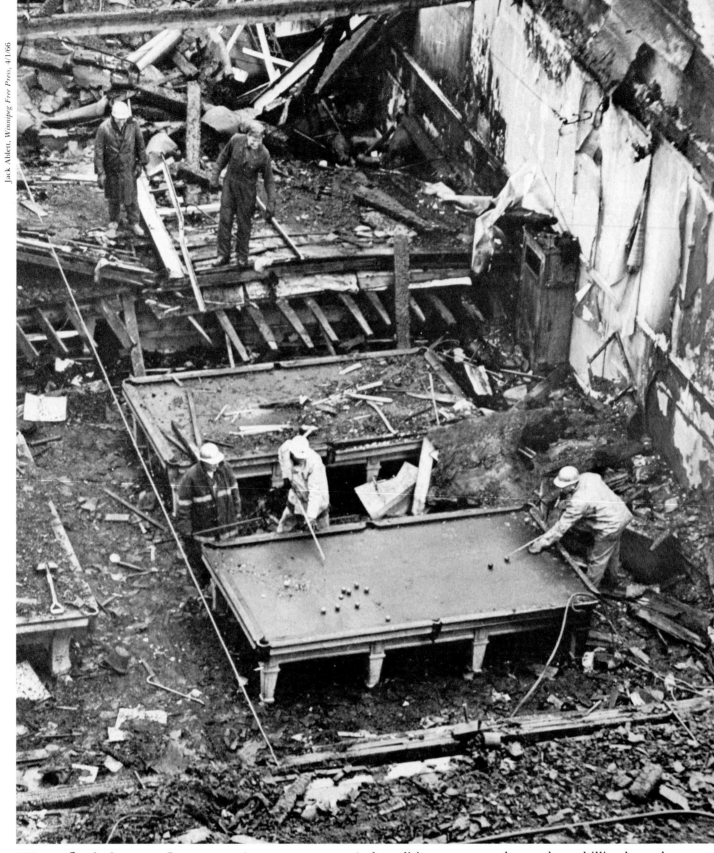

Jack Ablett, Winnipeg Free Press, 4/1/66

Exploiting the Ruins

A demolition crew at a burned-out billiards parlor
spots an intact table and takes the cue.

Dennis Rowedder, 11/23/59

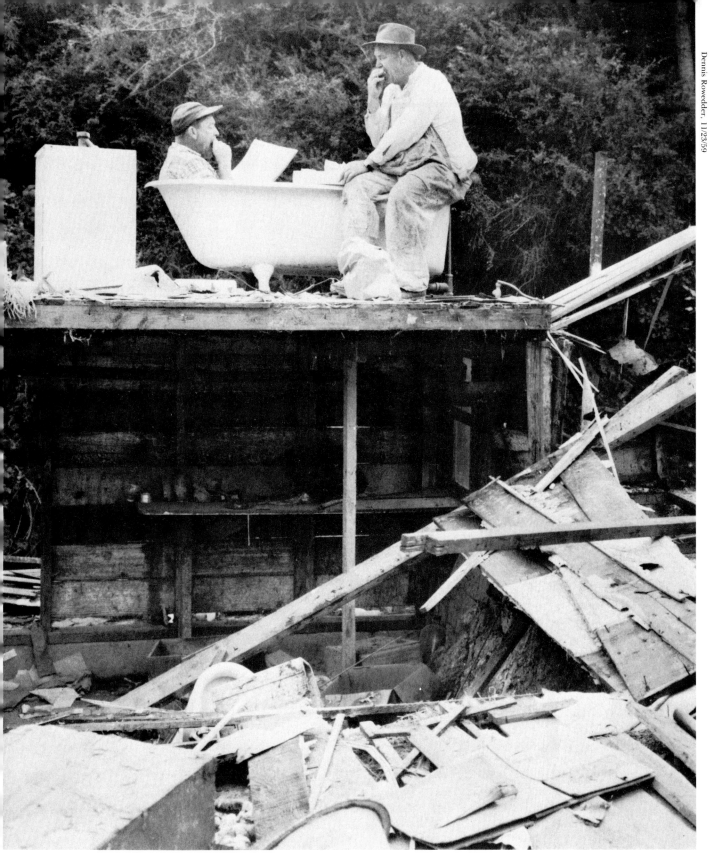

Good reason why these wreckers left the bathtub till last.

Here's Mud in Your Eye

Breaking ground for a new clubhouse at a California golf club, participating officials call a spade a spade.

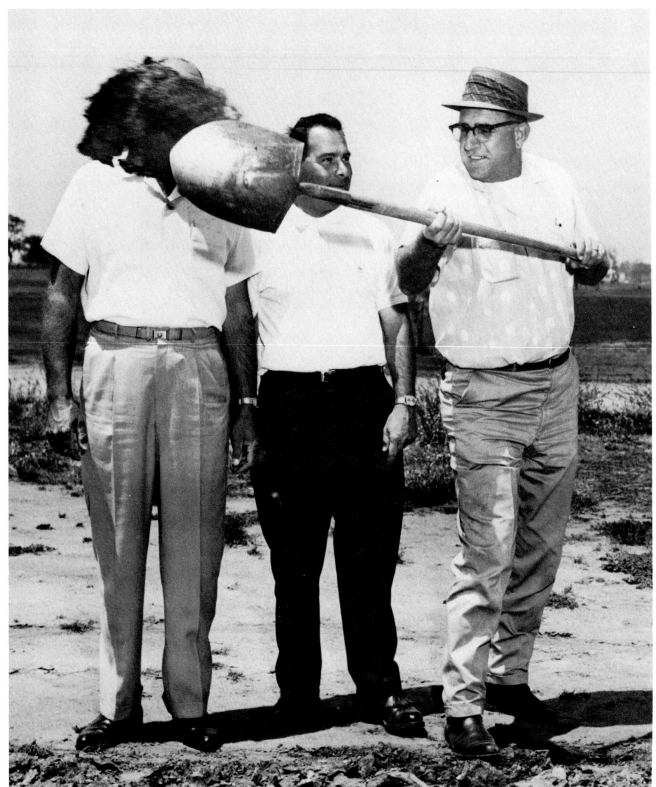

Leonard Covello, 8/13/65

Philip Halpern of Springfield, Pennsylvania, tries to turn the other cheek.

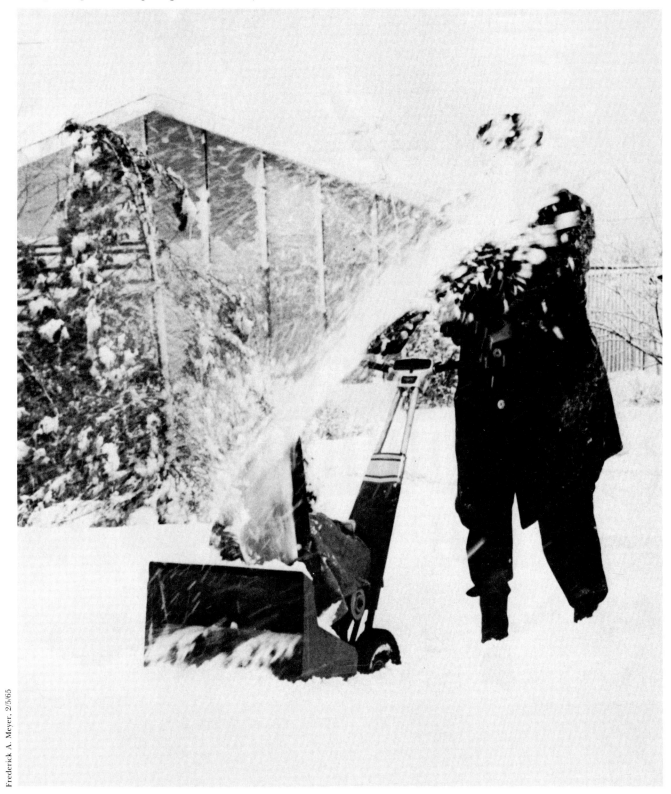

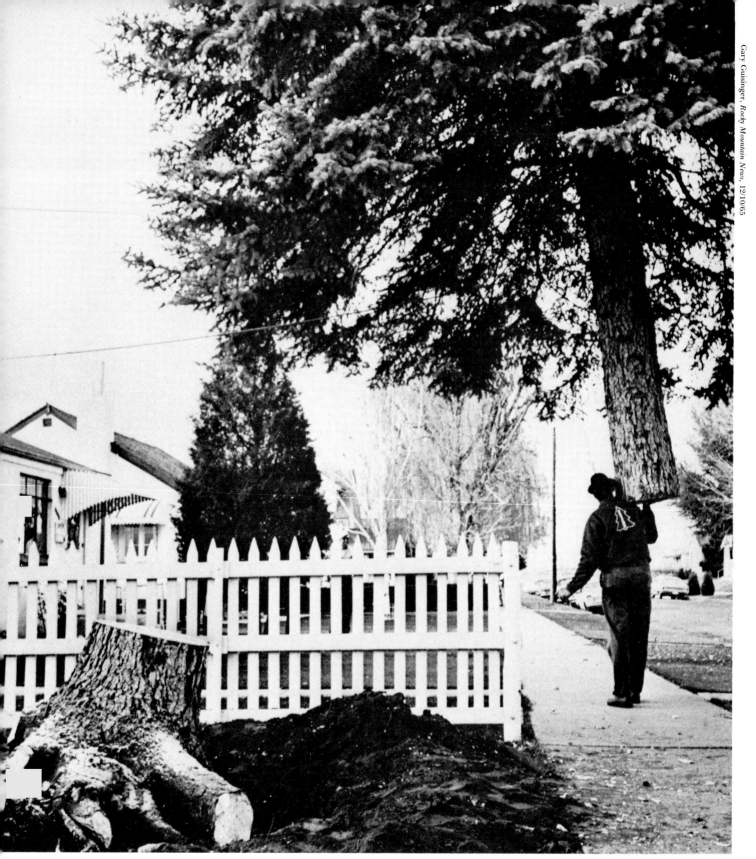

Gary Guisinger, *Rocky Mountain News*, 12/10/65

Sprucing Up

Ray Keesen of Denver hefts a 3½-ton tree he has just cut. An out-of-sight crane is helping a little.

Francis Stoppelman, 9/20/68

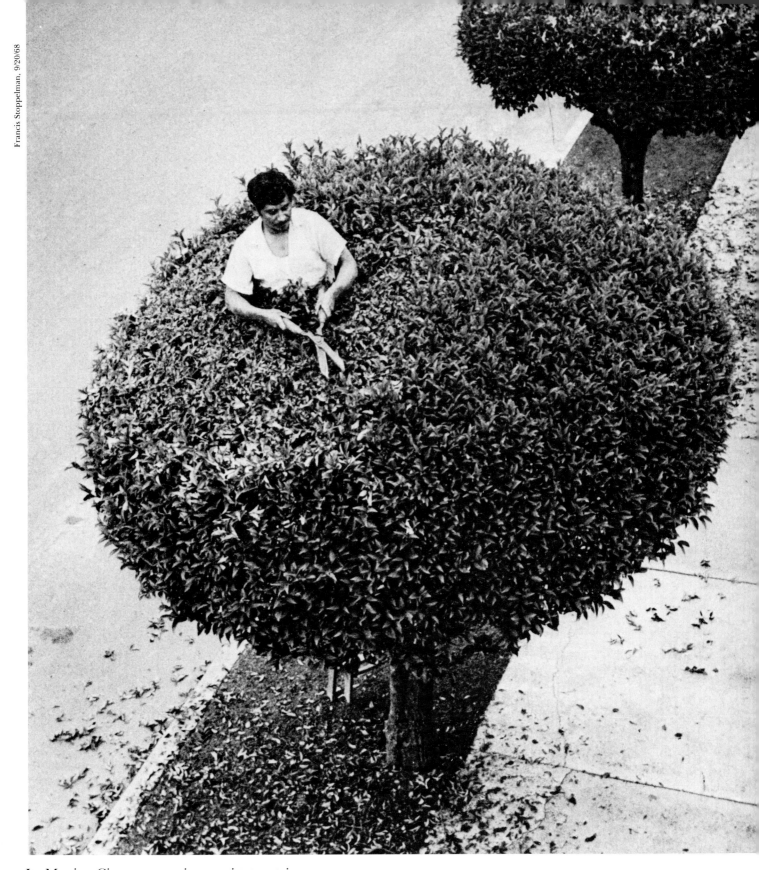

In Mexico City, a tree trimmer in top trim.

Danger from the Rear

How does that grab you?

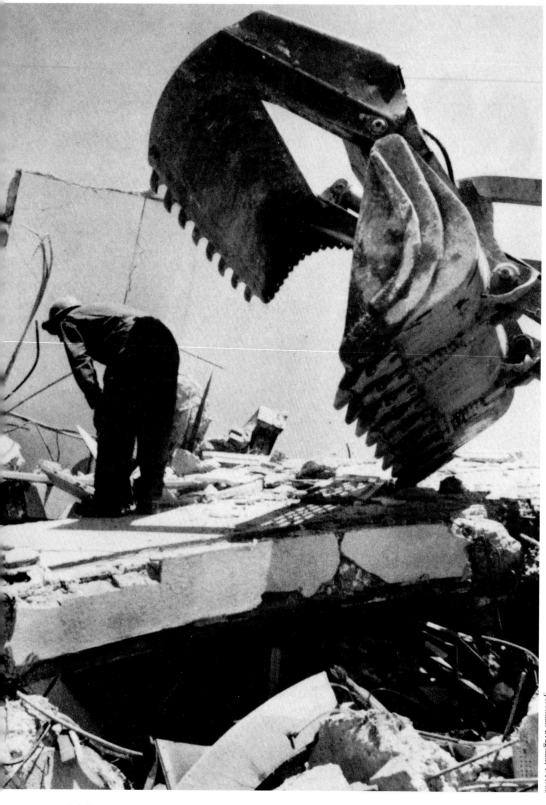

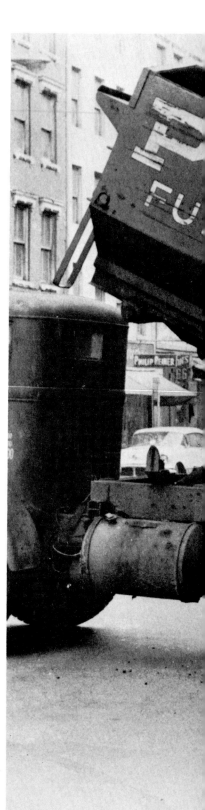

Jeremiah Bragstad, 1/17/69

Michael Gold, 9/29/67

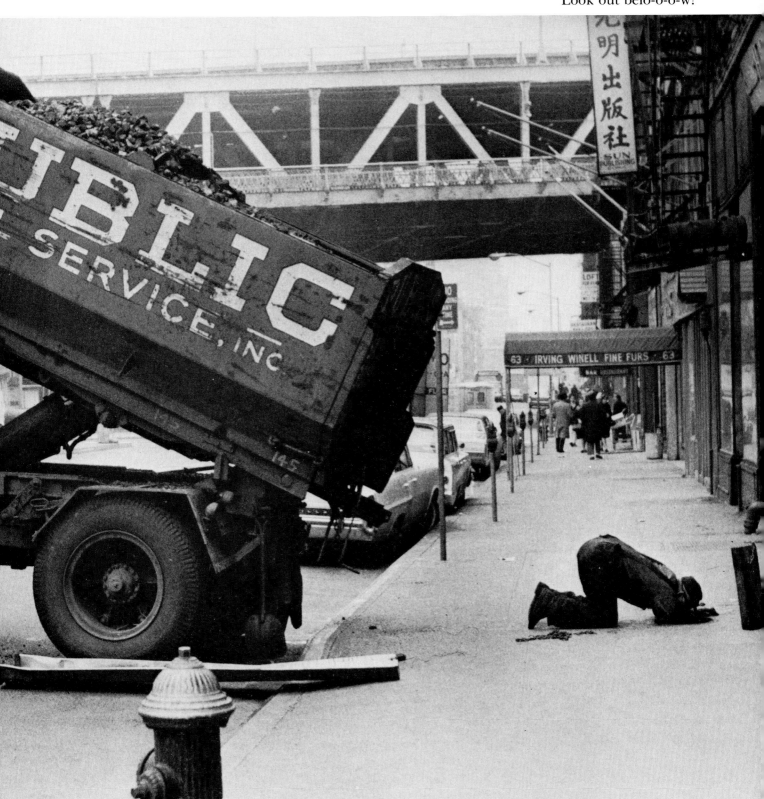

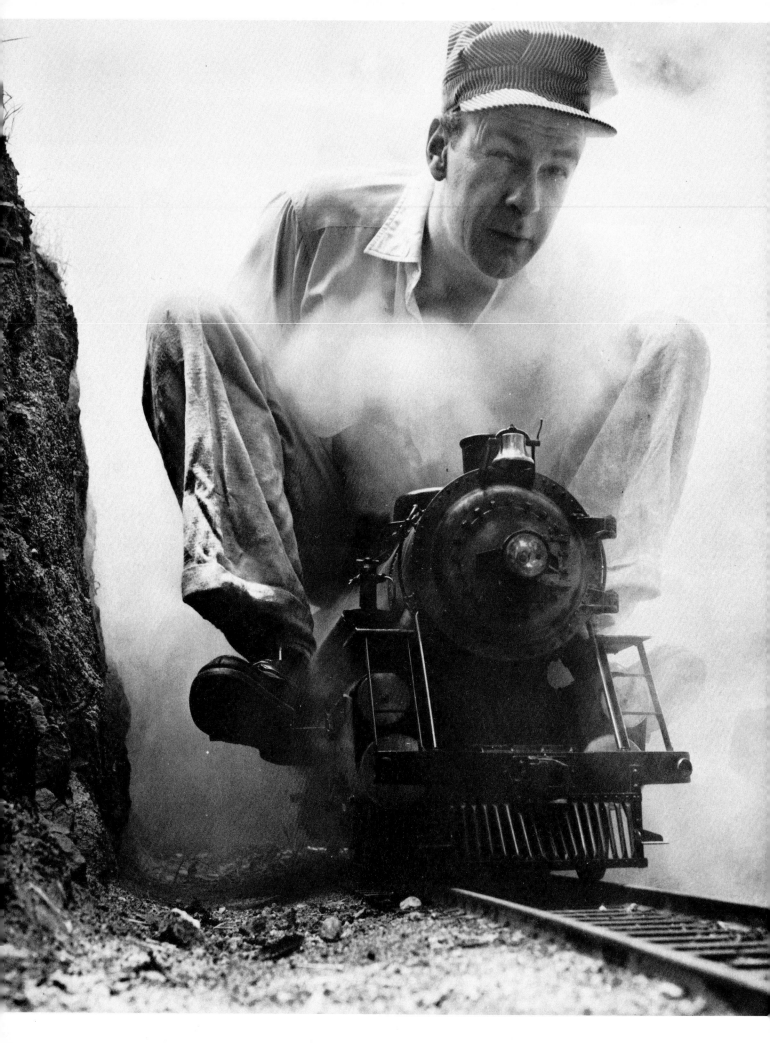

Rail-Splitters

Giant engineer Ollie Johnston
and his midget engine.

What a spot
to put a pole!

The engine that never could make up its mind.

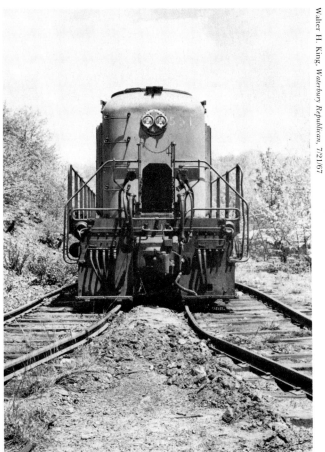

Richard Hartt, 8/1/62

Walter H. King, *Waterbury Republican*, 7/21/67

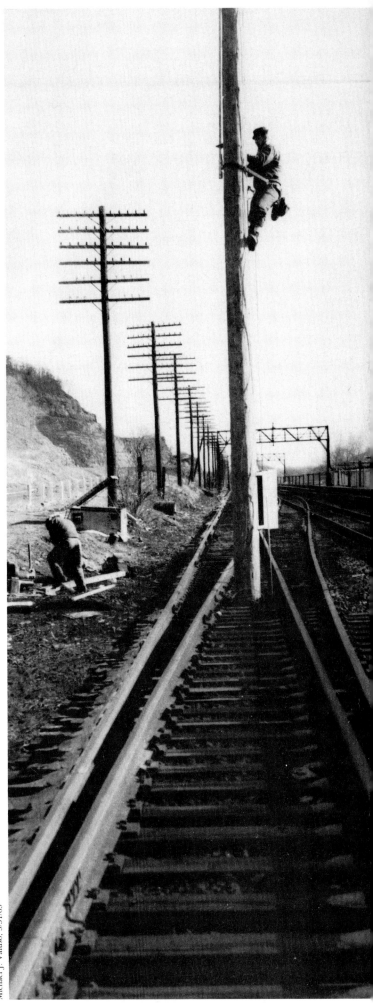

Michael J. Vaiuso, 5/31/63

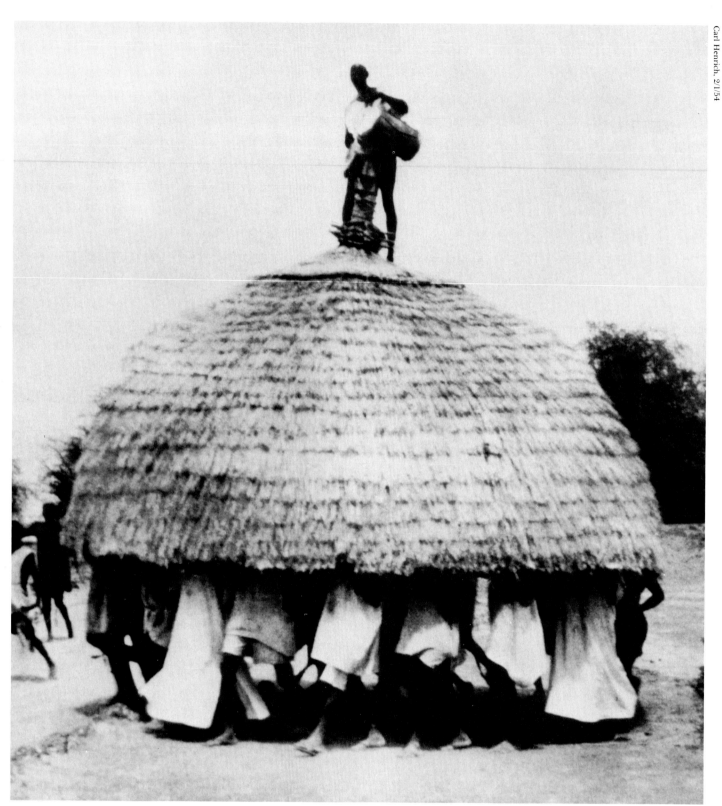

Moving Day

In Nigeria, relocating is done by the neighbors.

Bill Homan, 4/21/58

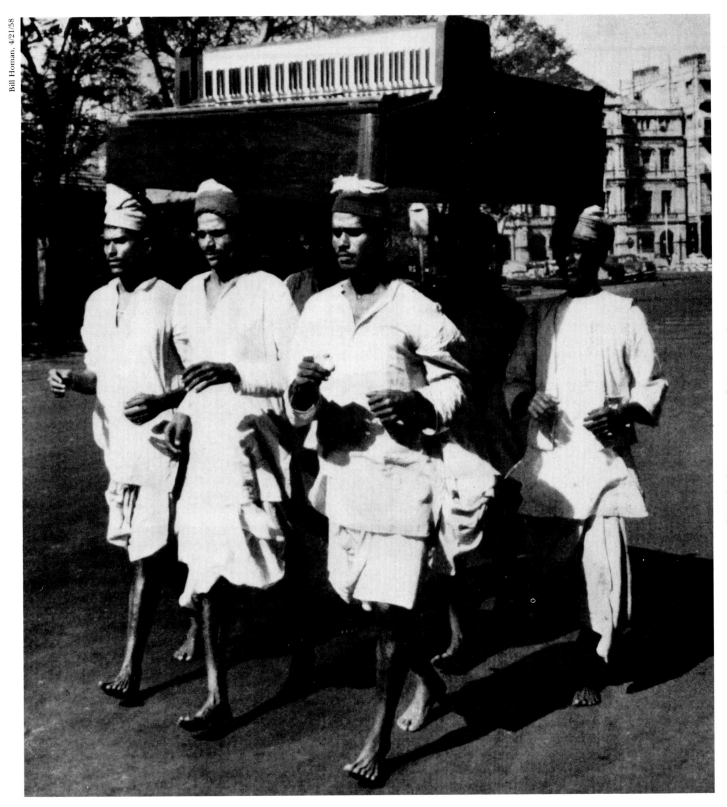

In Bombay, delivery men demonstrate an easy way to carry a tune.

Sleight of Hand

Keystone, 2/3/67

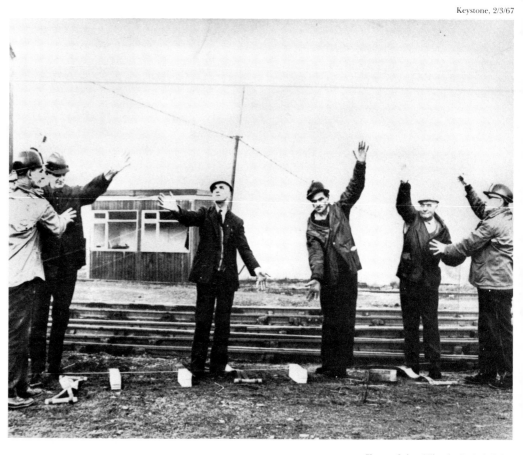

All these guys are doing something transparent—they're carrying glass.

Clarence Leino, *Milwaukee Sentinel*, 8/4/58

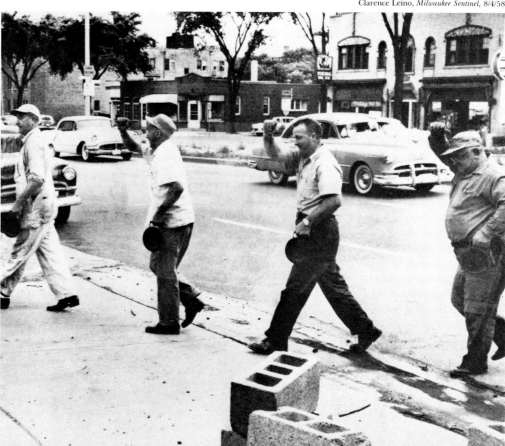

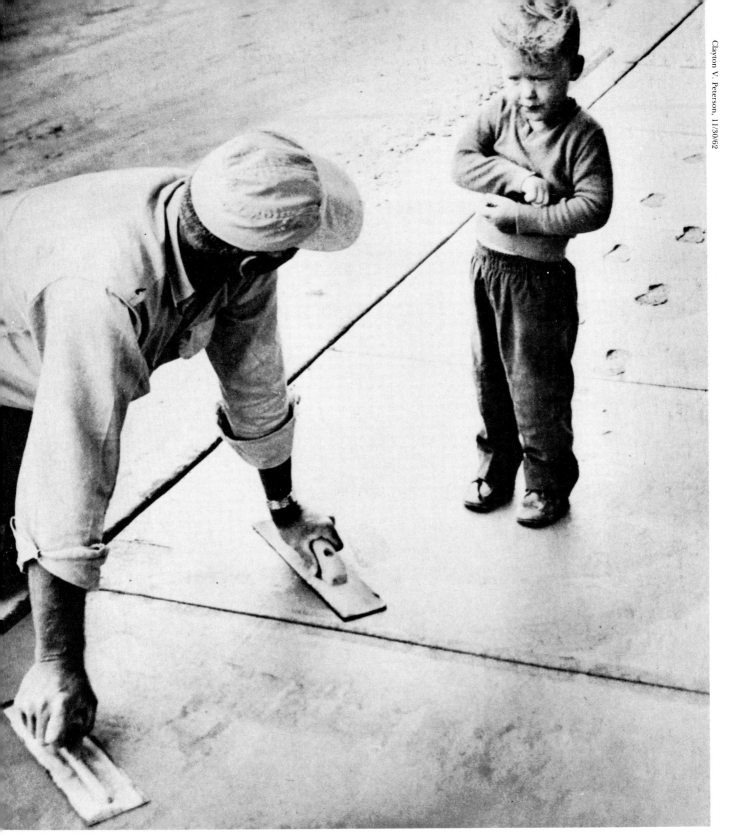

Clayton V. Peterson, 11/30/62

and Plight of Foot

Three-year-old Grant Angove of Salinas, California, doesn't know why mason Hugh Myers is gnashing his teeth.

CHAPTER 7
is
FOR THE BIRDS

OK Now, Watch the Baby!

In New York City,
Danny Fry's parakeet
poses for his picture.

Ilsa Hofman, 3/17/58

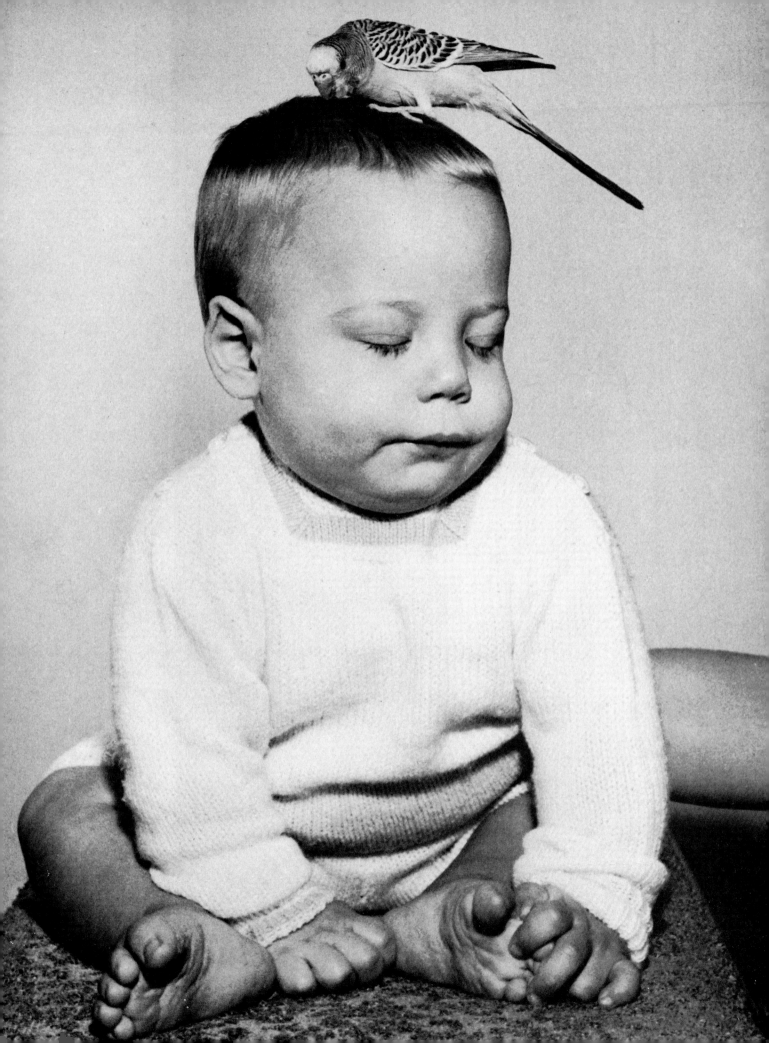

Handy Beaks

In Huntsville, Alabama, a jay named Blue Brummell has a smoke, a nasty habit he picked up at Thomas Dilworth's house, but Mrs. Dilworth swears B. B. never inhales.

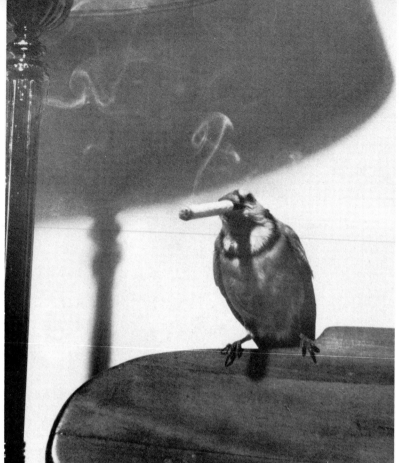

Joyce Jones, 12/8/52

This Amazon parrot named Captain Hook likes to sip rum butter from a spoon while keeping Charles Godsal company in their London house.

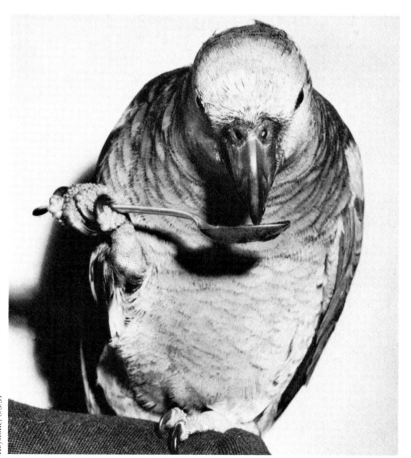

Keystone, 8/5/57

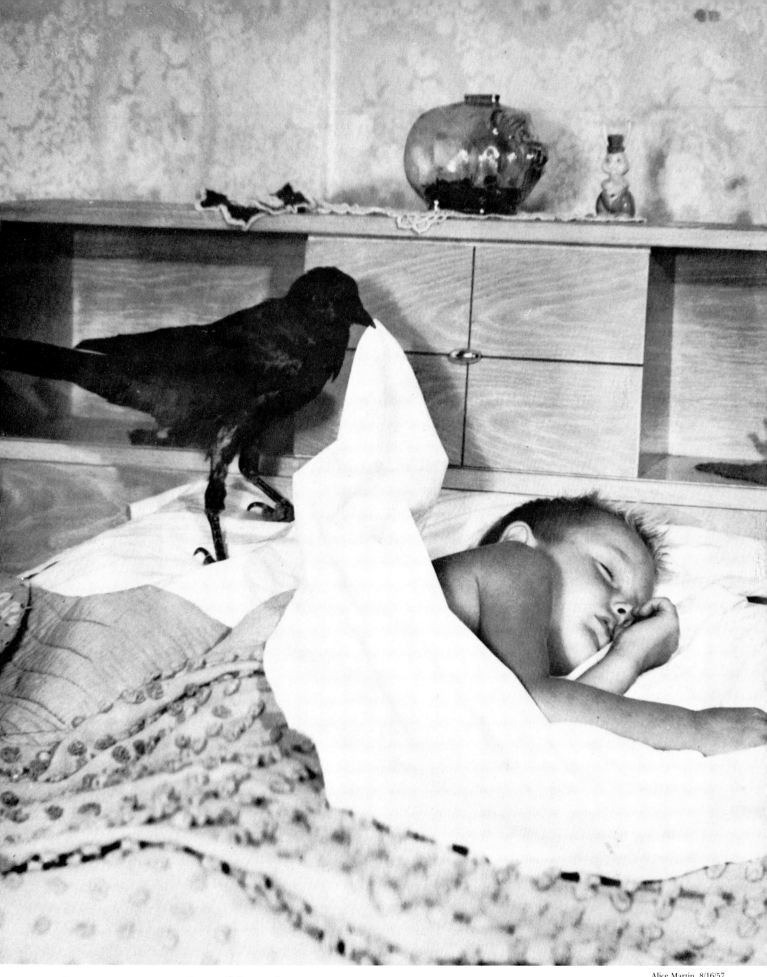

Each morning with a piece of fancy beakwork Jim, a crow,
wakes up Linnual, a child, at the Denton home in Post, Texas.

Alice Martin, 8/16/57

Wide World Photos. 12/8/72

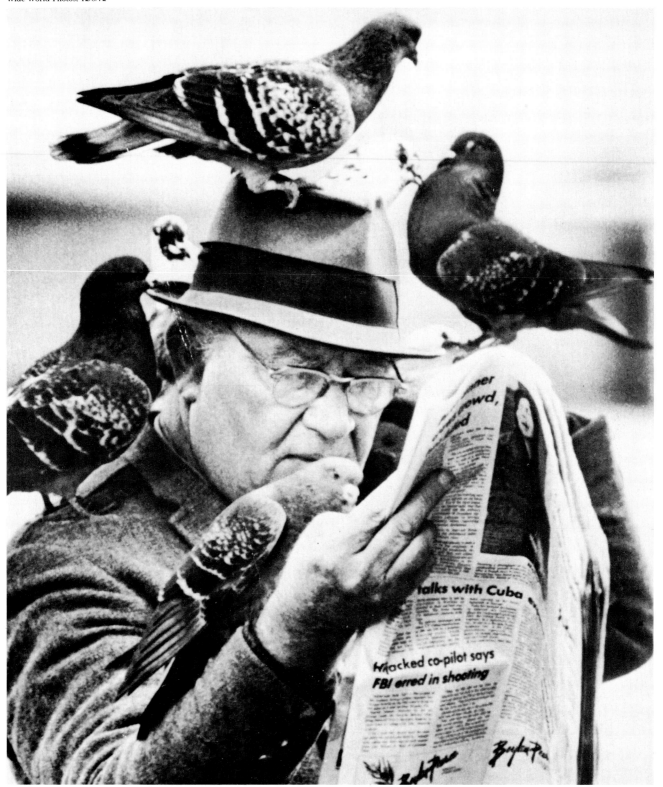

Birds of a Feather

Peanut vendor Jesse Broyles of Raleigh, North Carolina, thinks his flock of pigeons is a feather in his cap.

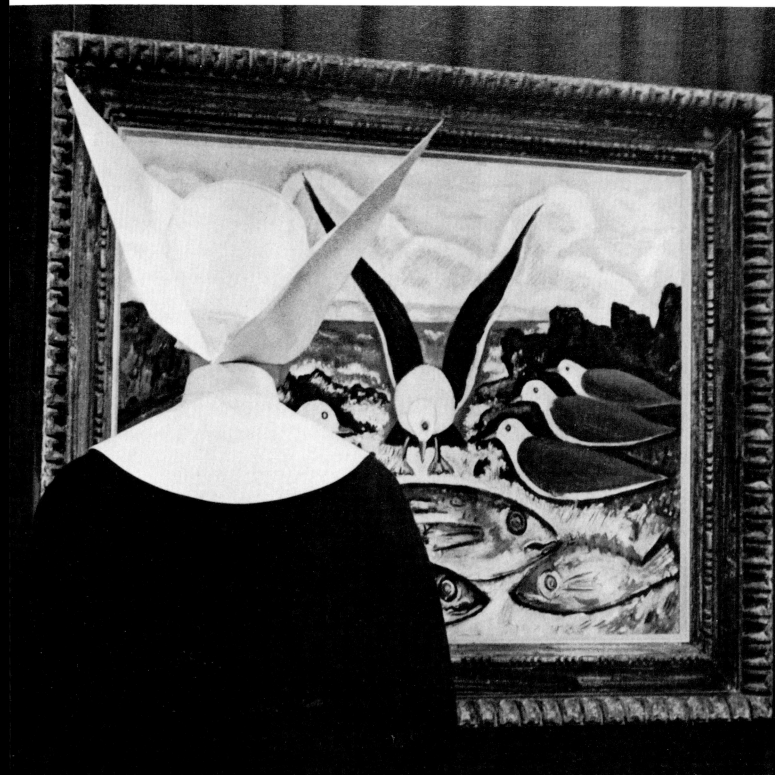

For some reason this Sister of Charity in Waterville,
Maine, is drawn to a painting of a seagull taking wing.

Eyes Front!

At a V-E Day celebration at Bourges, France, Private First Class
Fouldeau presents arms and incidentally presents a pigeon, too.

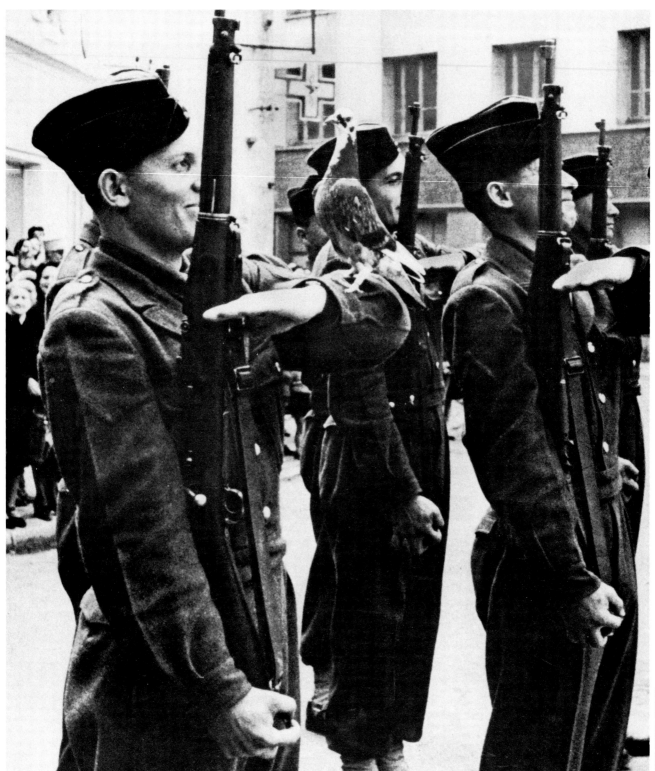

Bernard Hilbert, 6/8/53

120

At Annapolis graduation, as midshipmen stand at rigid attention, a starling presses Peter Hughes's shoulder into service.

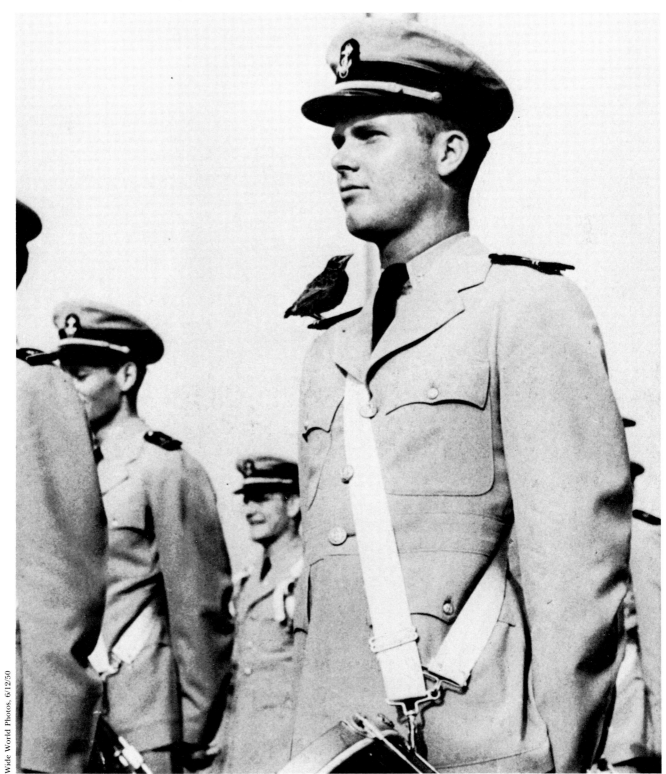

Wide World Photos, 6/12/50

Air Defense

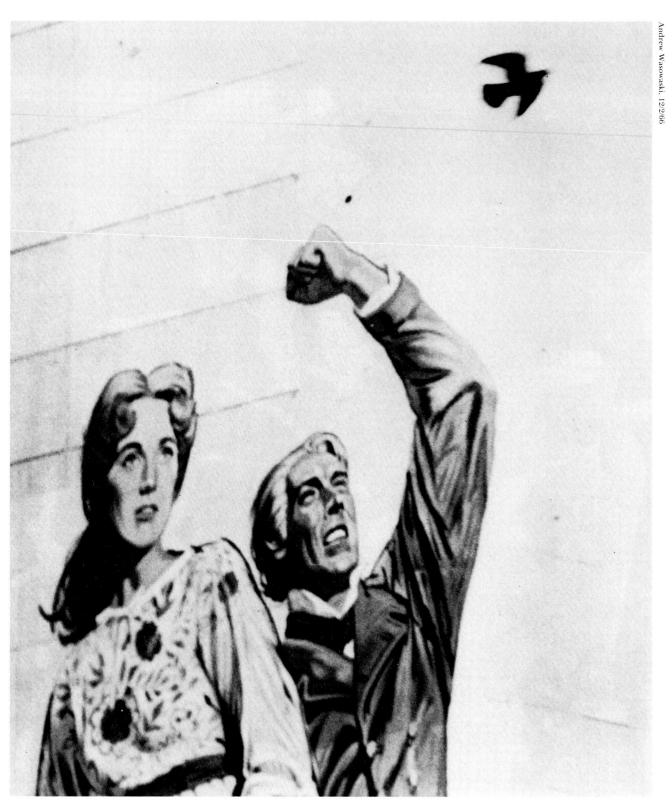

Andrew Wasowski, 12/2/66

A Times Square pigeon beats a fast retreat from a movie poster's angry fist.

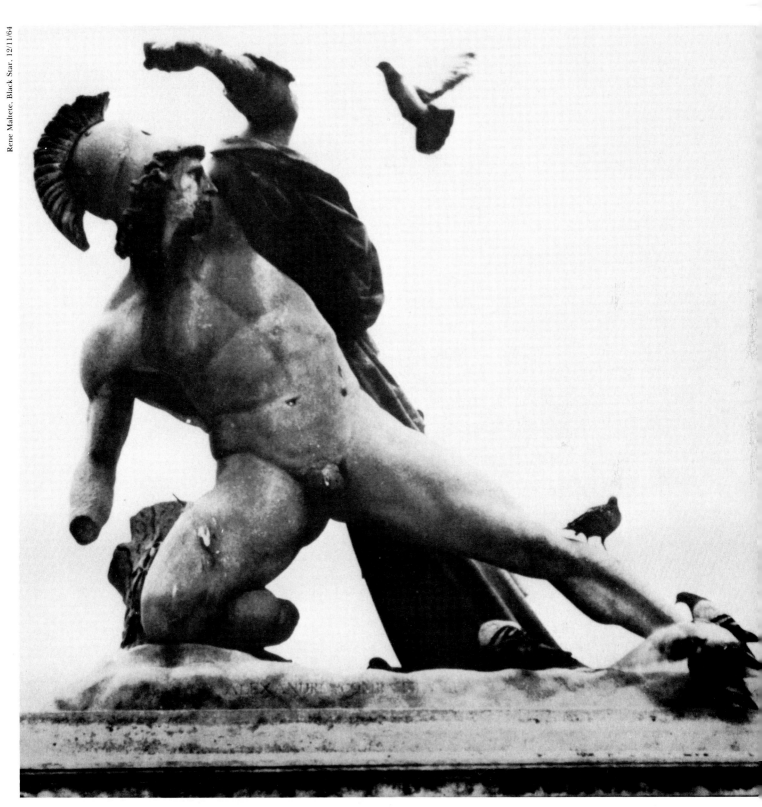

It matters not a crumb to this brash Paris pigeon that the man
with the left hook is Alexander the Great.

A Bird in Hand . . .

A little bit closer and this tempting Swiss morsel will be one dead pigeon.

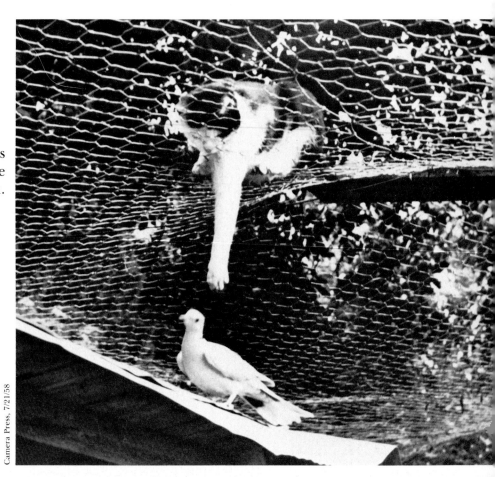

At the San Francisco Zoo a hippo named Puddles thinks this gull is a swallow.

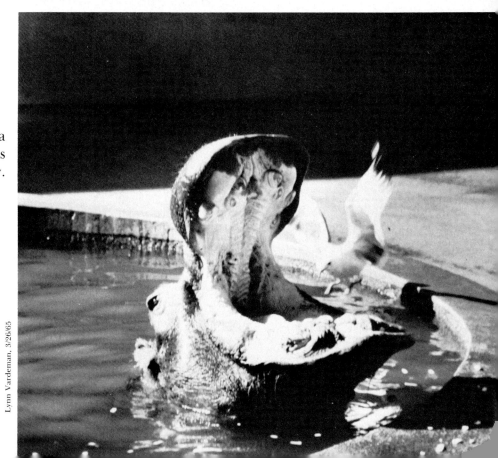

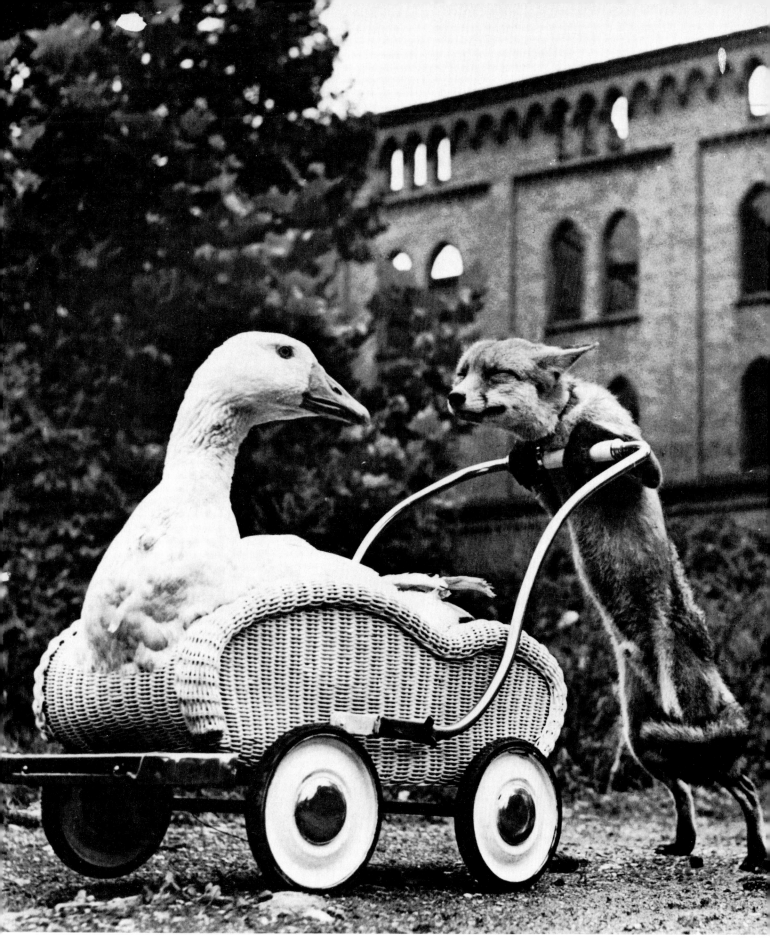

In this German circus trick the fox is supposed to push the goose
around lovingly in a baby carriage. Don't count on it! By the chop-
licking leer on nursy's face, it looks as if his goose is cooked.

Henry Brueggemann, Associated Press, 9/20/54

Not Giving a Hoot

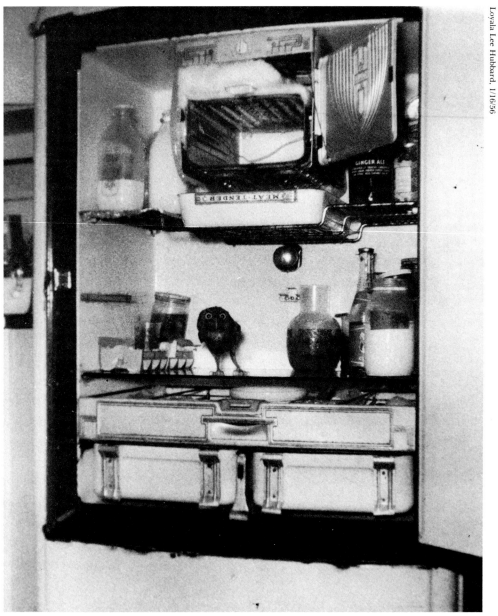

Loyala Lee Hubbard, 1/16/56

Donald M. Kerr, 11/22/68

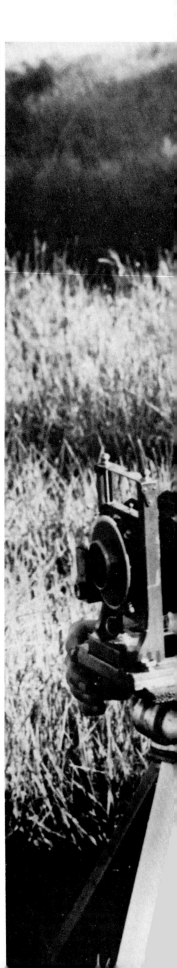

One day Mrs. Wynant Hubbard of Miami decided to defrost the fridge. Look what flew into Mrs. Hubbard's cupboard.

All right now, everybody,
hold still and watch the owl.

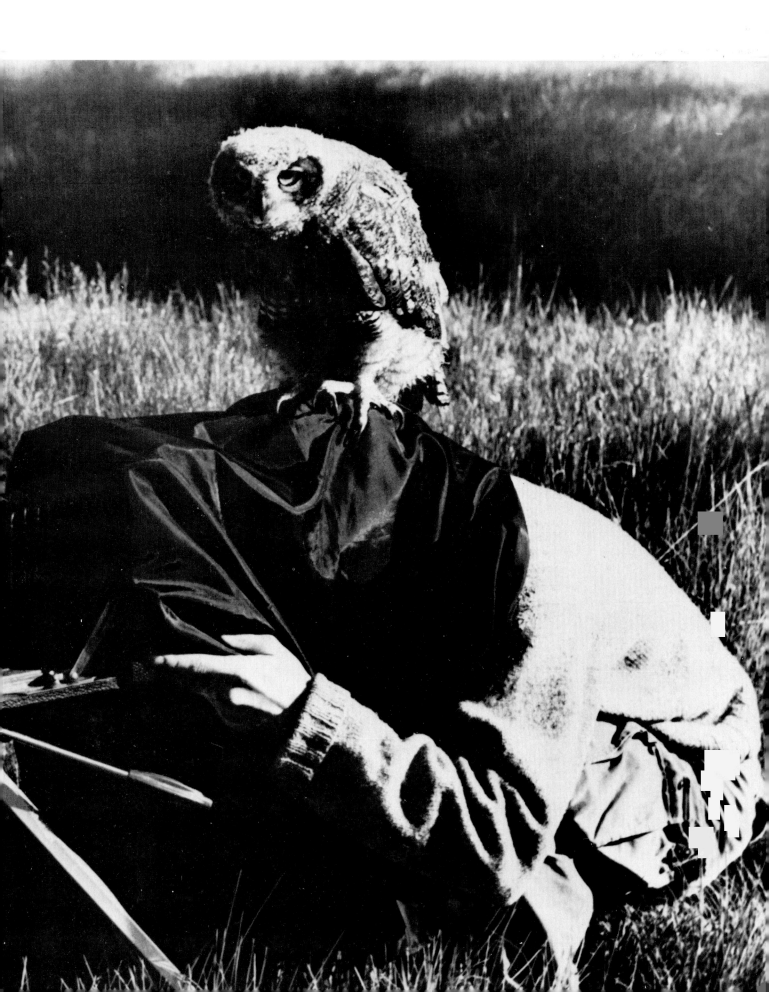

CHAPTER 8
celebrates
BOYS AND GIRLS

Battle of the Sexes

At the site of a traffic mix-up in Sacramento, California, each driver claims the other is at fault, while an eyewitness waits patiently for the road to clear.

Don D. Minnick, 6/30/67

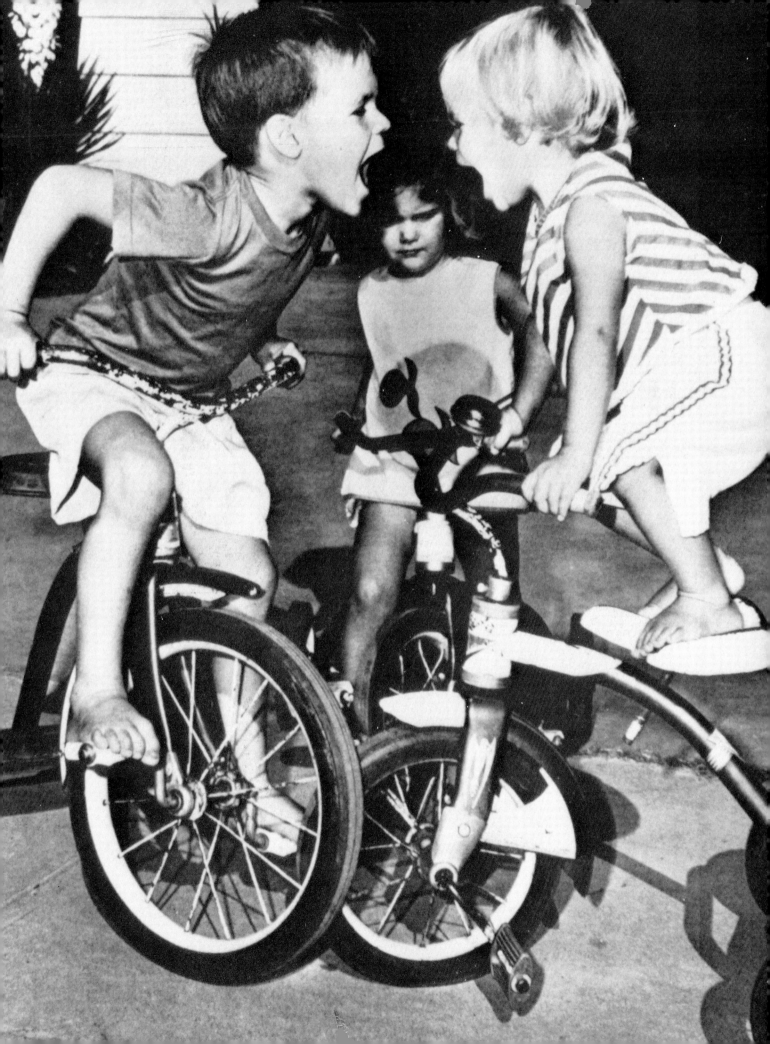

William H. Mortimer, *Baltimore Evening Sun*, 8/4/61

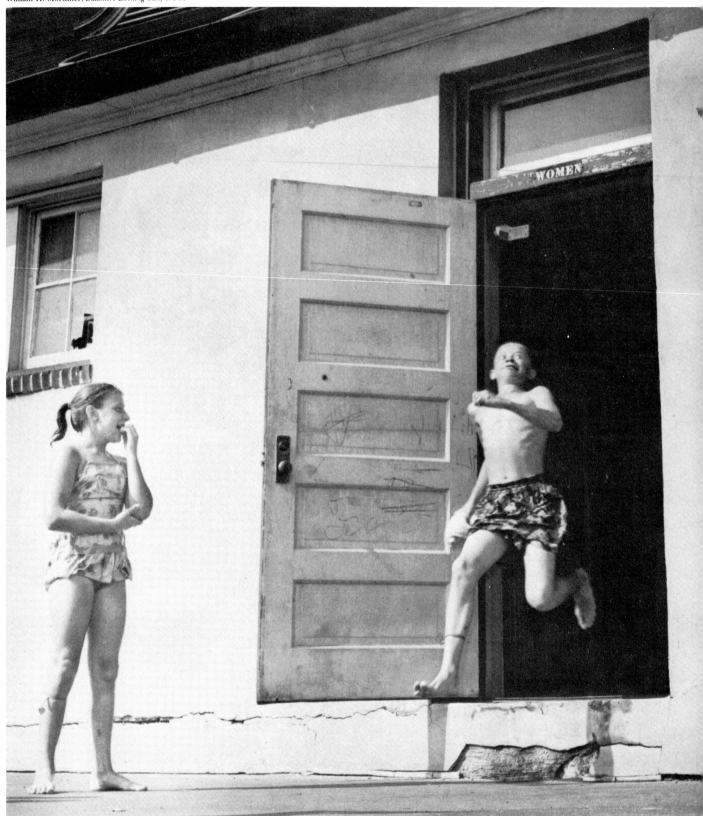

The Facts of Life

Realizing his big mistake, out he comes in sheer panic, to the vast amusement of the opposite sex.

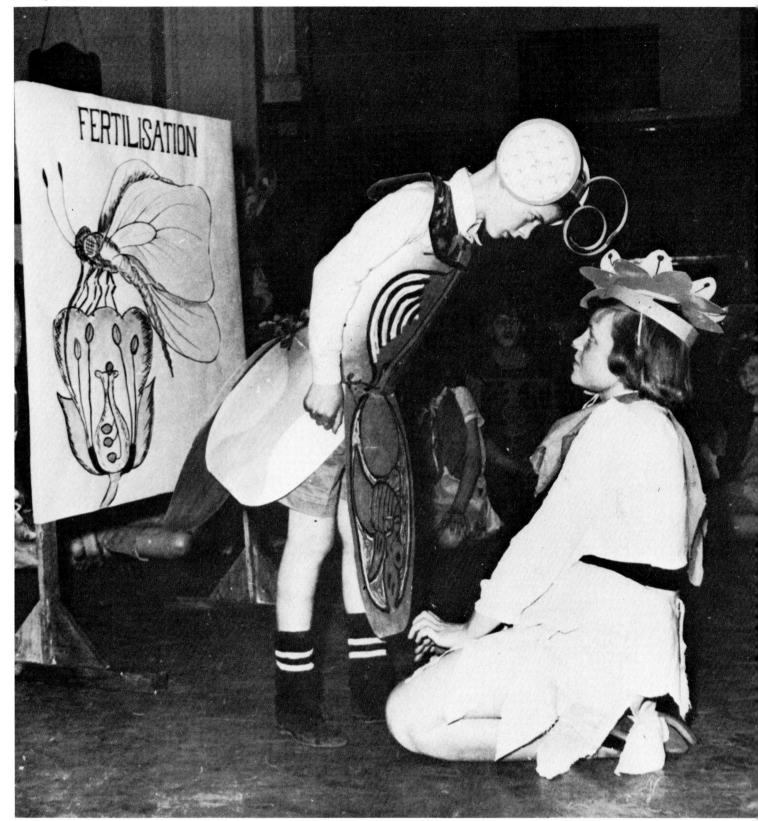

In a science class in Scotland, a boy dressed up
as a bee demonstrates how to fertilise a flower.

Underhanded Petting

Look, Ma, three hands!

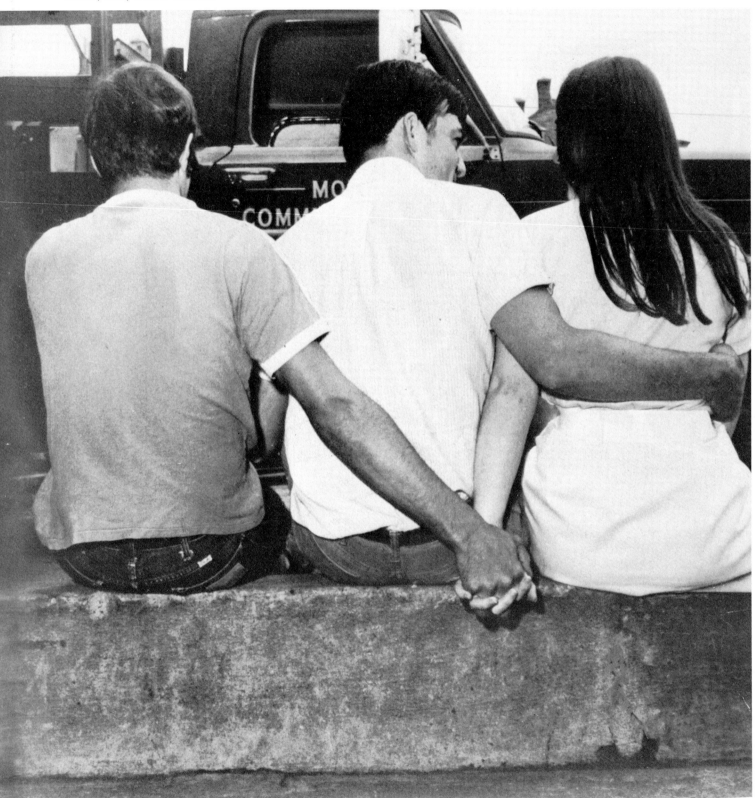

Anthony Bruculere, 7/26/68

I gotta hold your paw!

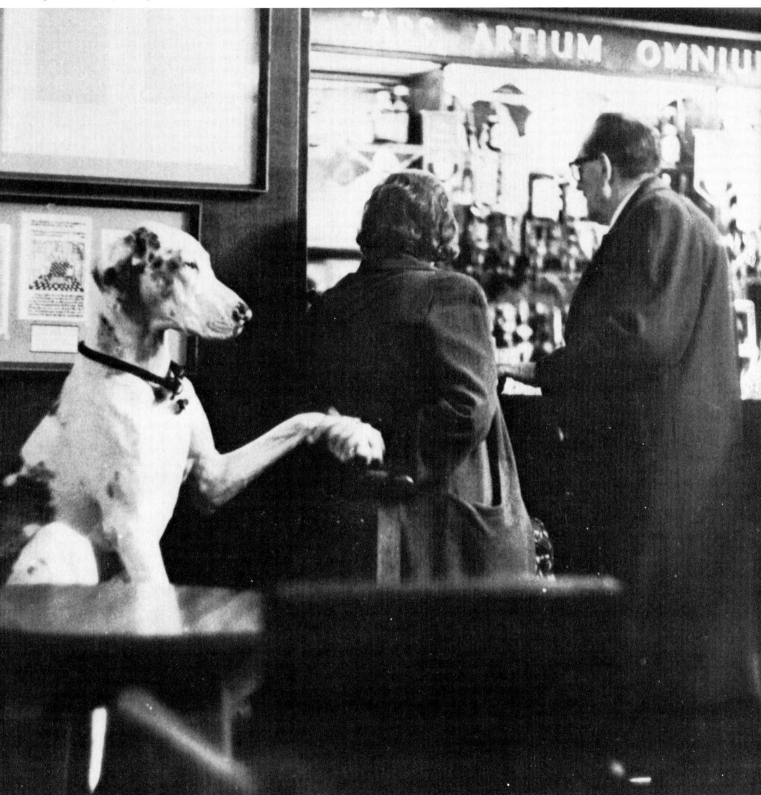

Michael Irwin, 1/5/68

Central Press, London, 4/21/61

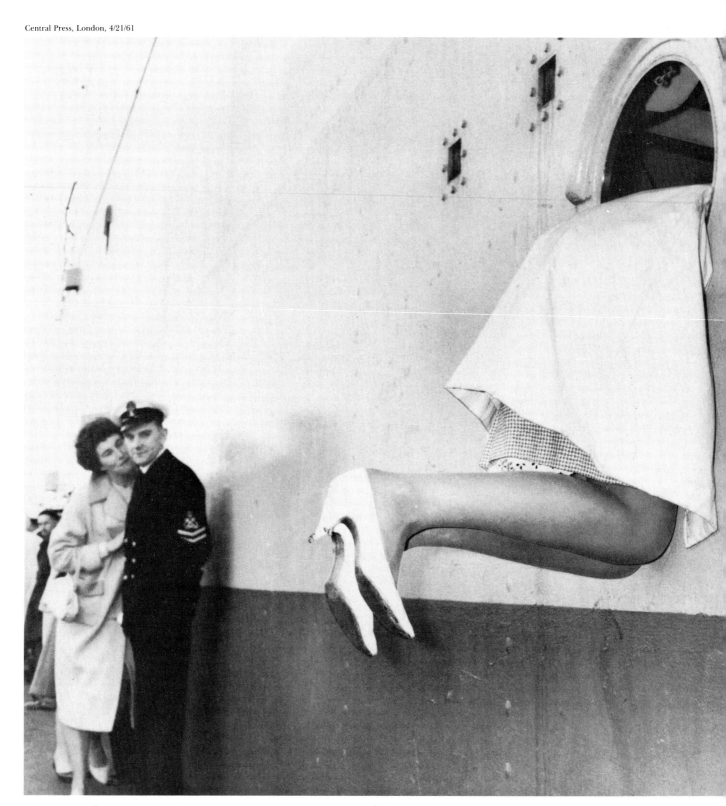

Royal Welcomes

After waiting fifteen months when he was away on Her Majesty's carrier Ark Royal, she spots him through a porthole and takes immediate action.

Press Association, Ltd., 4/8/66

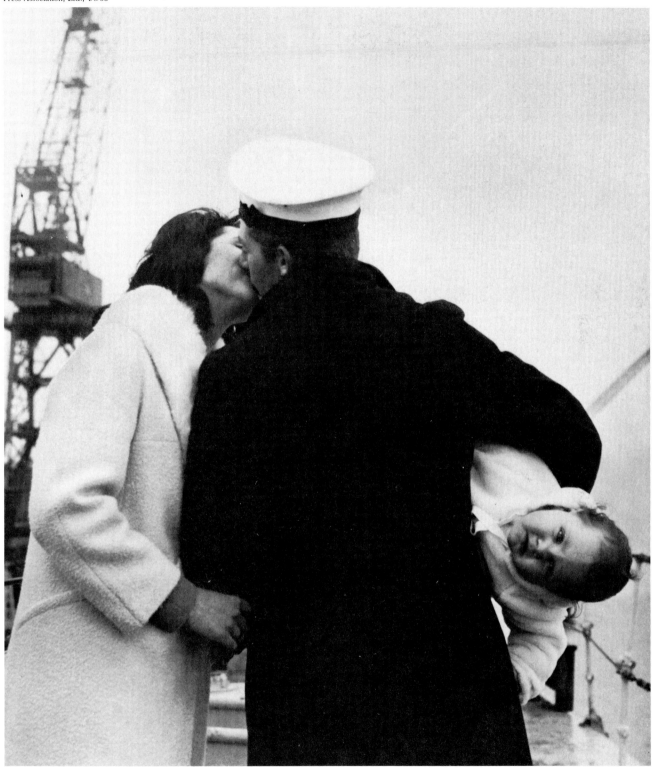

After fourteen months at sea on Her Majesty's
frigate Whitby, seaman Anthony Bennett
meets his baby for the first time.

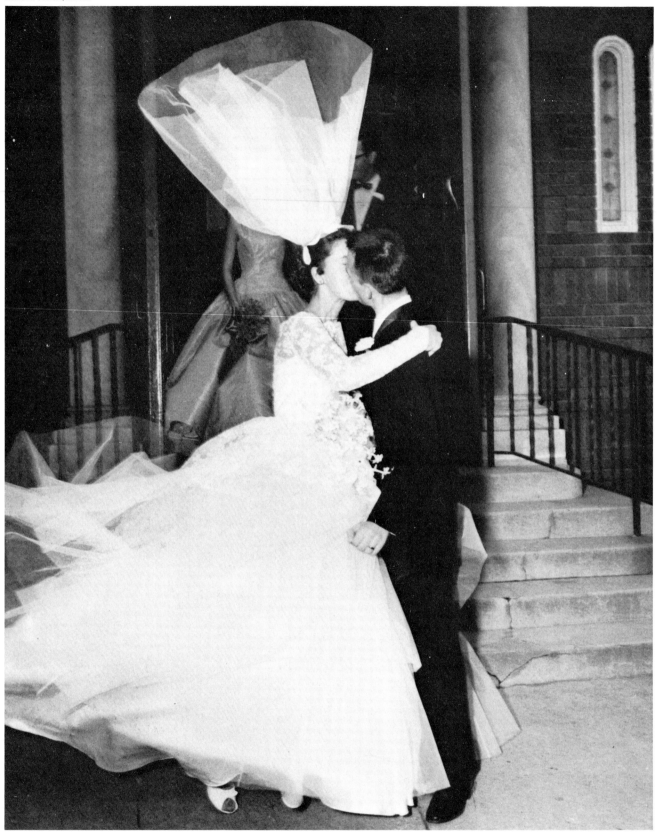

Blowing in the Wind

The groom may think his church-step kiss is having an electric effect on his bride, but it's really a gust of Herrin, Illinois, wind that's doing the generating.

Ed Gilkey, *Spokane Spokesman-Review*, 7/22/66

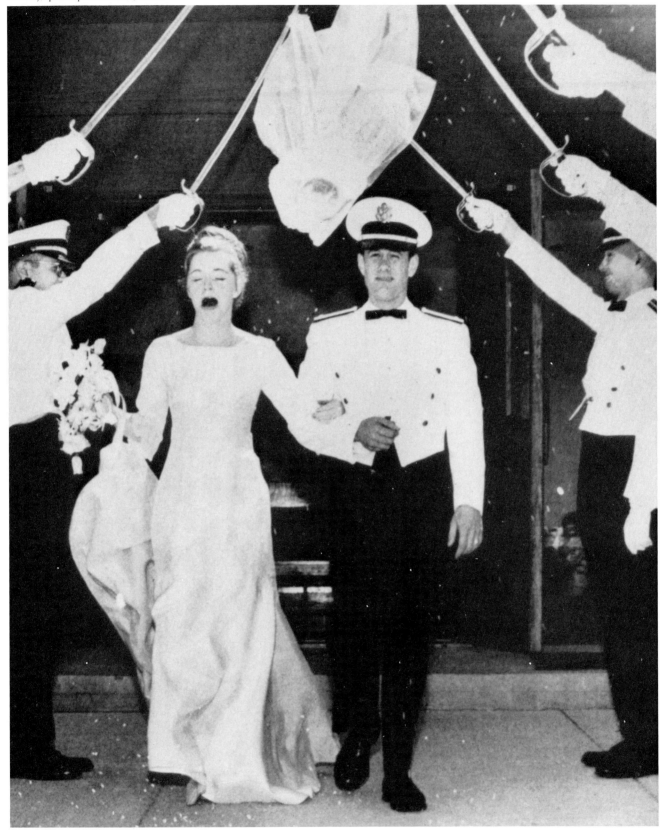

Wind is also the culprit outside the Fairchild Air Force Base chapel in Washington as the new Mrs. Michael W. Cole seems to lose her veiled composure to a phalanx of upthrust sabers.

Going, Going, . . .

Newlyweds Anne and Frederick Warder, Jr., pick the wrong time to get heavy-handed.

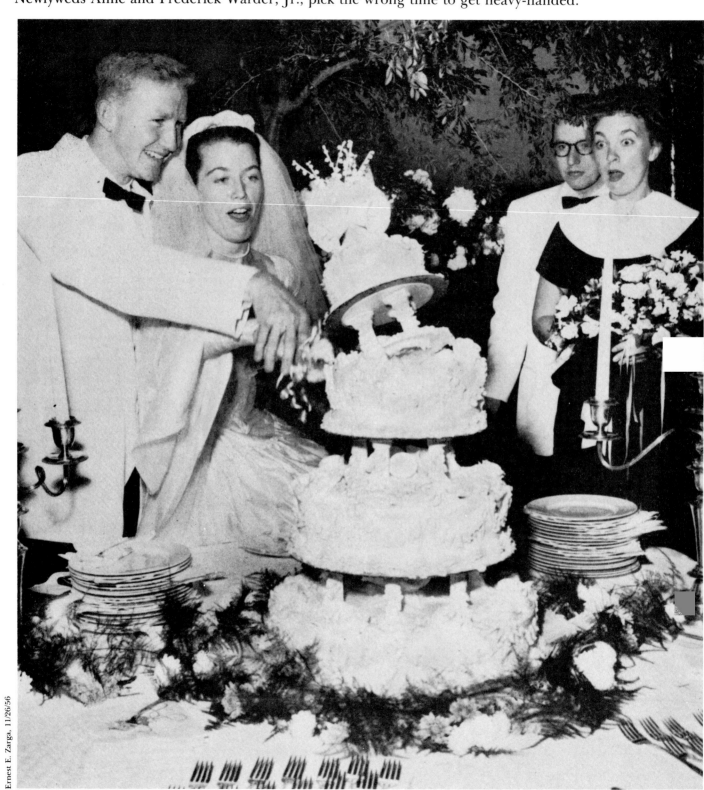

Ernest E. Zarga. 11/26/56

138

Gone!

Try as they may, Eleanor and Paul Sherry just can't get their cake to rise.

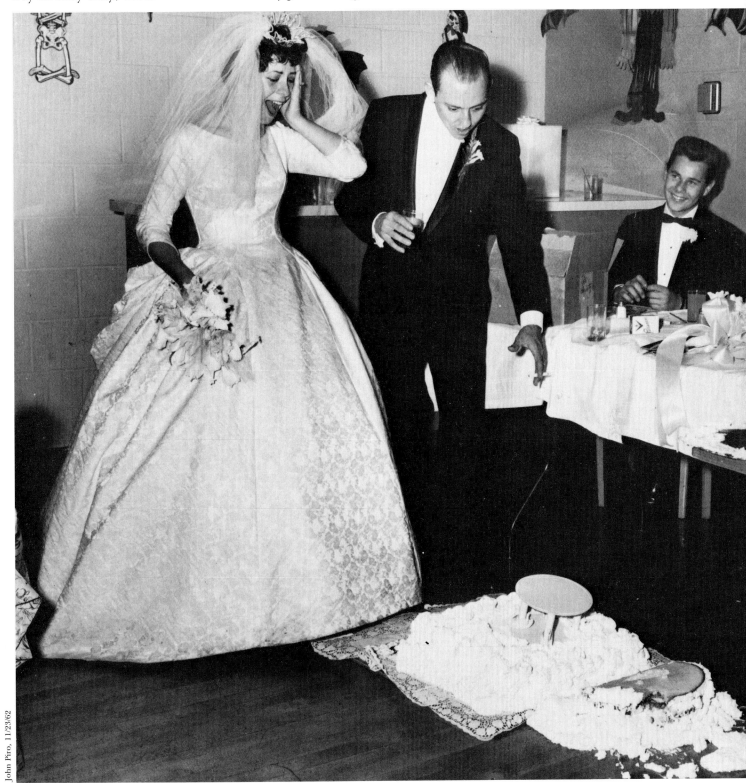

John Piro, 11/23/62

Fred Ward, Black Star, 2/18/66

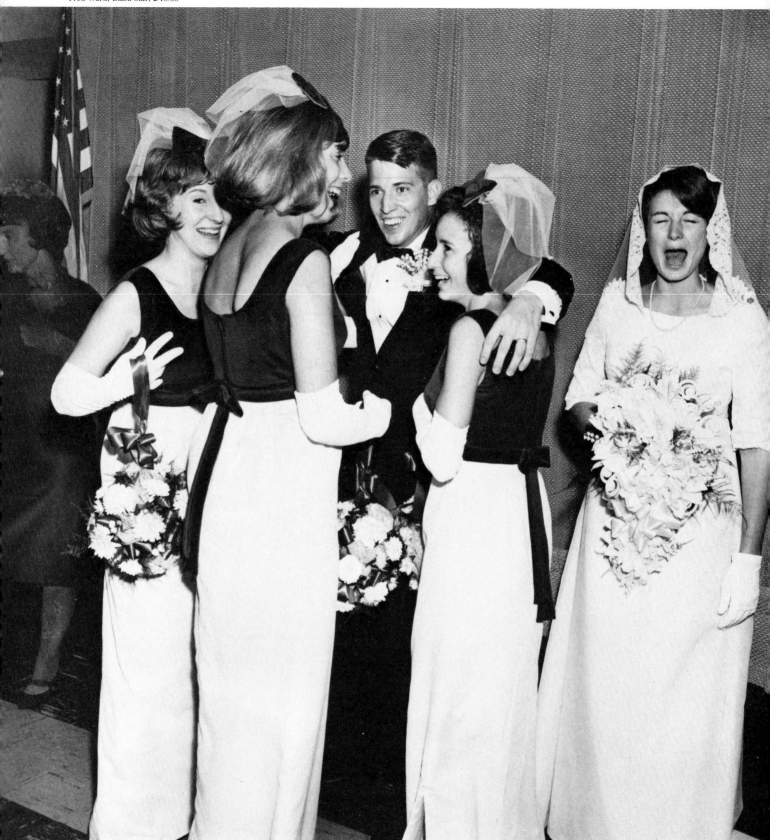

A Woman Scorned

In the considered opinion of bride Judy Hendrix, her bridesmaids are definitely too well groomed.

Mildred Totushek, M. Photo Cr., FASP., 5/31/54

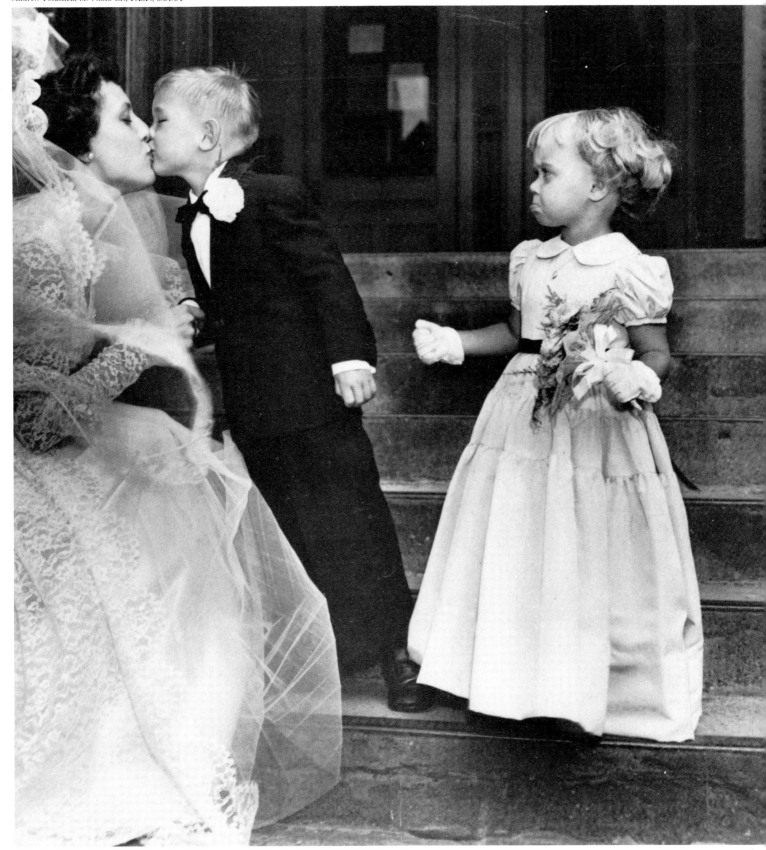

Flower girl Jan Schlueter takes a dim view of ring bearer
Ricky Lofy's bussing any other woman, even the bride.

CHAPTER 9
is
ALL WET

Don't You Ever Knock?

Face it, girl, if you've made it to
a big-time zoo, your privacy is nil.

Juerg Klages, 9/7/62

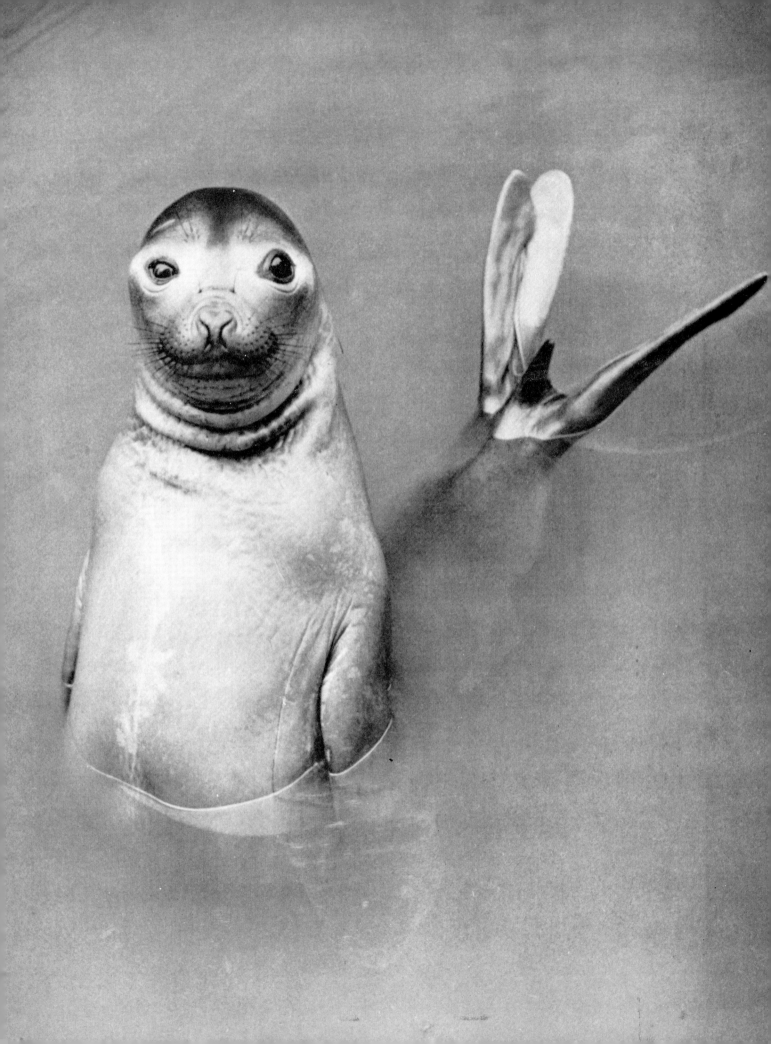

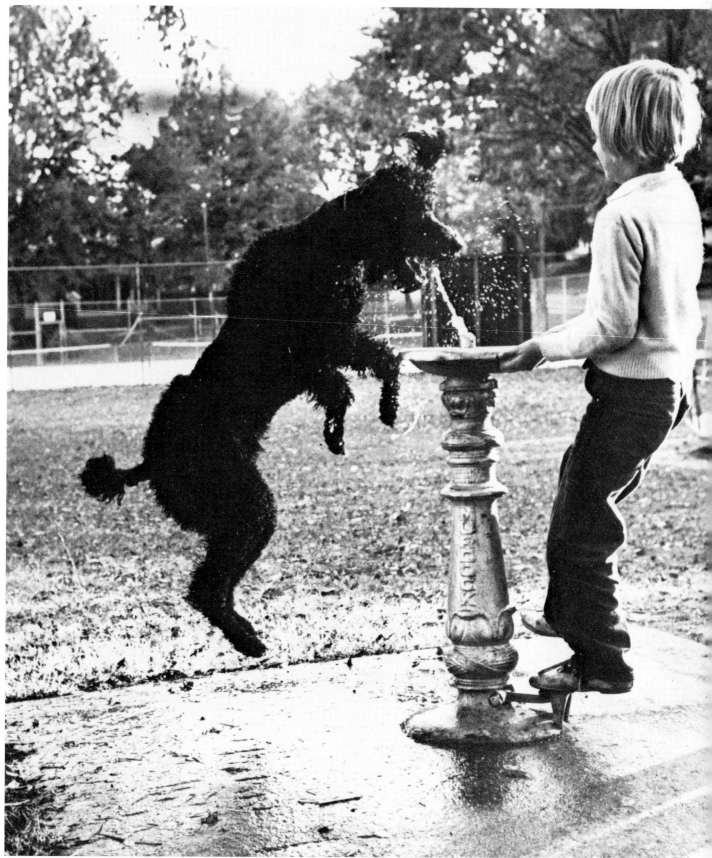

Wetting the Whistle

In Charlotte, North Carolina, Pierre will jump through a hoop for a refreshing squirt of aqua.

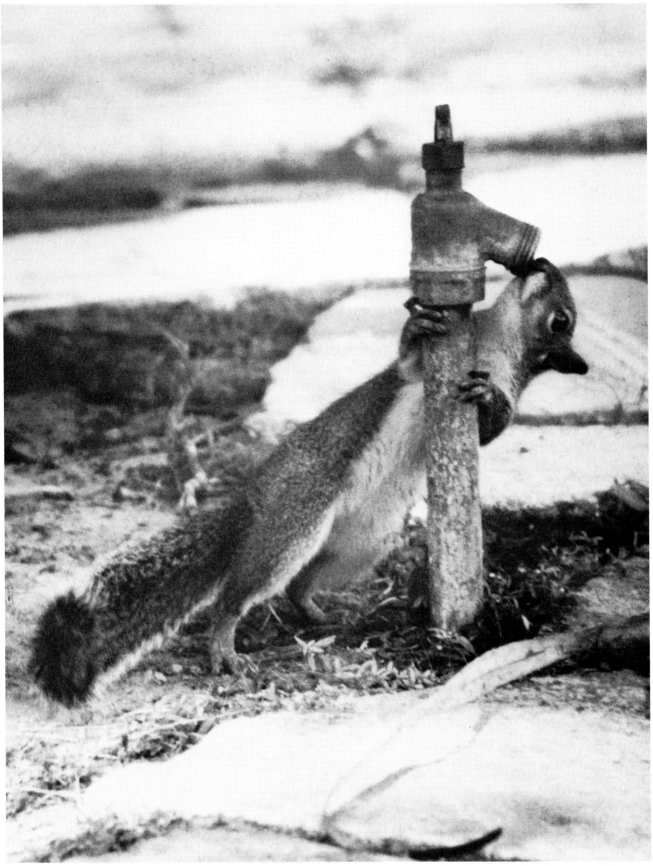

In Orlando, Florida, a squirrel uses a dripping faucet as his own private fountain.

Wash 'er Down and Fill 'er Up

Has Ervin Szocinski been washing his car so long that he's filled up his South Bend, Indiana, street? Enough's enough, Erv—even if it did rain last night.

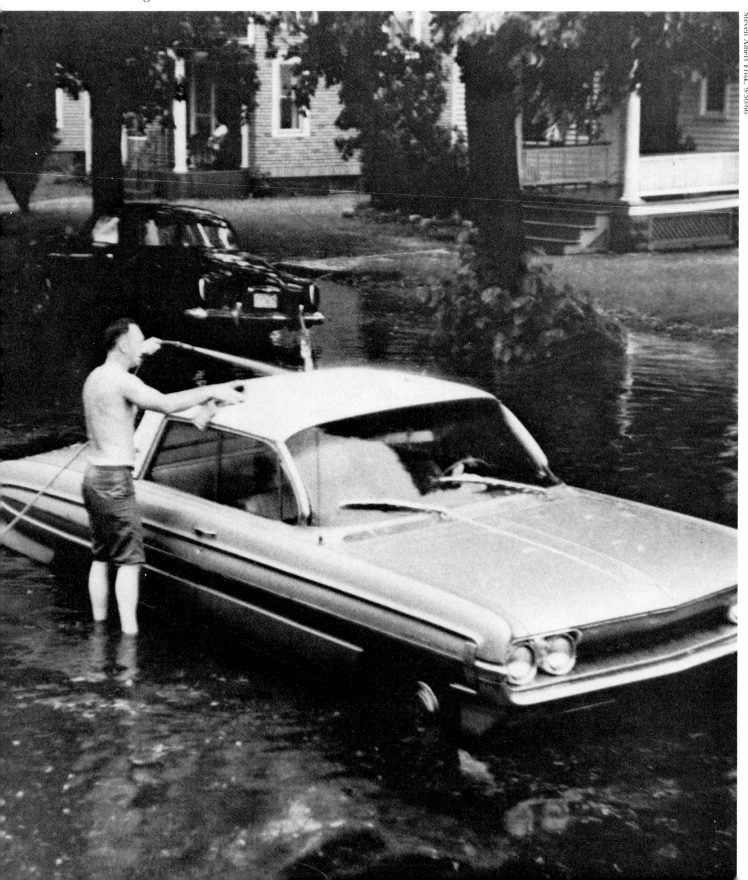

It's a different story in the great Indian Desert north of Jodhpur
where water is scarce, comes from hump-high faucets, and goes for
2½ cents the bagful.

European, 4/12/54

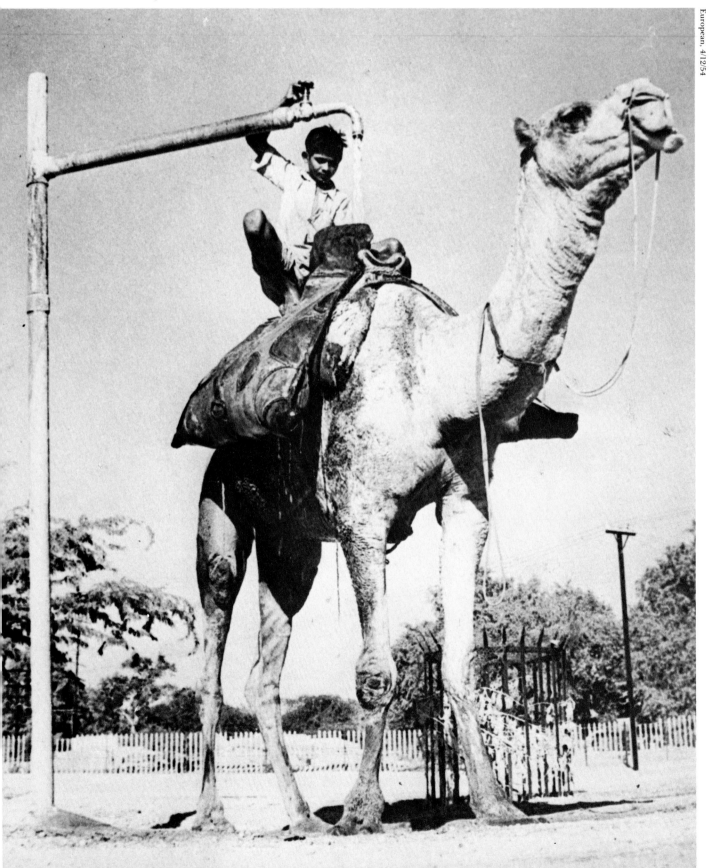

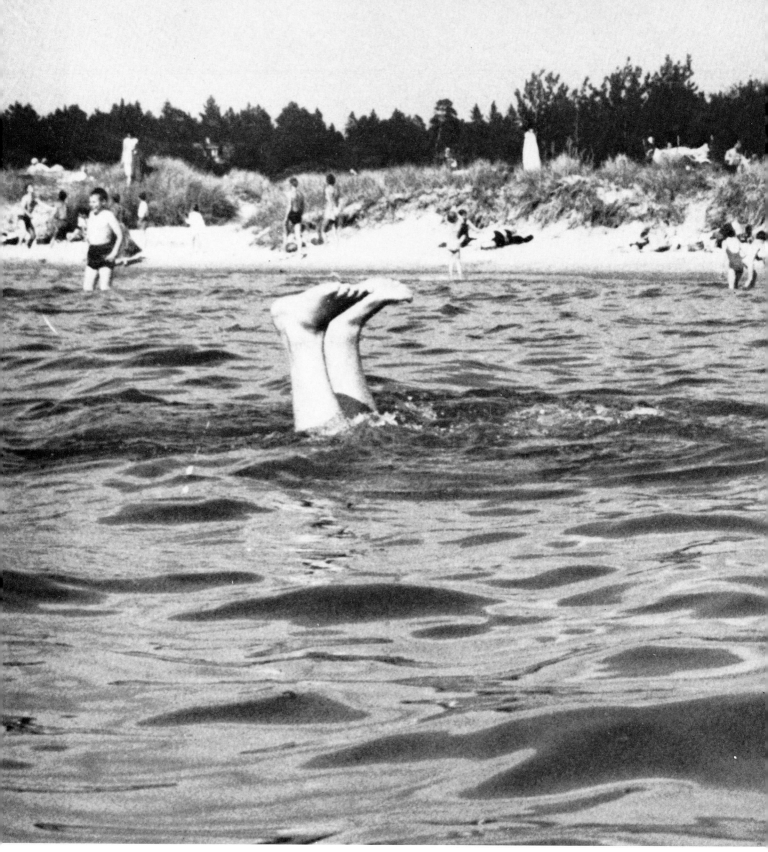

Tommy Wener is stretching out his vacation on the Baltic as long as he can.

Extenuating Circumstances

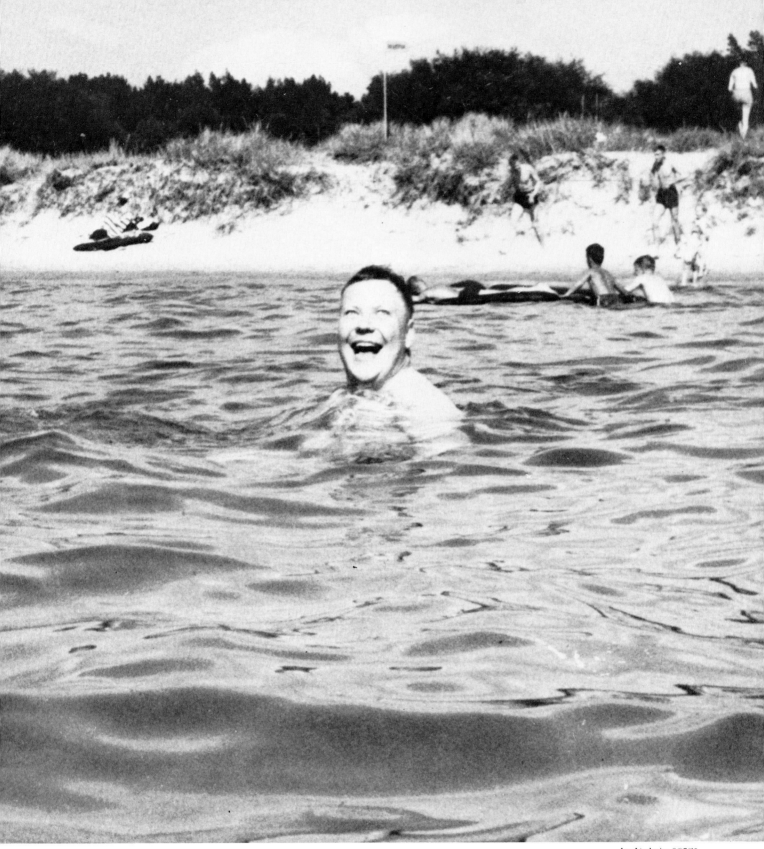

Jan Lindqvist, 8/27/65

149

The Jet Set

In Marion, Illinois, Herb Ashley helps quench a blaze.

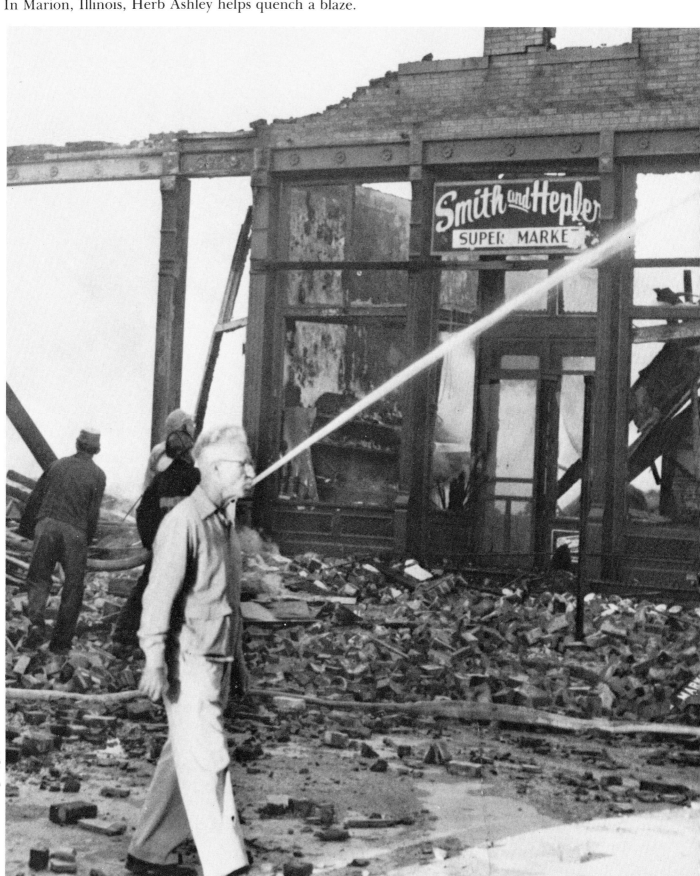

Charles A. Ingram, Jr., 11/5/56

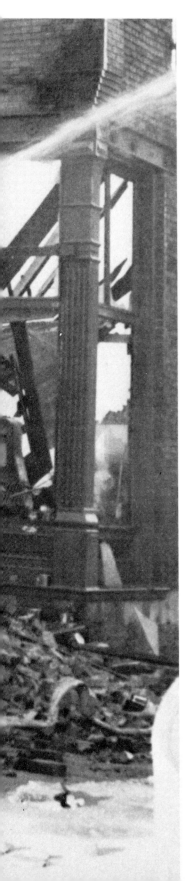

In Washington, D.C., fireman Donald MacDanel practices getting up on burning roofs without a hook-and-ladder.

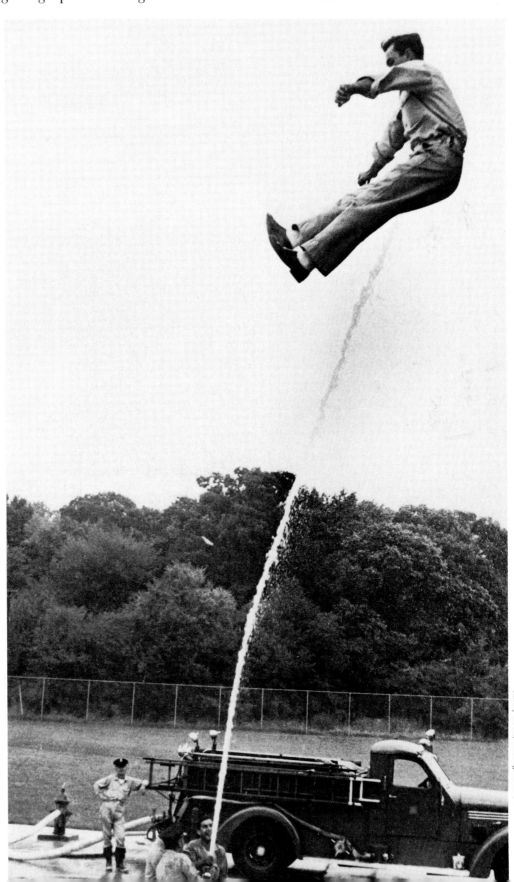

Ranny Routt, Washington Star, 9/21/62

Under Pressure

At a motel fire in Pittsburgh, a firefighter experiences his worst fear.

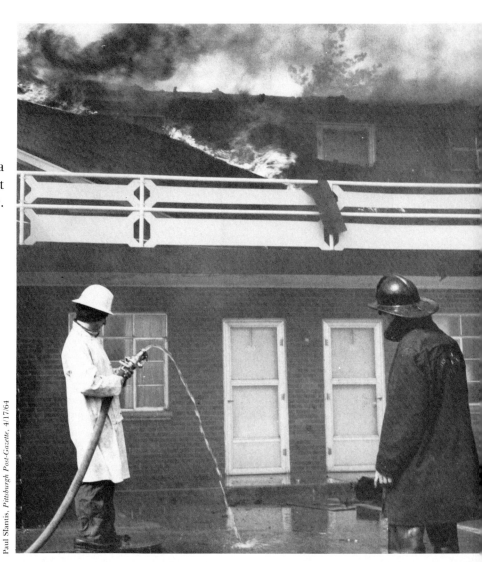

Paul Slantis, *Pittsburgh Post-Gazette*, 4/17/64

At a conflagration near a Long Island food depot, a fireman shoots from the hip and gets his just dessert.

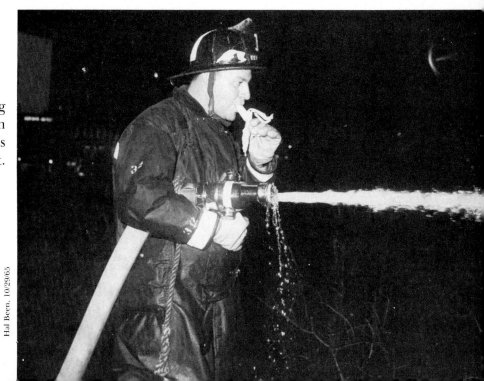

Hal Been, 10/29/65

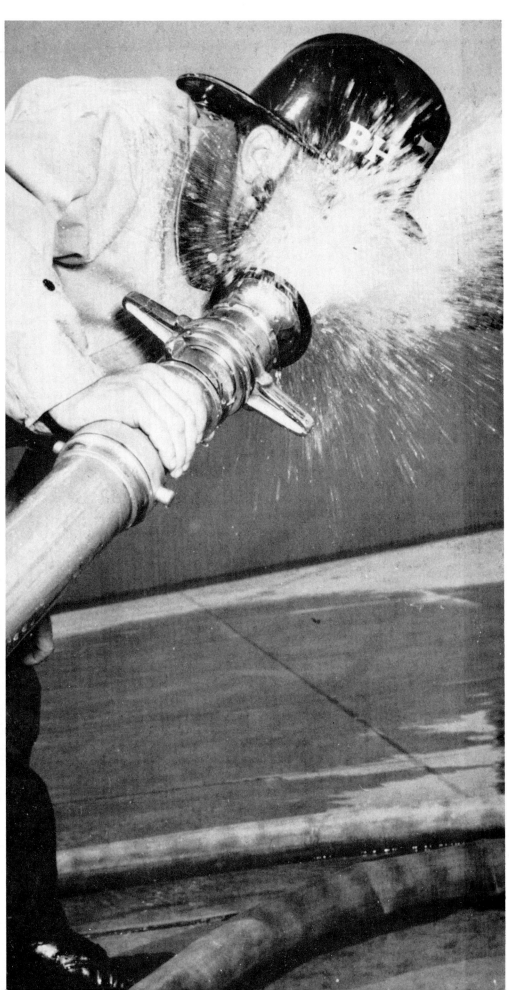

While the fire department instructor in Beverly Hills shows new recruits how not to look down a hose for the water, someone turns it on.

Mary Nogueras Frampton. 8/17/59

153

It Just Won't Hold Water

In Omaha, Ann Holley tries to hold back five feet of rain a cloudburst has dumped against her sunken cellar door.

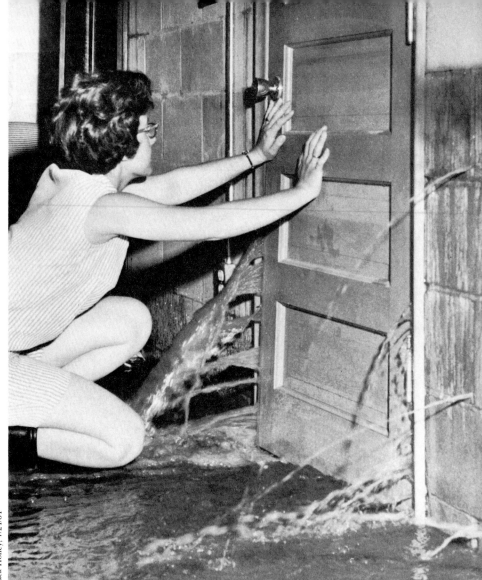

Jack Holley, 7/24/64

In Farmingdale, New York, Wade Garnett is trying to get a drink from the family pool, but unfortunately his cup runneth under.

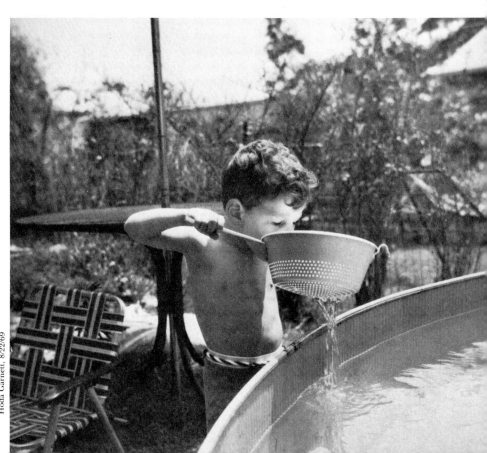

Hoda Garnett, 8/22/69

Five-year-old Sean Sweeney is irrefutable proof of the summertime brain drain in Detroit.

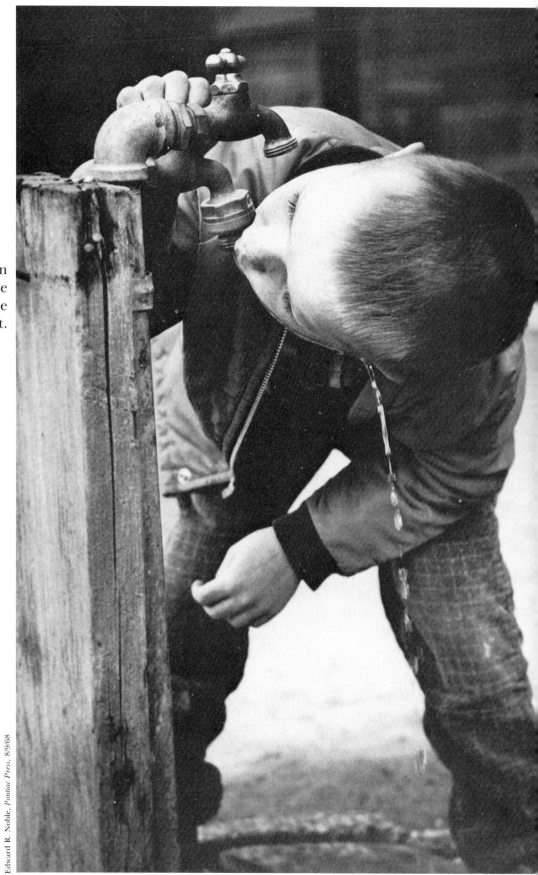

Edward R. Noble, *Pontiac Press*, 8/9/68

A Sinking Sensation

His boat's already thrown him and
Jimmy Parks of Charlotte has made it
safely to shore. Now what?

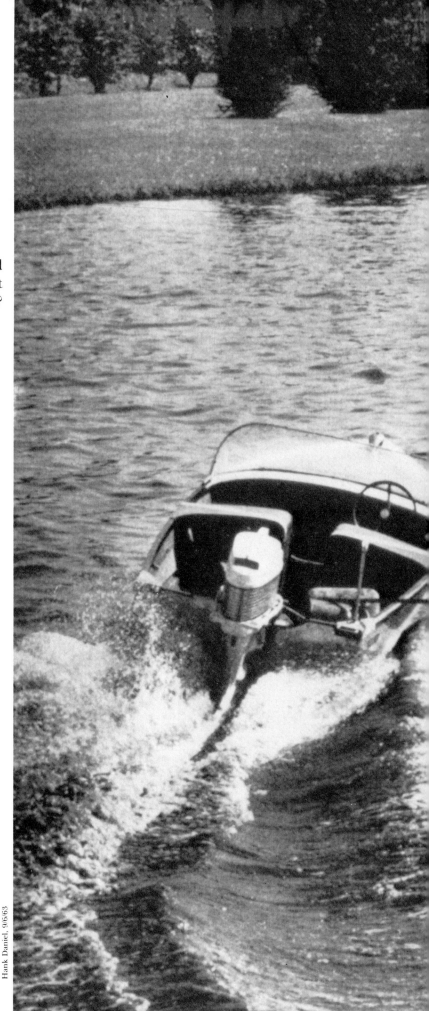

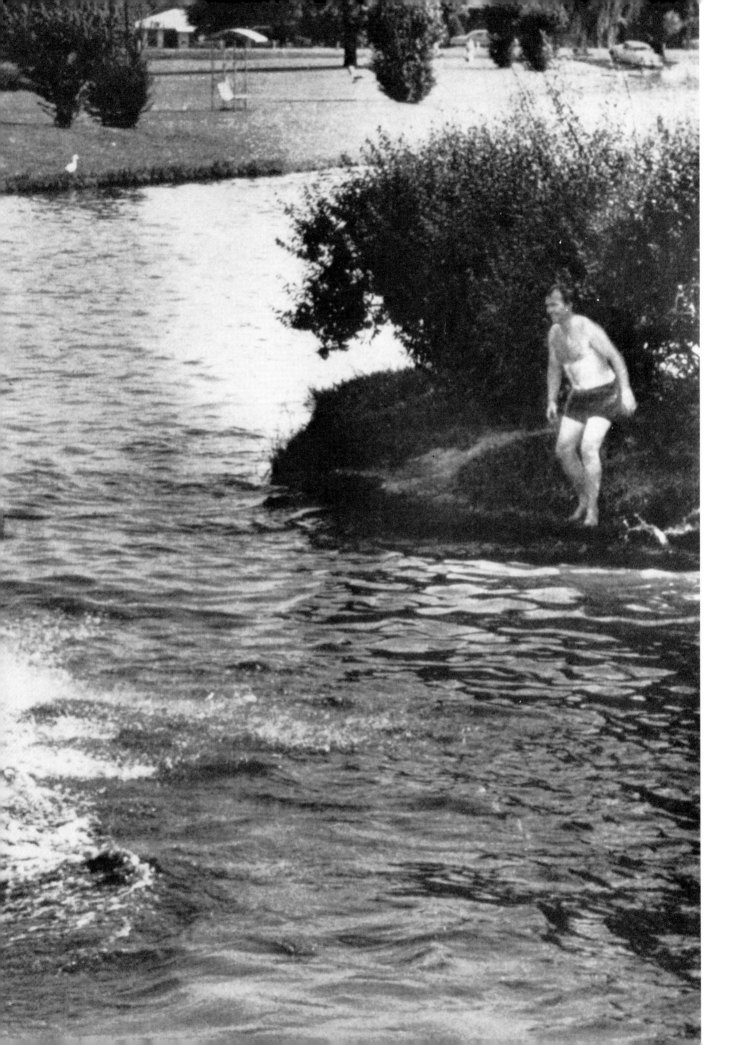

CHAPTER 10

repeats a few examples of

SMALL TALK

"Don't You Speak That Way to My Sister!"

Meet the Chihuahua siblings—
Missy and Sambo.

Robert C. Winter III, 2/2/62

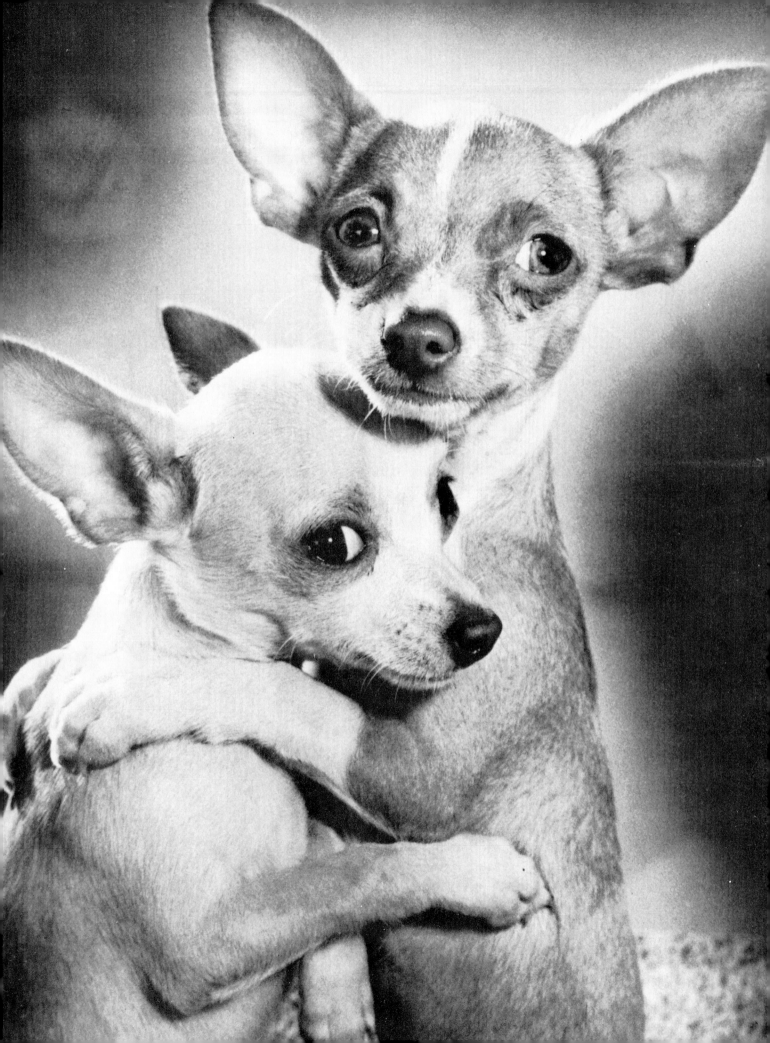

"Open Wide . . . Now Say Ahhhhh"

Sir Francis Chichester and
Percy the pelican from
England's Plymouth Zoo.

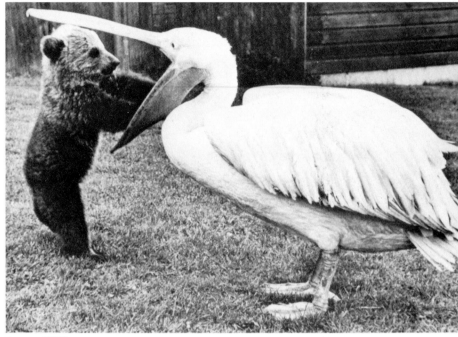

Keystone, 5/19/67

Ralph Crane, LIFE, 2/14/69

Shamu, a 3500-pound killer whale,
got a medical checkup as part of
his act, until he came down with
the flu and was advised to avoid all
human contact.

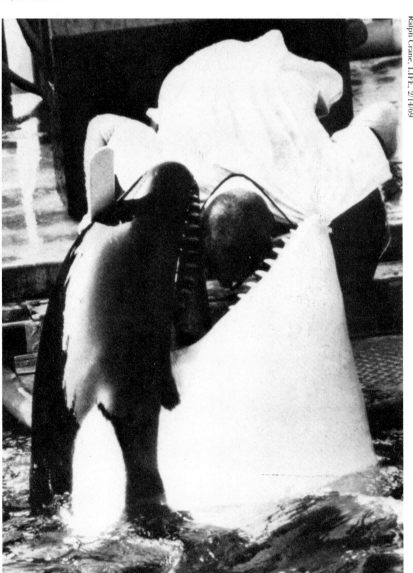

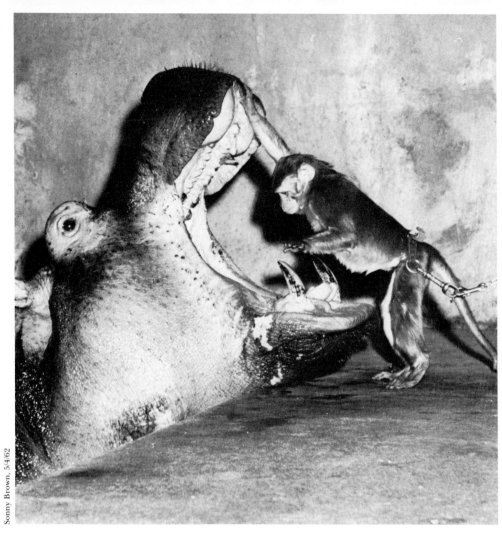

At the Mesker Zoo in
Evansville, Indiana,
Bashful first checks
out the tonsils and
then rummages
around the maw for
leftovers.

Old Doctor High-
brow tends a
patient at the
London Zoo.

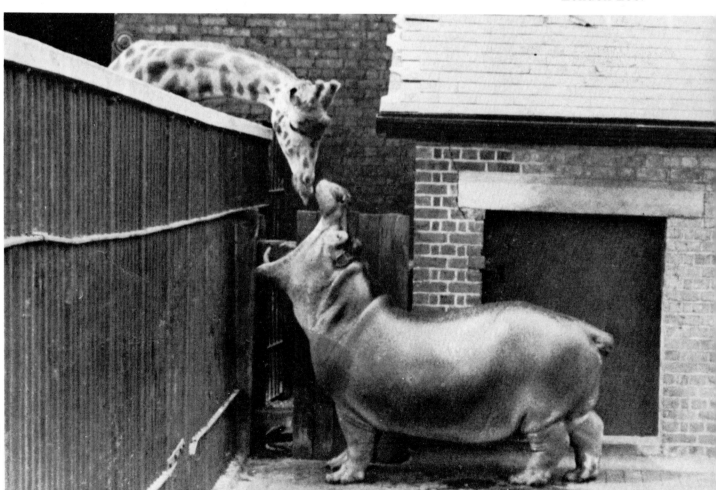

Howard Borvig, 9/6/68

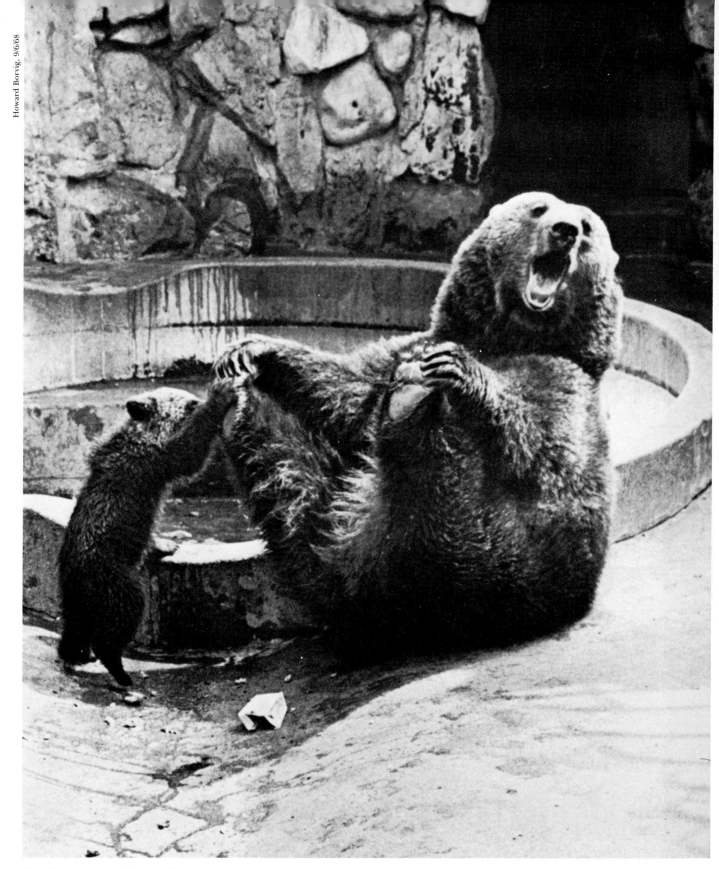

A cub torments its mother.

"Stop, I Can't Bear It. I'll Try It Myself."

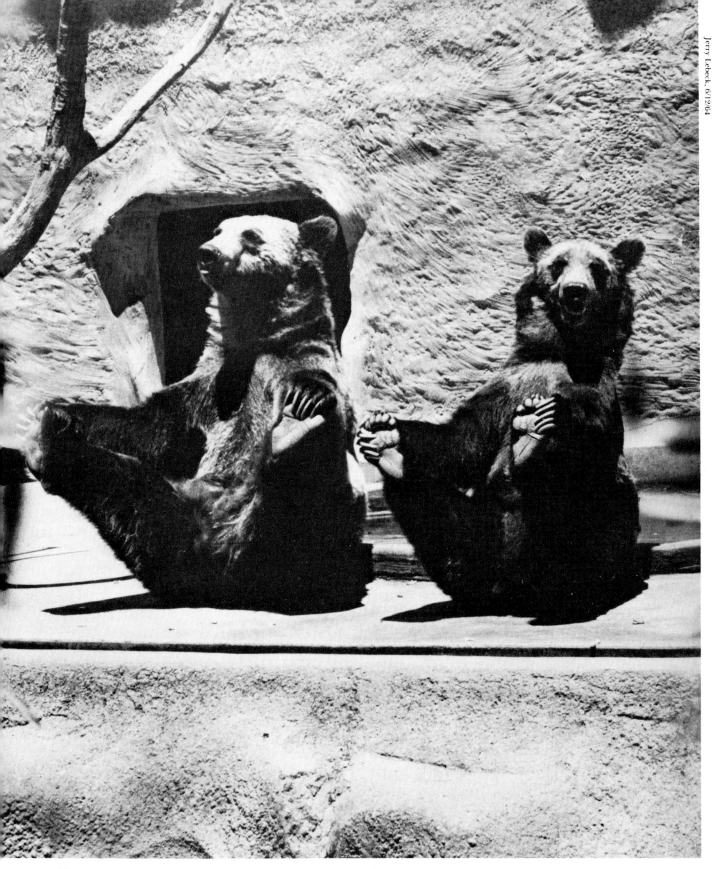

Jerry Lebeck, 6/12/64

Show-offs at the Sacramento Zoo baring their soles.

"Oops . . ."

Princess Christina of Sweden prefers to forget this award.

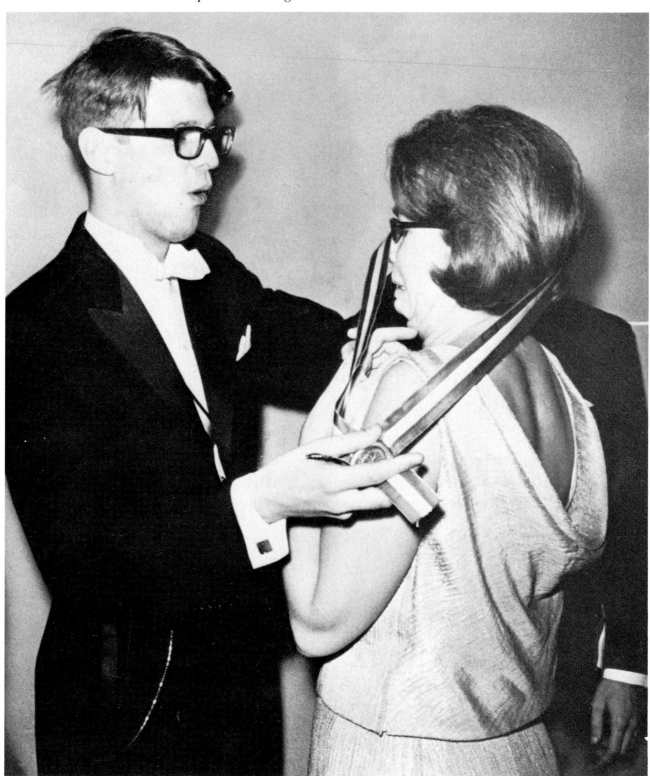

In the act of graduating from Central Washington
State College, honor student Gale Smoke gets an
unexpected face job from his own medallion.

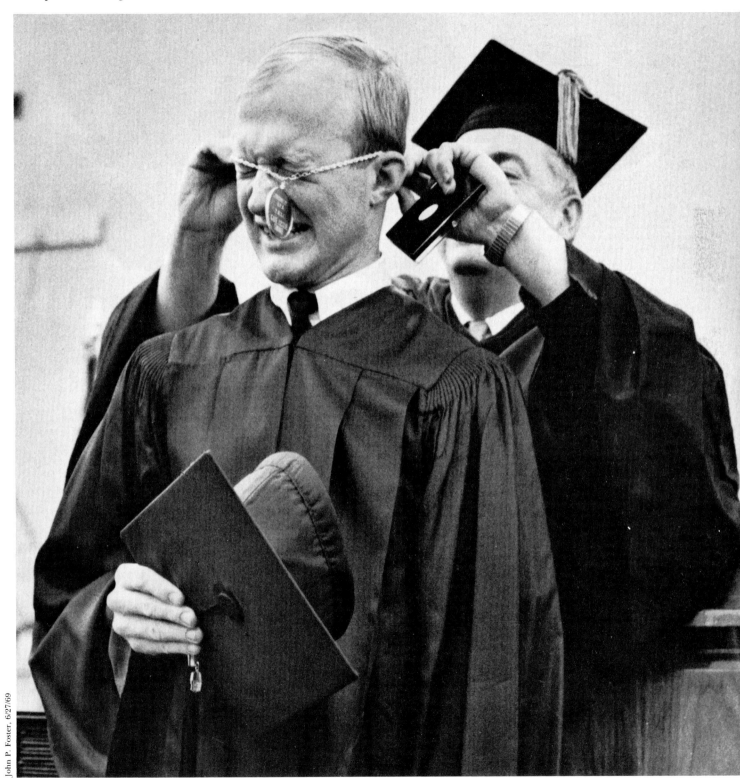

John P. Foster, 6/27/69

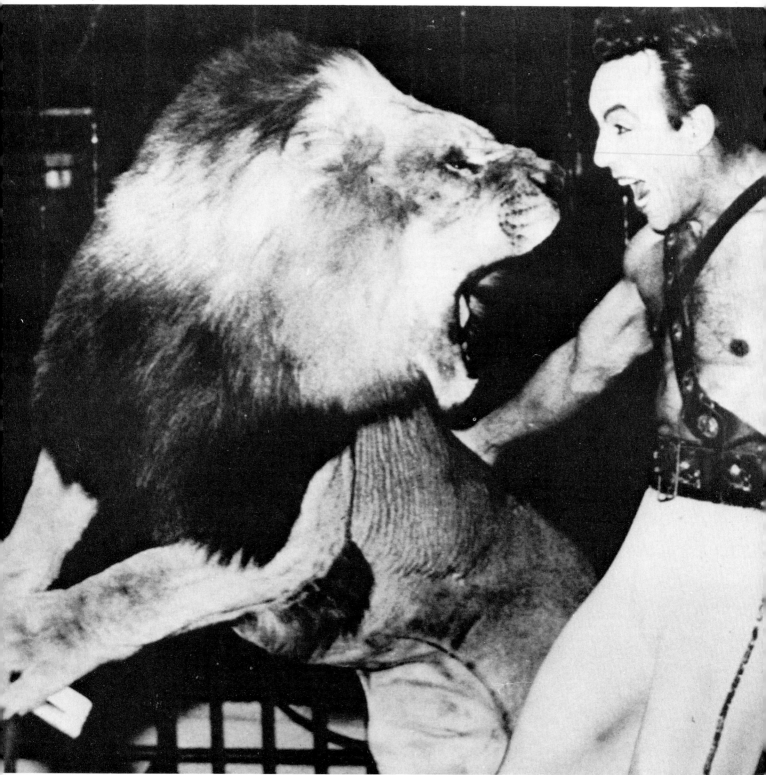

"Grrrrrr Yourself"

In Manchester, England, Luigi Garardi
and Leo tell each other off.

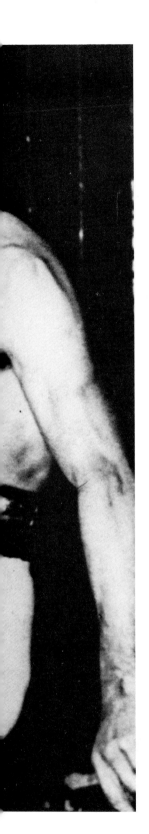

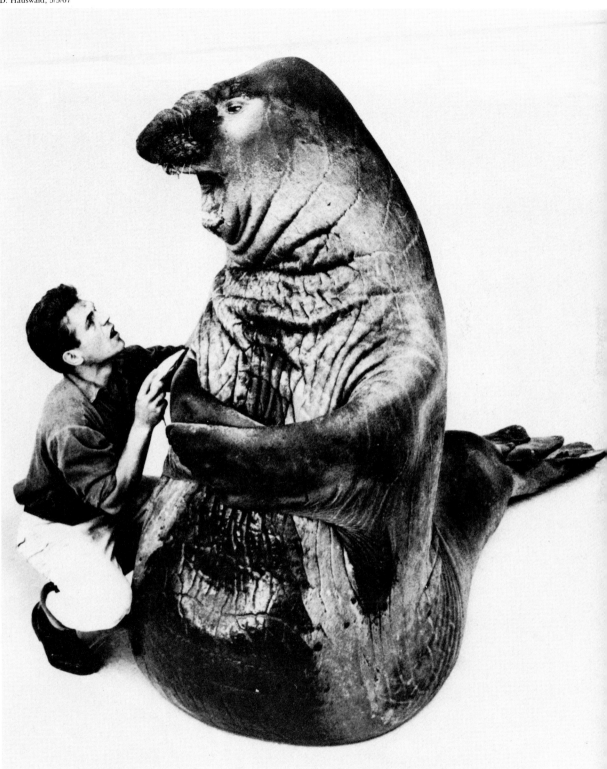

And then the haughty elephant seal spoke again: "I don't care what you say, you broke your promise and you'll have to pay."

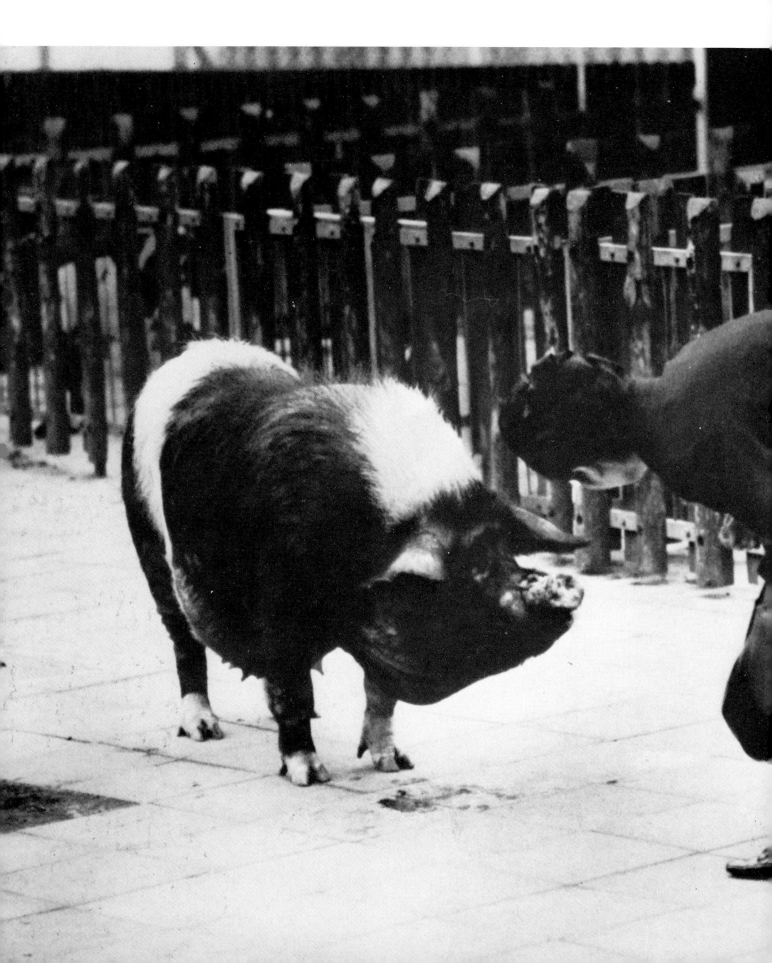

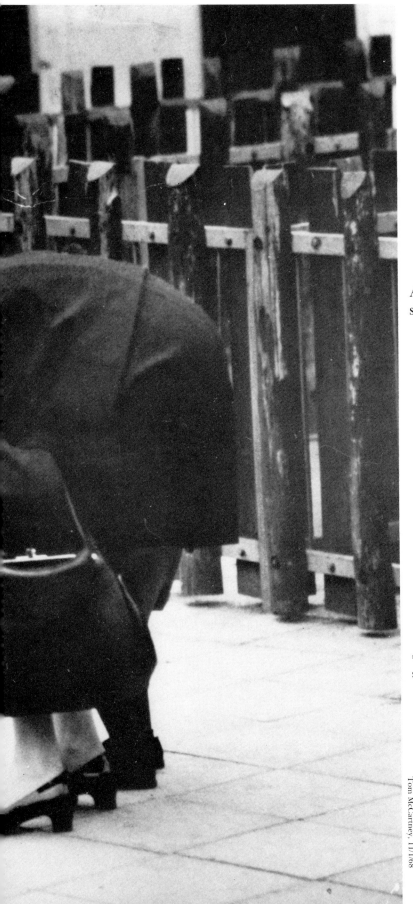

でも　ちょっと　さ
あたしが　彼に
あんたの言ってる事
話したら　さ
彼ったらさ・・・*

At the Tokyo Zoo, a housewife and a pig share the morning gossip.

* "But my dear, when I told him what you said, he said. . . ."

Tom McCartney, 11/1/68

169

"Don't Worry. This Won't Hurt a Bit."

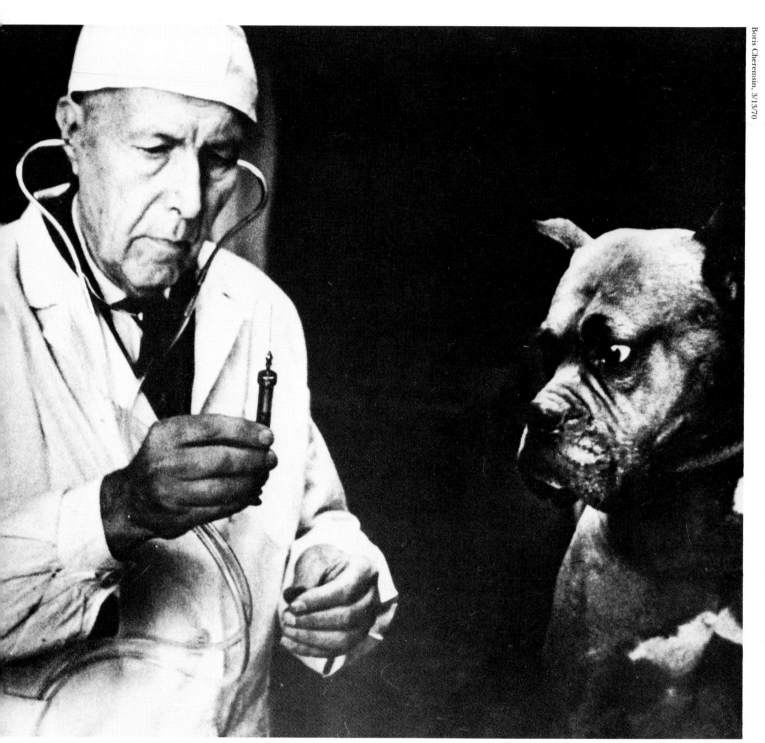

Boris Cheremsin, 3/13/70

Horrified thoroughbred in Russia.

170

Alarmed mongrel in Oakville, Ontario.

Charles Osland, 6/11/56

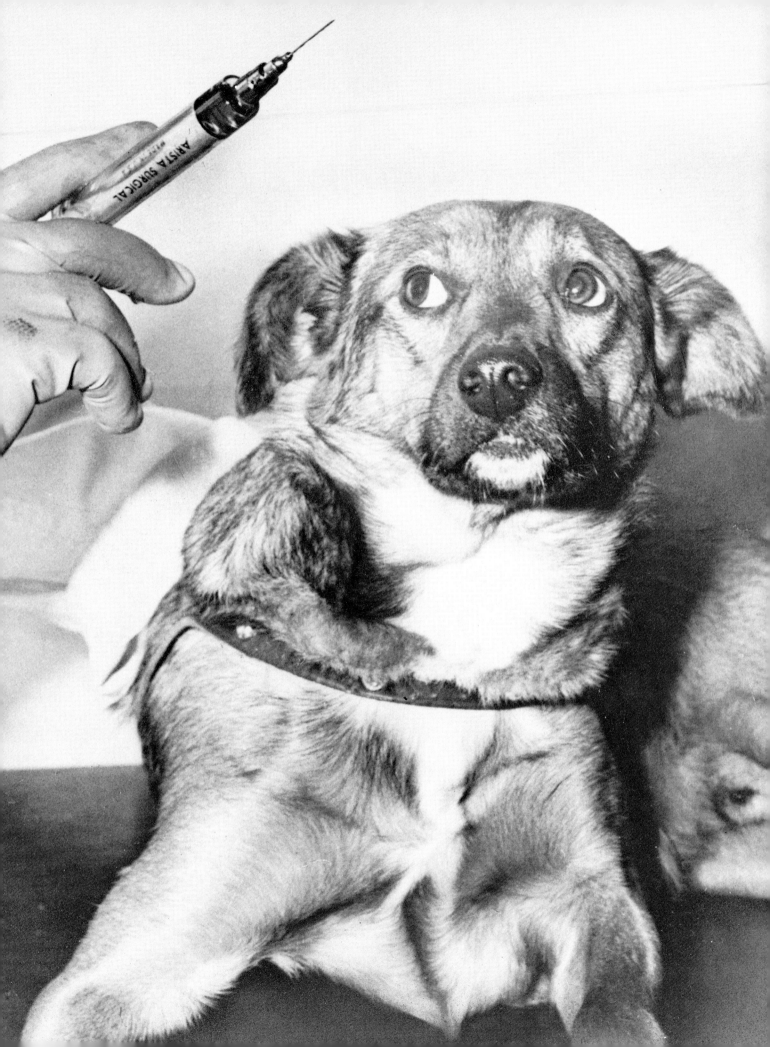

"OK Now, Get Off My Back!"

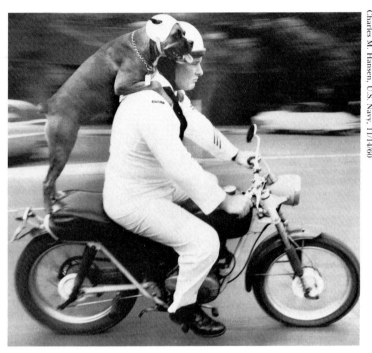

Charles M. Hansen, U.S. Navy, 11/14/60

Katie obeys the hardhat law when she rides with Franklin Driscoll in Hawaii.

A pelican pulls at Ellen Longworth's pony-tail at Casey Key, Florida.

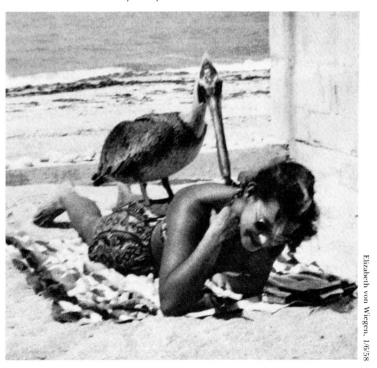

Elizabeth von Wiegen, 1/6/58

Joan Powell, 6/13/60

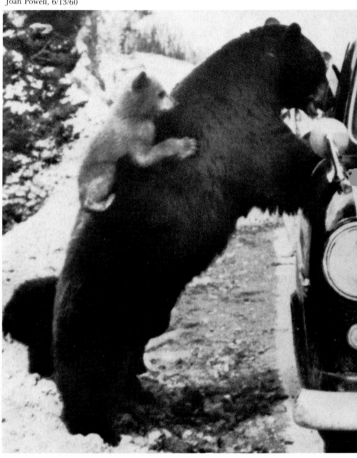

This Canadian bear has learned that homey scenes like this produce healthier handouts.

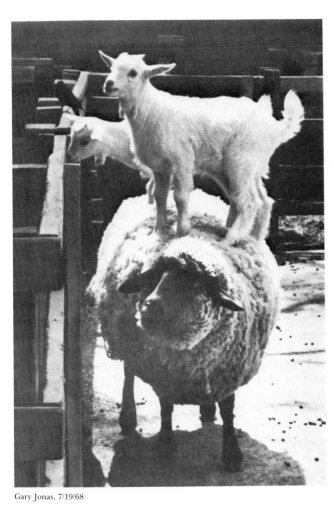

A sheep puts up with two curious kids.

Gary Jonas, 7/19/68

Ted Castle, 10/10/60

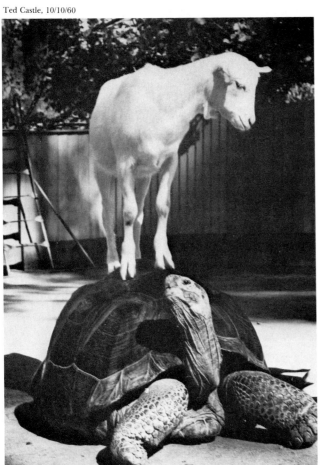

At the San Diego Children's Zoo a goat takes the high ground.

Ted Church, 11/29/68

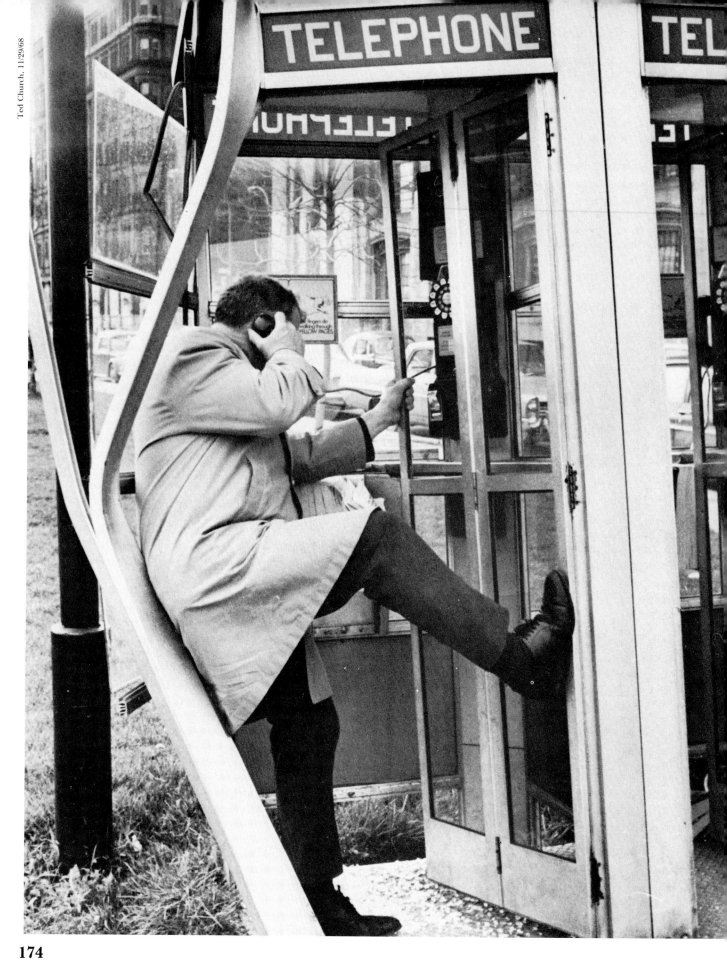

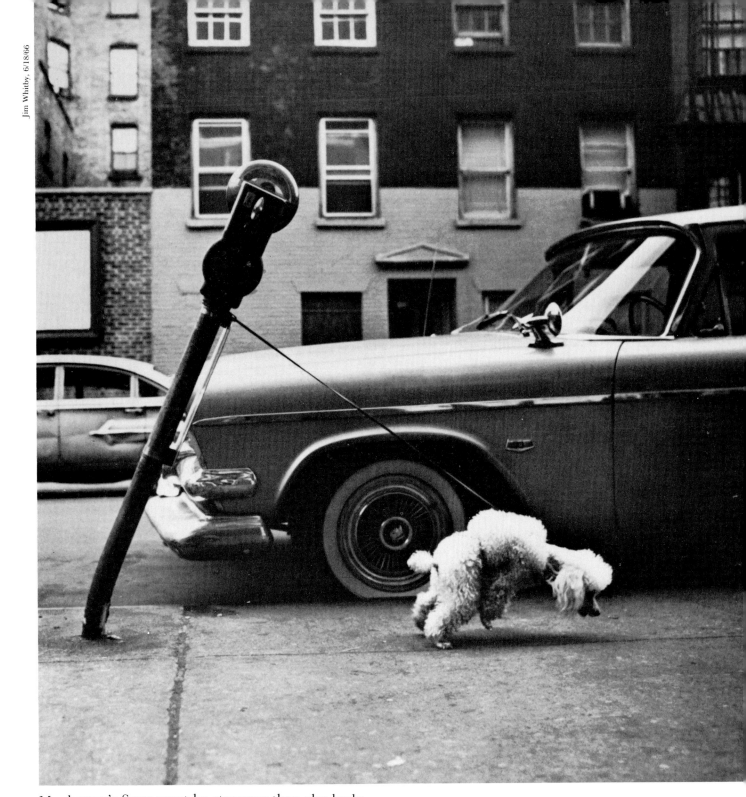

Manhattan's Suzy must be stronger than she looks.

"Whaddaya Mean, Still Busy? My Meter's Running Out."

Come on, fella, no call's that important.

"Tell You Something If You Don't Repeat It: His Bark Is Worse Than His Bite."

Ten-year-old Ch. Mighty Mo II from Flossmoor, Illinois.

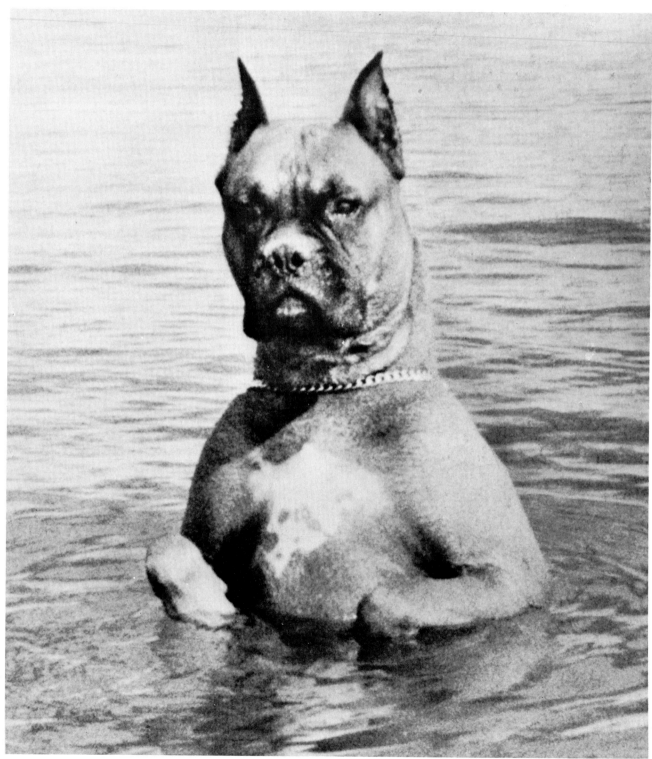

B. I. Ulinski; 3/23/62

A winking seal at the Copenhagen Zoo.

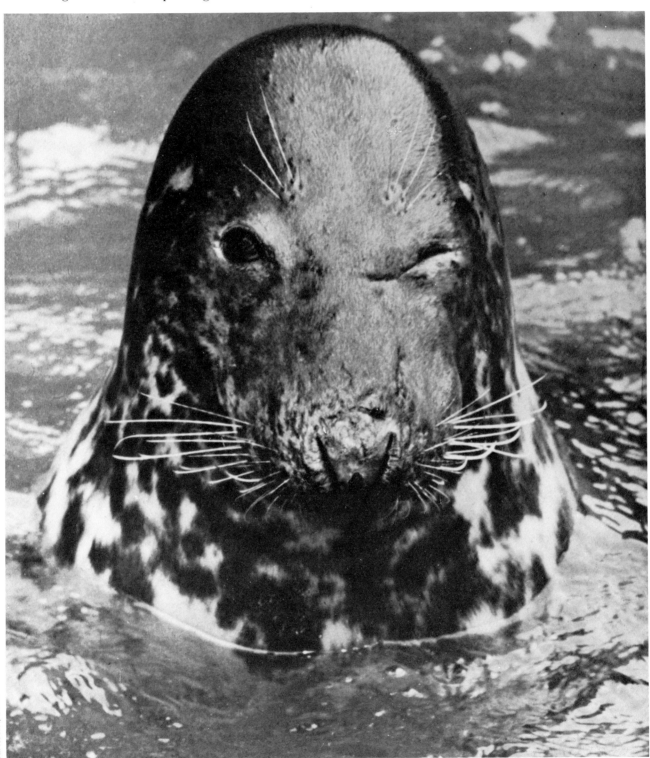

CHAPTER 11
takes pleasure in
THE SPORTING LOOK

Ringing Resolve

Even though 3½-year-old Danny Gillis from Michigan is not a regular at horseshoes, what seasoned pitcher could brandish better form or fiercer determination?

C. E. Westveer, 7/20/53

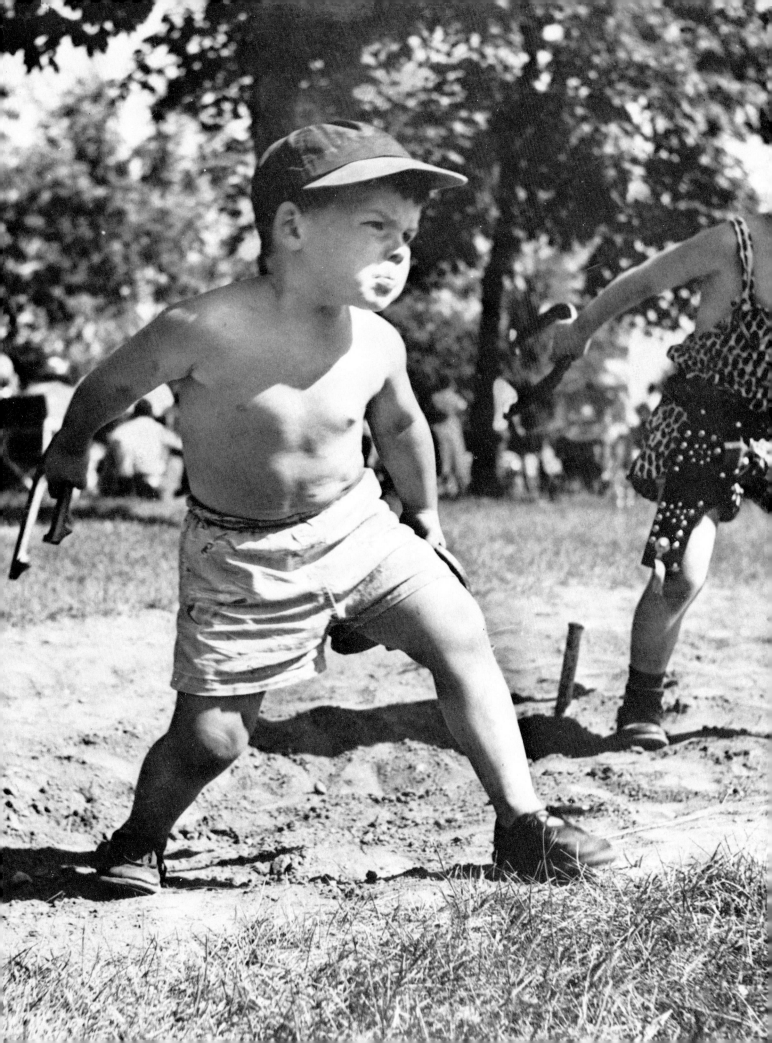

Underdogs

Washington Star, 5/2/60

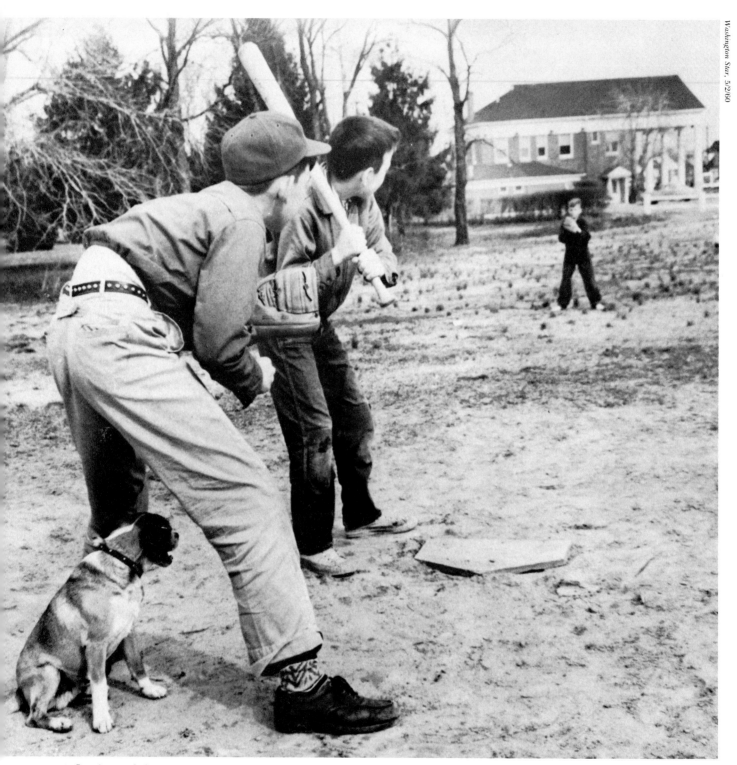

In Avondale, Maryland, sandlot baseball is a dog-eat-dog affair and the ump has to be careful not to play favorites, even if he's owned by the catcher.

Ed Wojtas, *Champaign-Urbana Courier*, 8/10/53

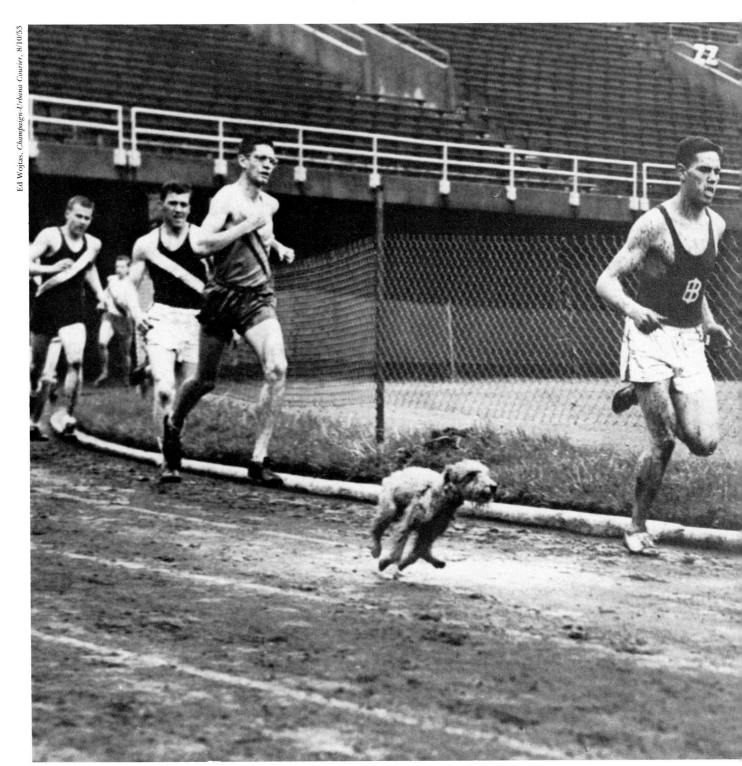

In Champaign, Illinois, Toggles isn't even entered in the high school mile, but he joins in anyway and makes the noncanines look as if *they're* dogging it.

Spanish Bull

In Seville, a small white bull resembling a cat terrorizes a torero.

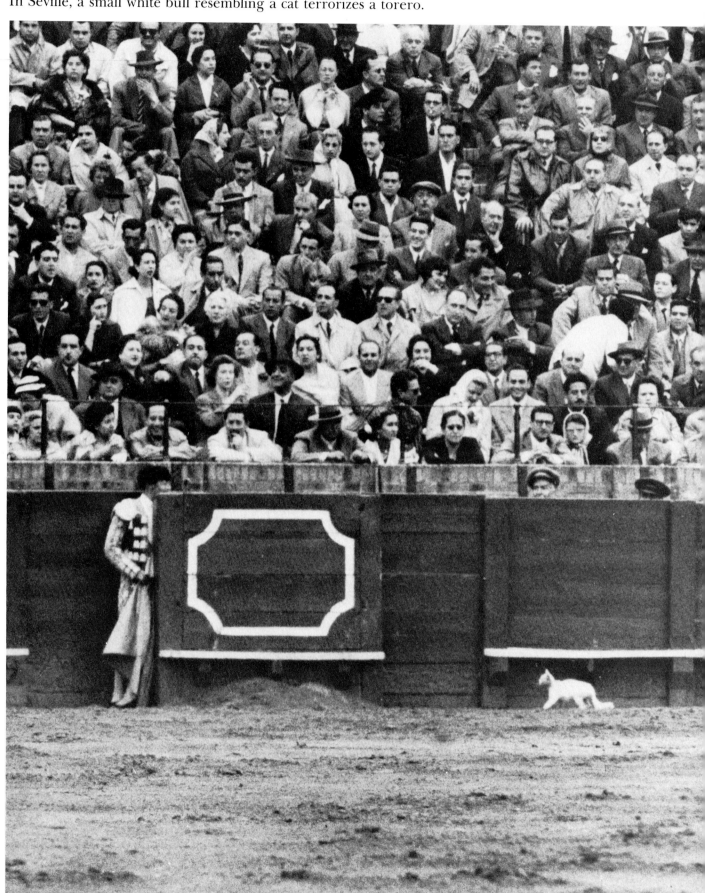

In Madrid, Aurelio Calatayud uses unconventional means to avoid the moment of truth.

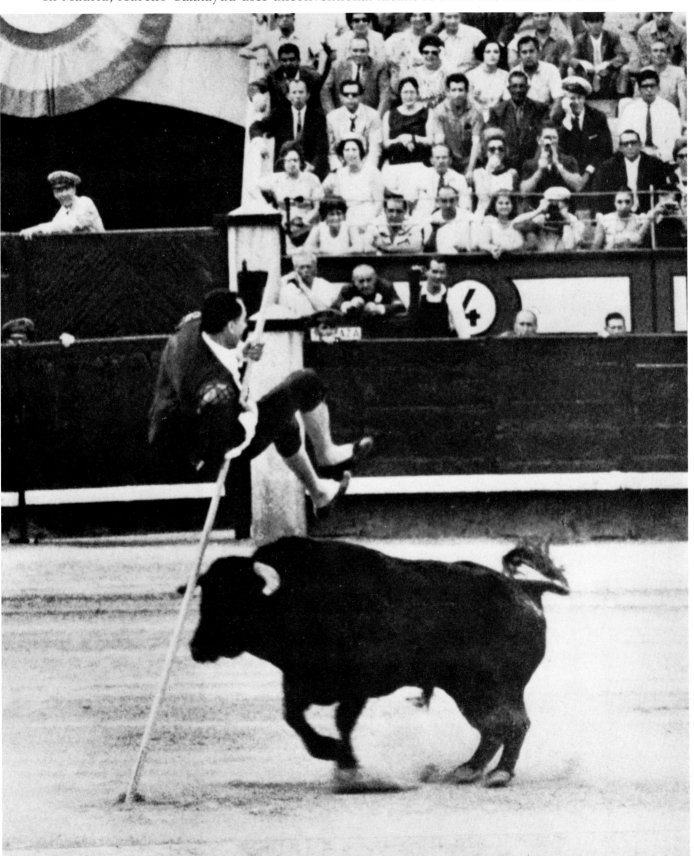

Bettmann/UPI, 3/6/70

The Detroit News, 6/15/59

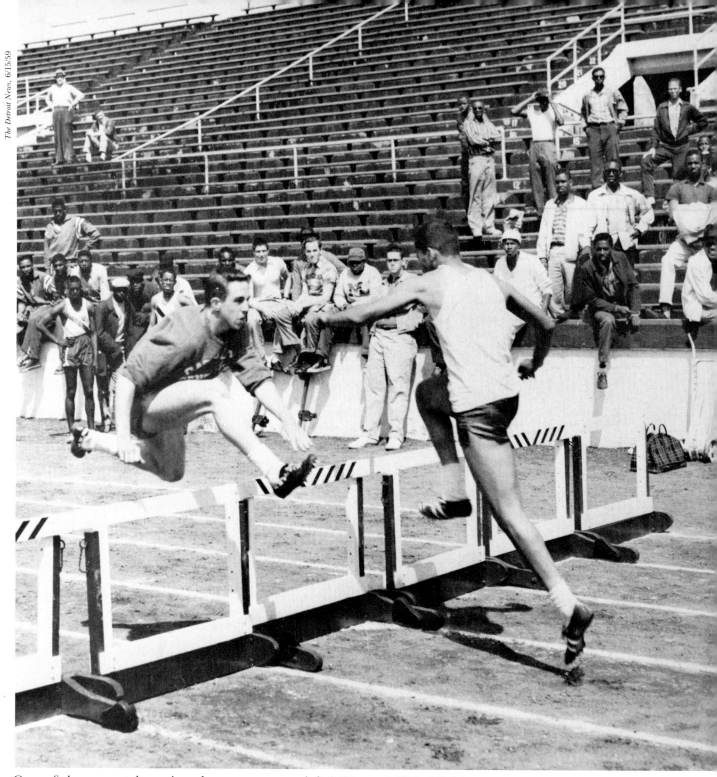

One of them must be going the wrong way, right? Wrong! This Michigan high school race is the 480-yard shuttle hurdles and each team has four runners. Dick Shenden of Catholic Central (left) is beginning the fourth and final lap while Harrison Baker of University of Detroit High is finishing the third and still has to tag his anchor runner who will then start in pursuit of Shenden. Get it?

Taking It All in Stride

Better nothing's said at all about this pushover.

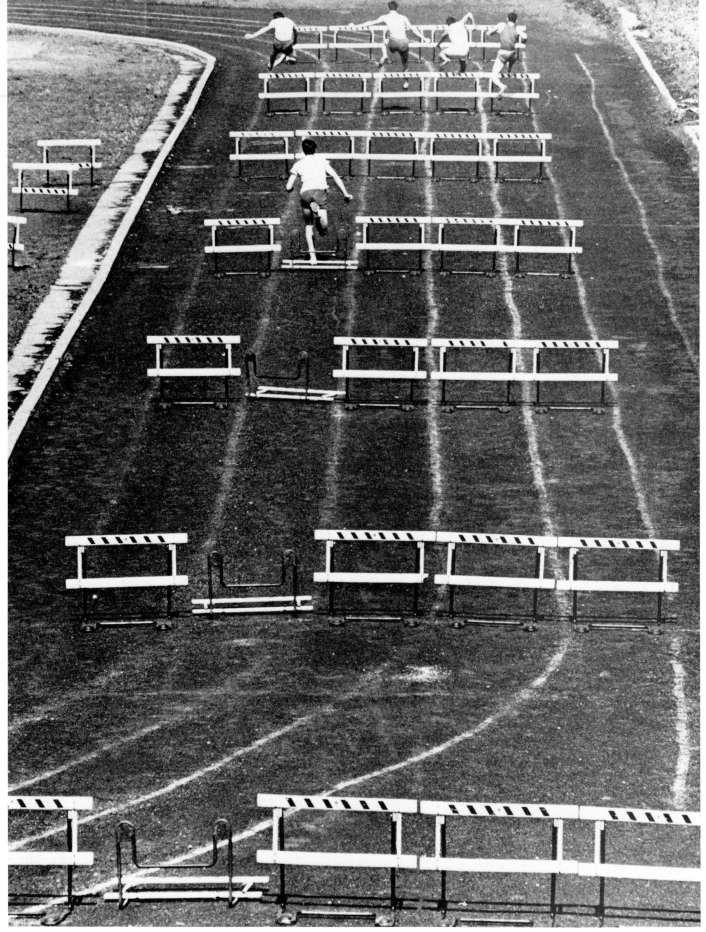

Bob Coyle, 6/13/69

Doing It the Hard Way

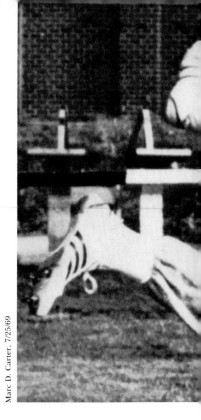

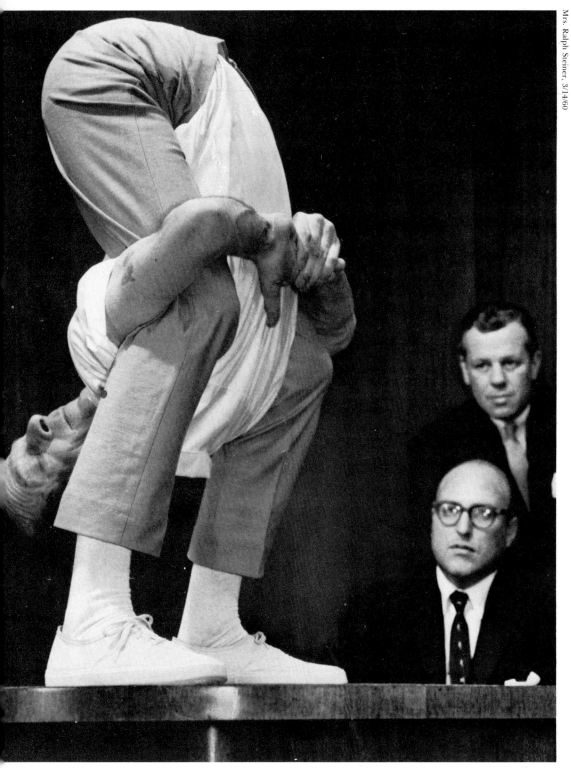

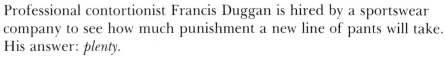

Professional contortionist Francis Duggan is hired by a sportswear
company to see how much punishment a new line of pants will take.
His answer: *plenty*.

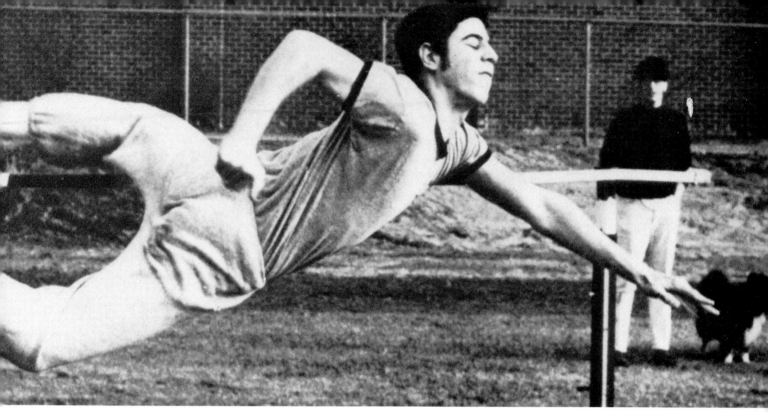

This high jumper makes it over the bar with inches to spare. His form? Spare us!

It took seventeen-year-old Diane Farley a full year to learn this impossible-looking cheerleader's leap. At the climax of a knee-bent jump facing the wall, Diane is clutching the pompon behind her back and swiveling her head 180 degrees, giving the illusion of being bent double the wrong way. But why?

At a high school championship wrestling match at Washington State University, referee Kirby Brumfield stays on top of the job.

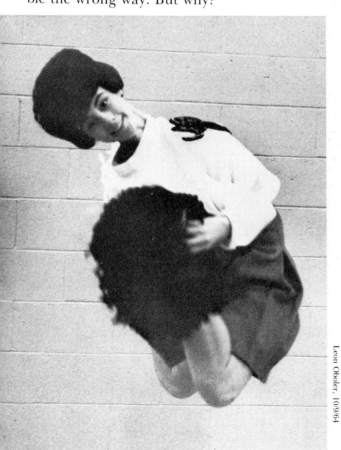

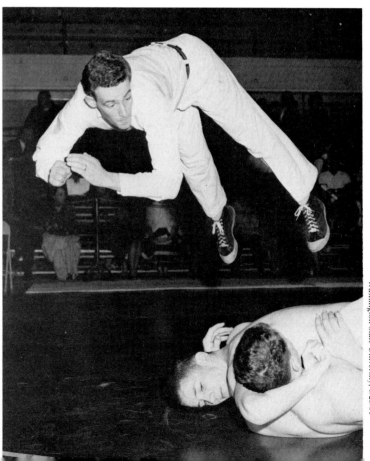

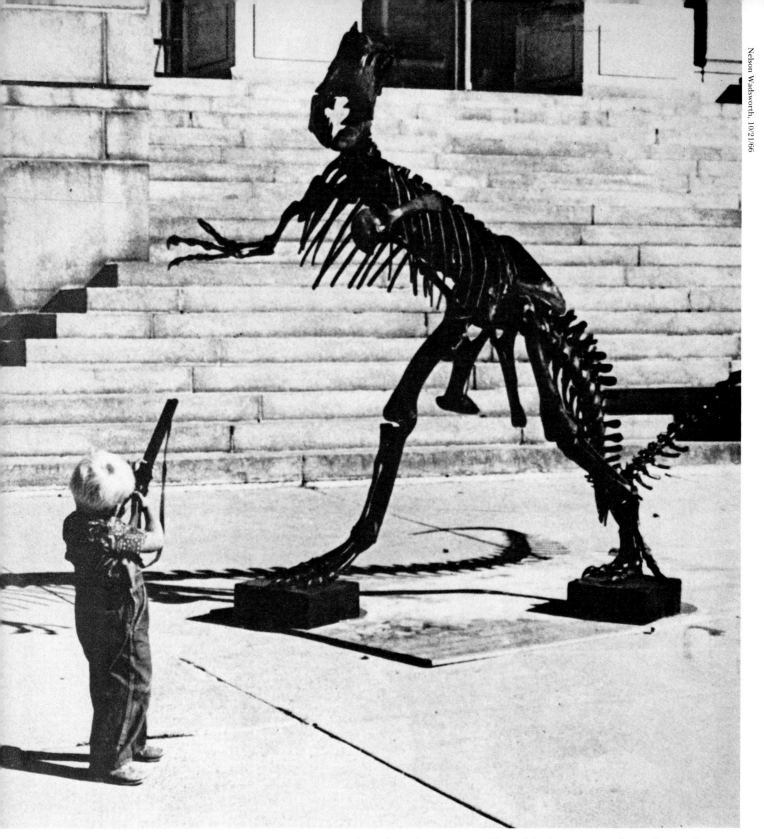

Big Game Hunters

On the University of Utah campus Chris Madsen, son of a paleontologist, takes dead aim at a thirty-foot-long allosaurus—or what's left of it.

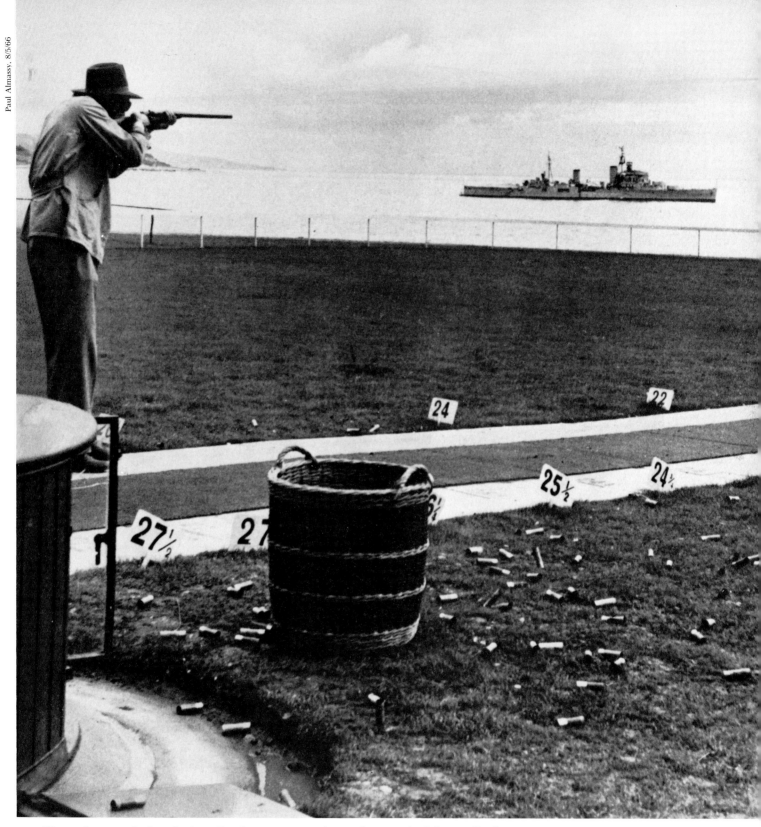

Paul Almassy. 8/5/66

Upset by an obviously hostile destroyer, a skeet shooter in Monte Carlo
seems inclined to put one across her bow.

Fancy Footwork

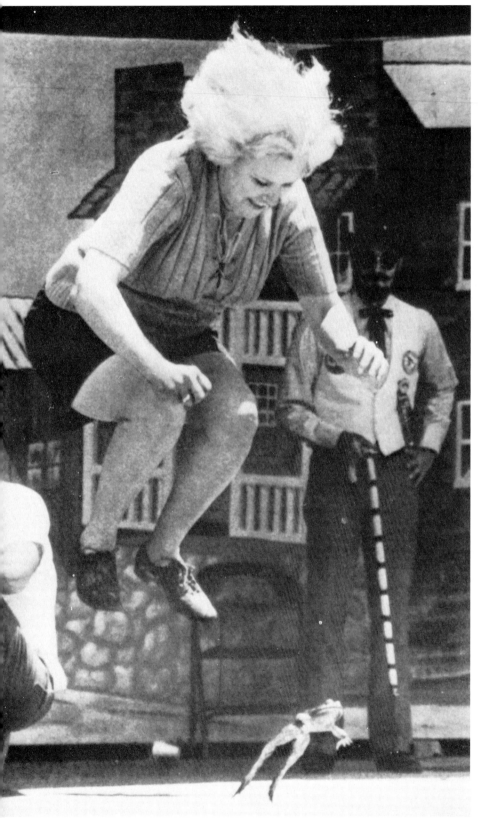

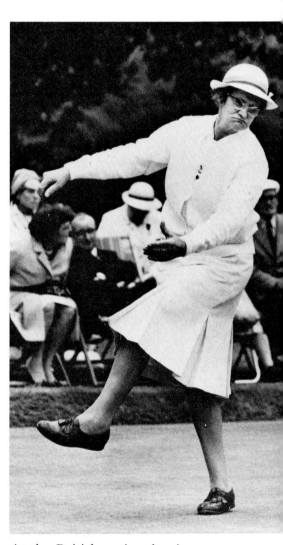

At the annual frog-jumping championships at Angels Camp, California, Lucille Offenhiser shows her entry how.

At the British national pairs championships of the Women's Bowling Association, a lady from Cumberland roots her ball home. Didn't you know? Everybody English uses body English.

Wide World Photos, 6/16/72

Gustav German, 3/13/70

Central Press, 10/15/65

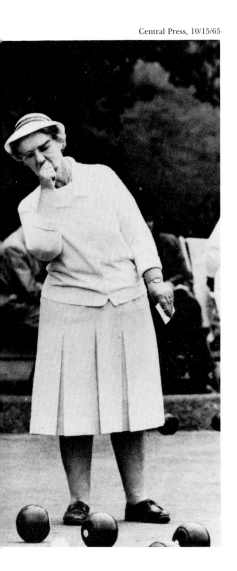

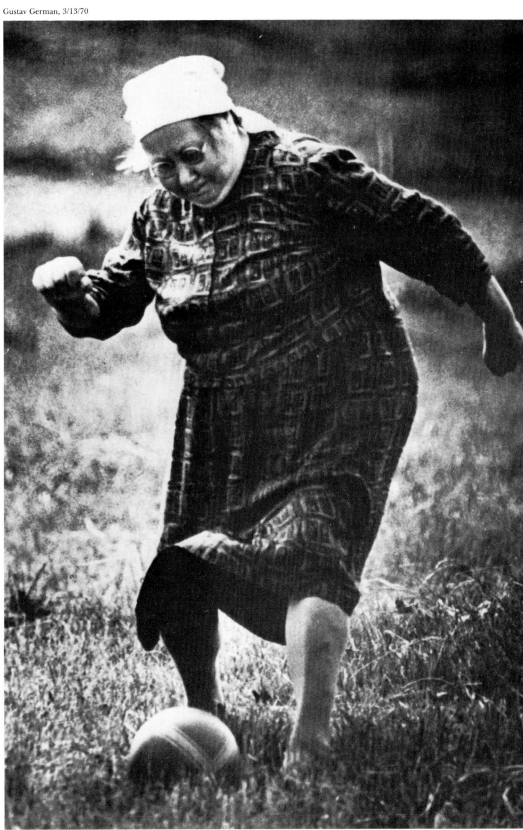

While the grandchildren
are at school a Russian
granny gets her dribble
down pat.

David Moore, Black Star, 11/5/65

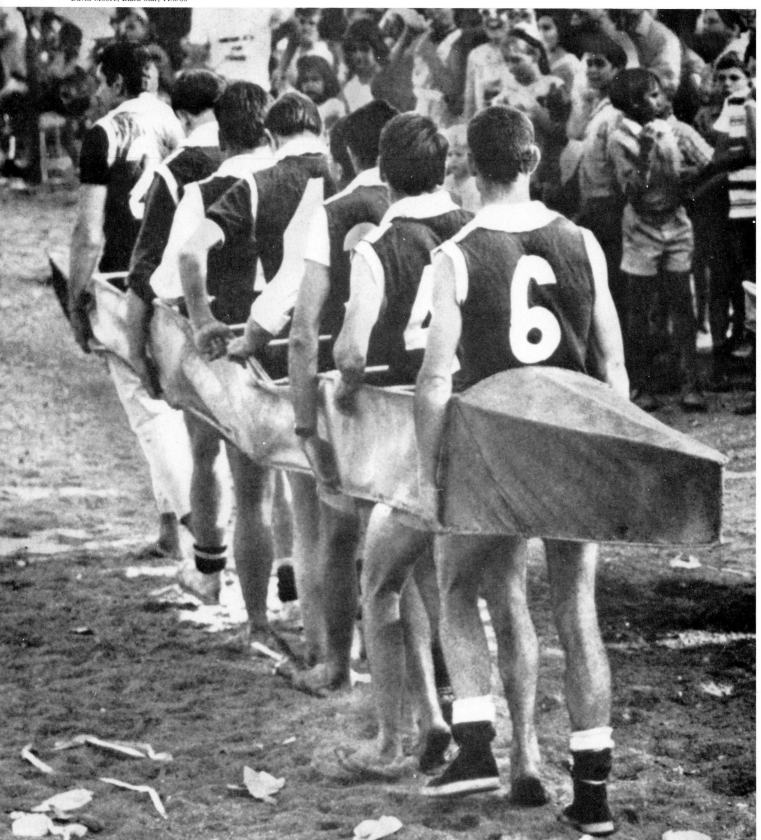

The Shell Game

At Alice Springs, Australia, this eighteen-foot, landworthy craft is about to compete in the dry-land Henley-on-Todd regatta.

Ken Oakes, *Vancouver Sun*, 8/26/66

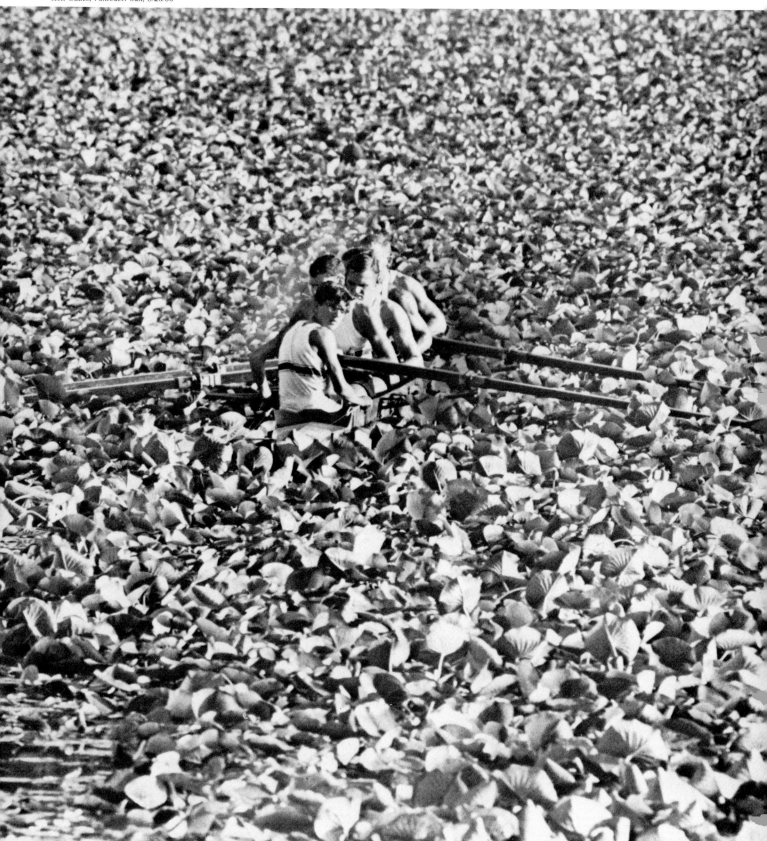

The carpet of water lilies this British Columbia crew
has to traverse is enough to give the cox a stroke.

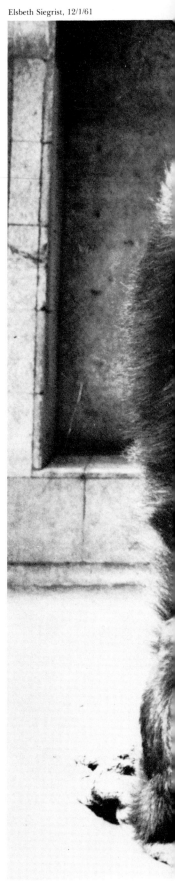

Elsbeth Siegrist, 12/1/61

CHAPTER 12
is a miscellaneous collection of
LAST LAUGHS

Mama's Boy

Twelve-day-old Iambo is smooth and sweet, but even in the Basel Zoo in Switzerland, raising little gorillas can get pretty hairy.

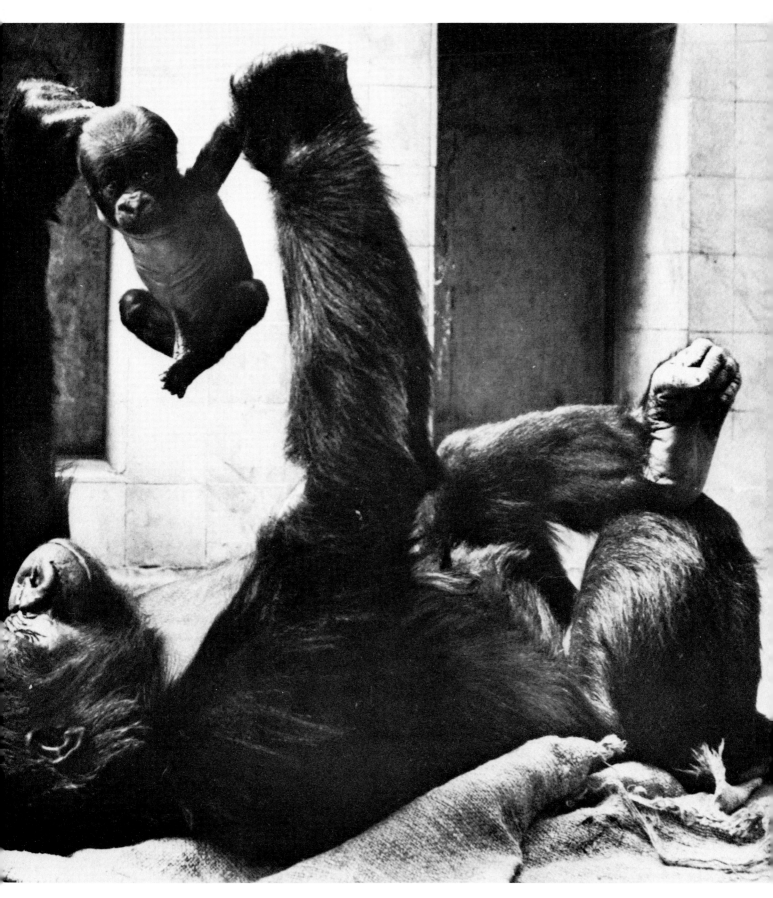

Getting Their Kicks

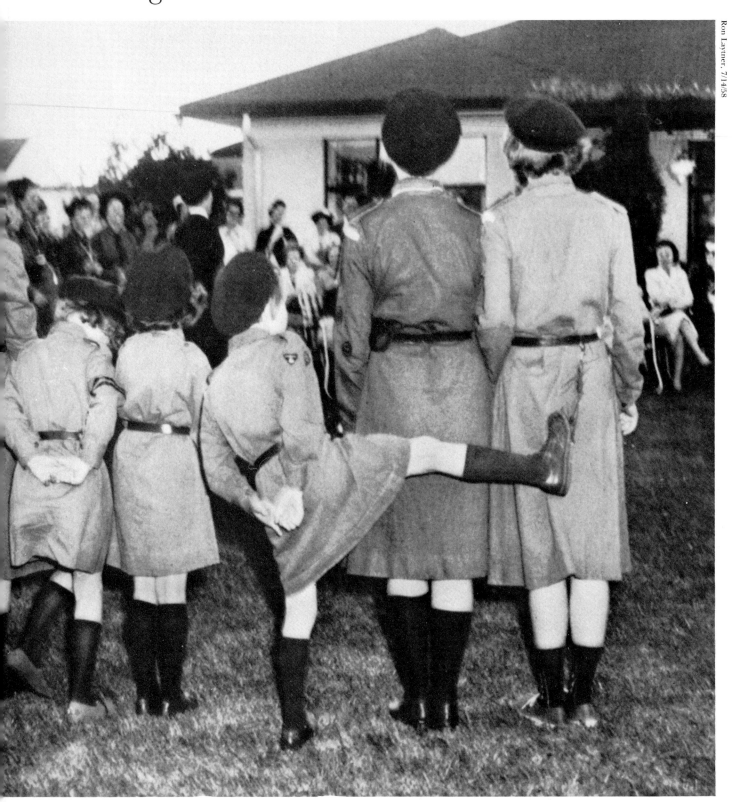

Ron Laytner, 7/14/58

In Toronto, a Brownie breaks the boredom of an awards ceremony
by sending a message to one of her elders.

Keystone, 8/20/56

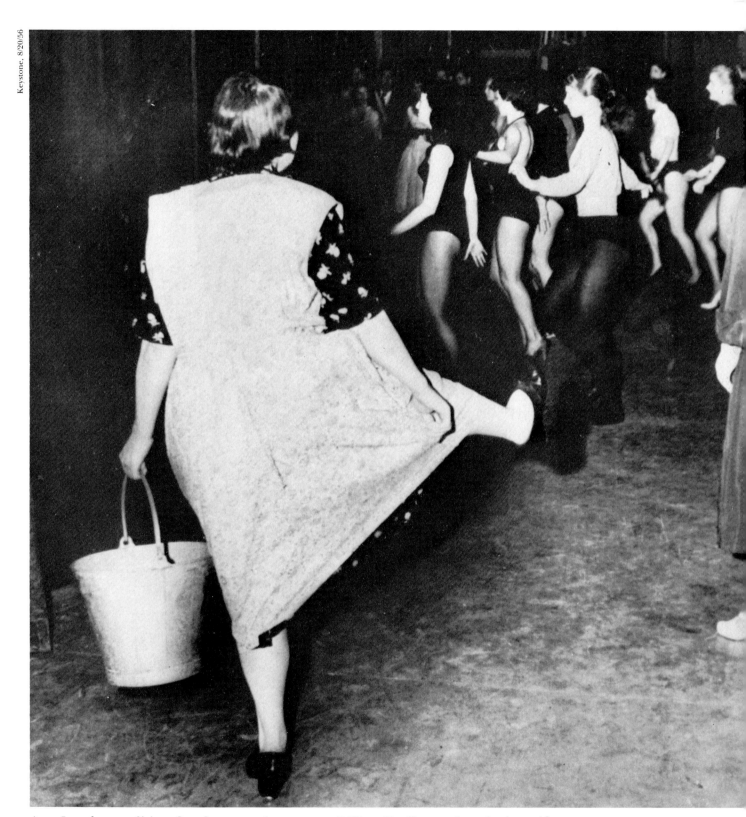

At a London audition for dancers, charwoman Lillian Dudley can't resist herself.

Fainting for the Crown

A soldier starts to buckle from the heat but is held in place
by a superior until the royal family passes by.

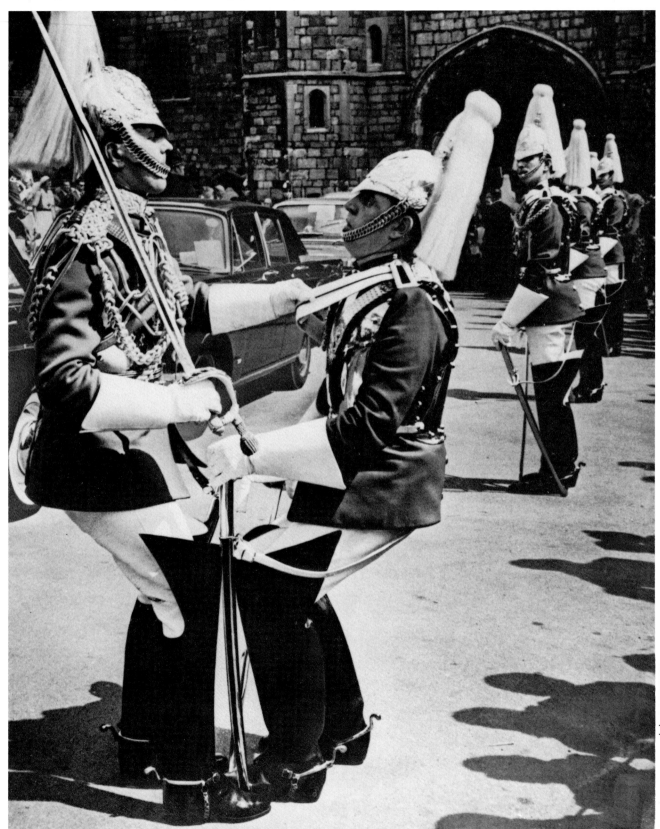

Associated Newspapers from Pictorial, 9/10/65

A bearskinned guardsman bites the dust, demonstrating that even
when he falls, a British soldier does so at attention.

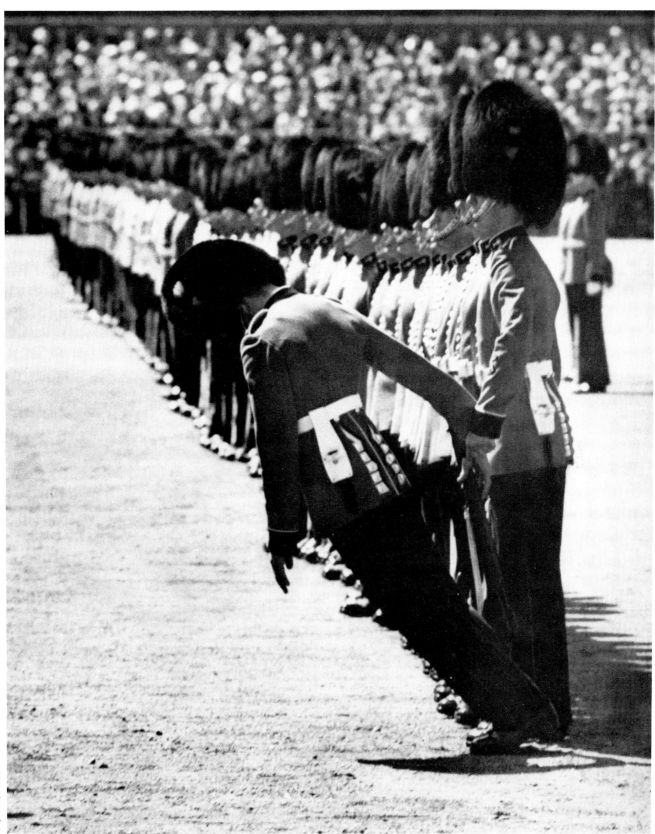

Towering Loads

In Saskatchewan, a two-hundred-ton grain elevator is trucked across the tunnelless Canadian prairie.

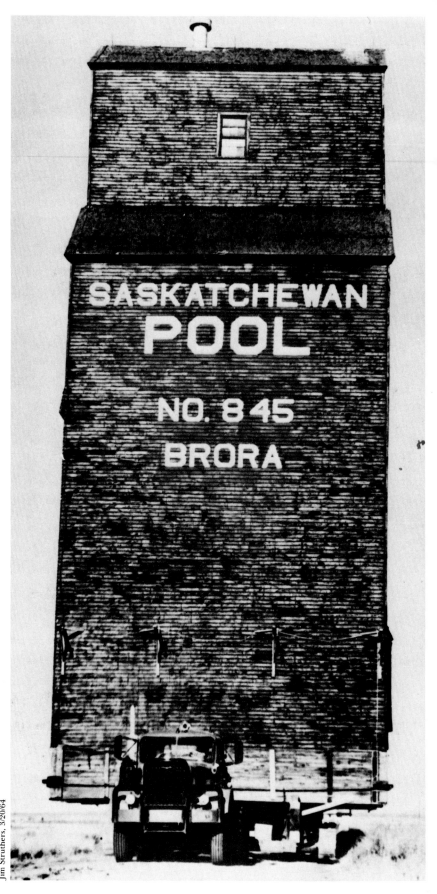

Jim Struthers, 3/20/64

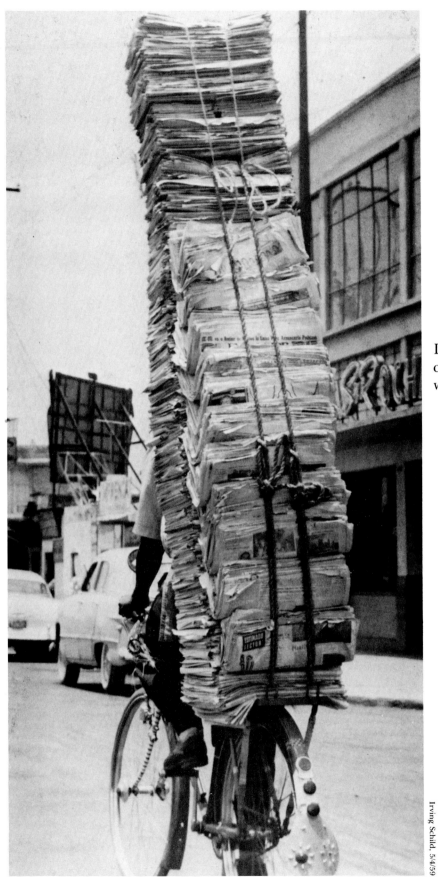

In Mexico City, all the news that's fit to carry is biked away by a courageous wastepaper collector.

Irving Schild. 5/4/59

Spanking Good Art

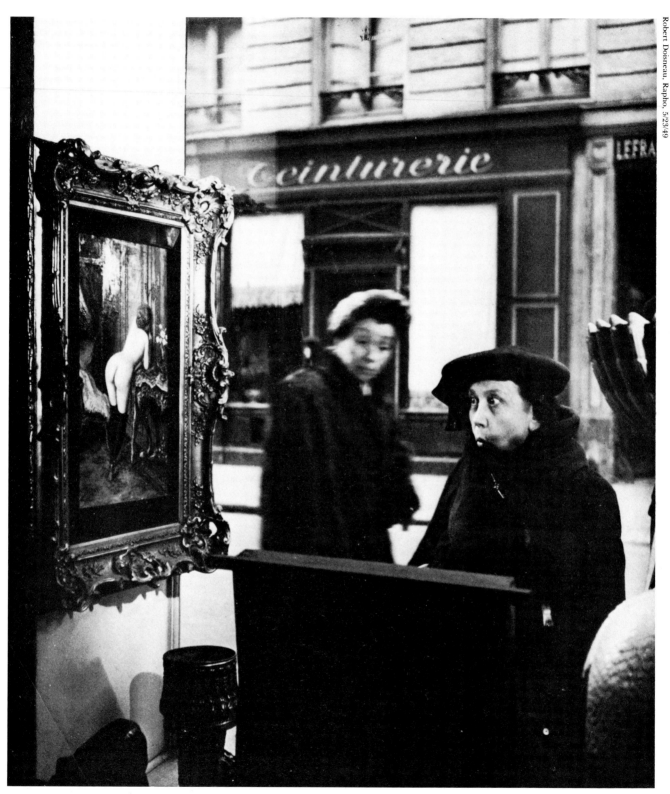

Robert Doisneau, Rapho, 5/23/49

A passerby is stopped in her tracks by a painting
in the window of a Paris antique store.

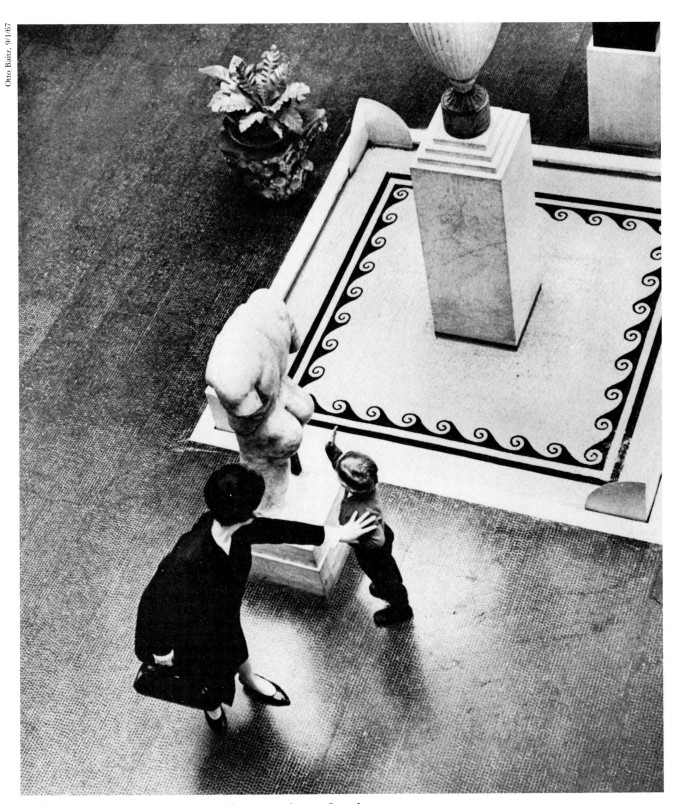

At the Santa Barbara Museum of Art, a piece of sculpture
appeals to a fledgling connoisseur.

Going Modern

In Paris, an artist idealizes his model.

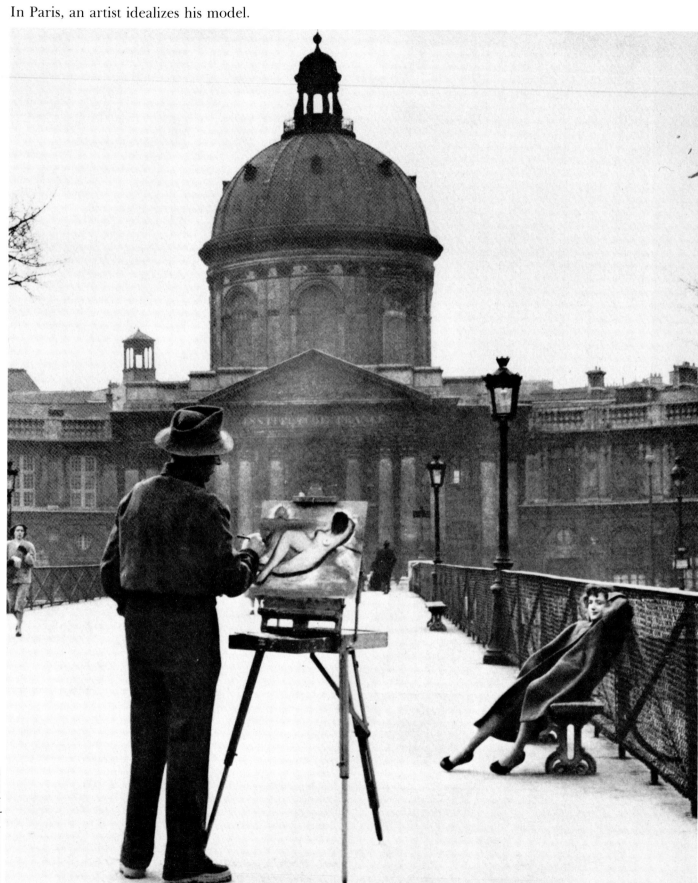

At the San Francisco Museum of Art, an abstract gets close scrutiny.

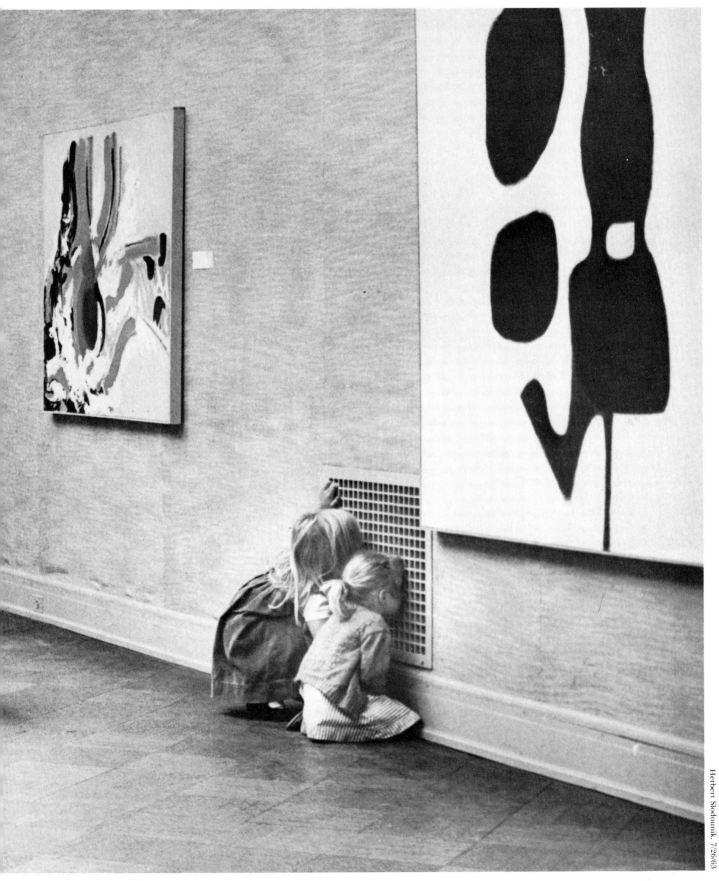

John Sadovy, 4/6/53

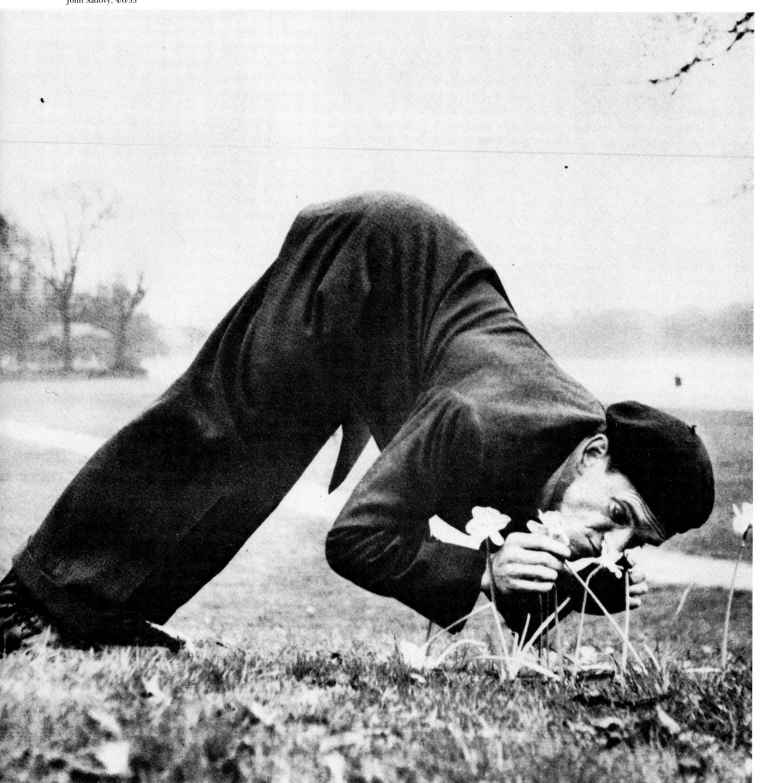

German contortionist Eddy Merky savors the daffodils of London's Hyde Park.

Spring in the Air

Bruce Roberts, 5/18/59

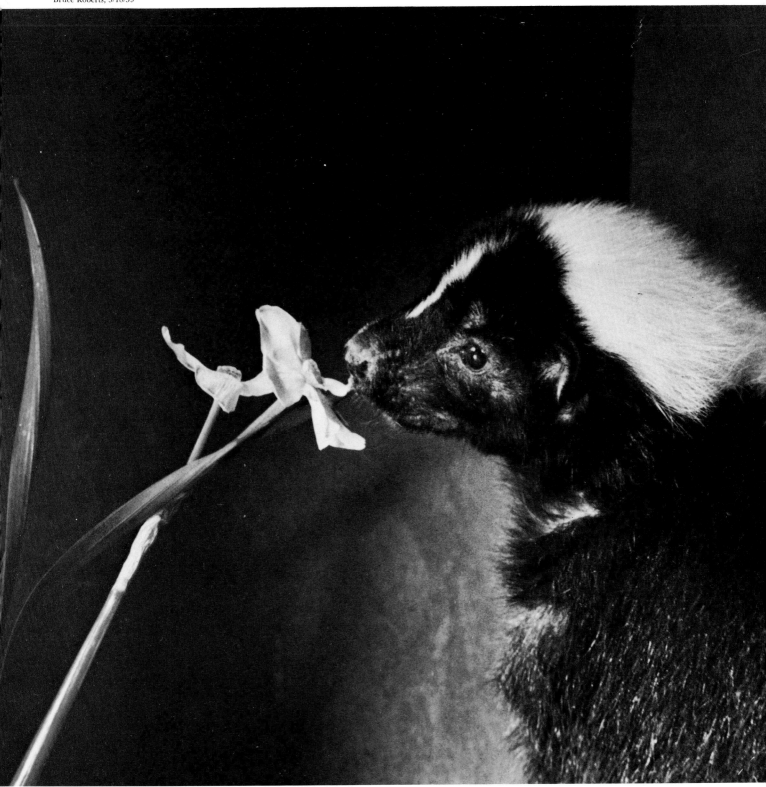

A specialist in smell considers a narcissus at the
Children's Nature Museum in Charlotte, North Carolina.

Knowing Looks

This is why some of the mail in Lancashire, England, never gets delivered.

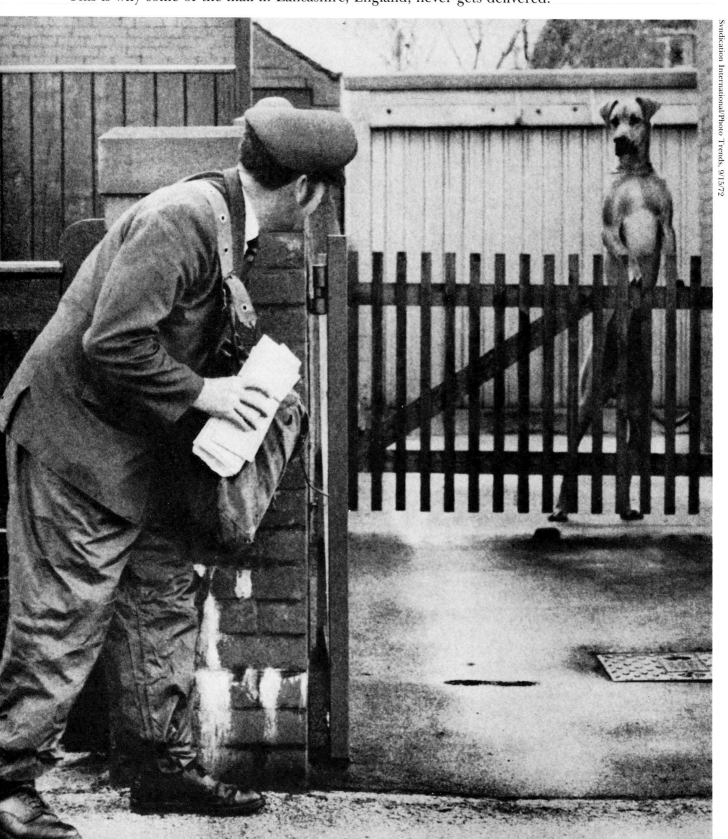

Syndication International/Photo Trends, 9/15/72

Hoping to shame his overweight orangutan into a diet,
the London Zoo's monkey house keeper, Bill Peckett, shows
Mr. Jiggs that his midriff measures forty-seven inches.

Combine, 9/5/55

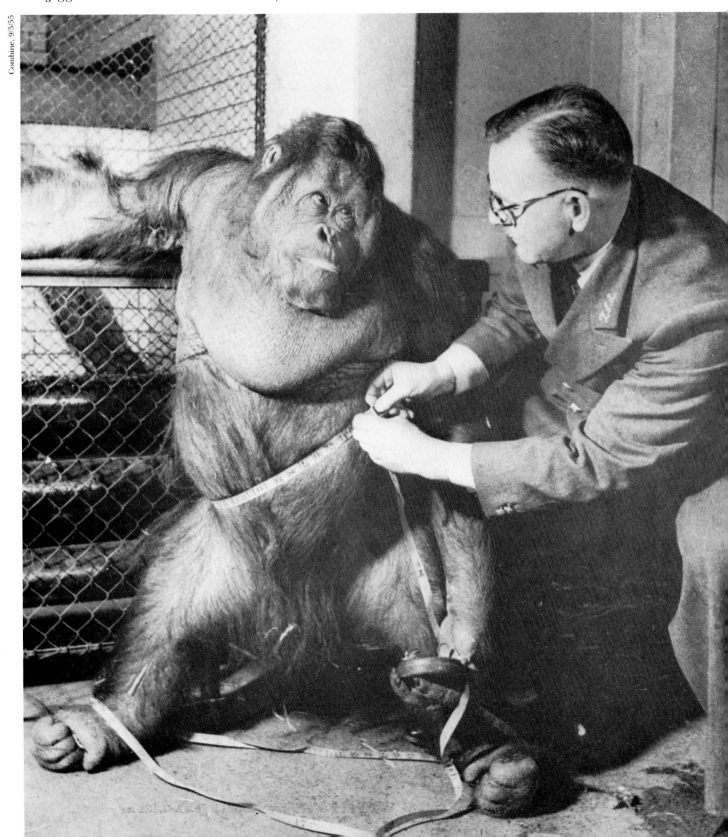

Problem Solving

A couple of Toronto kids search for the answer to a classic question.

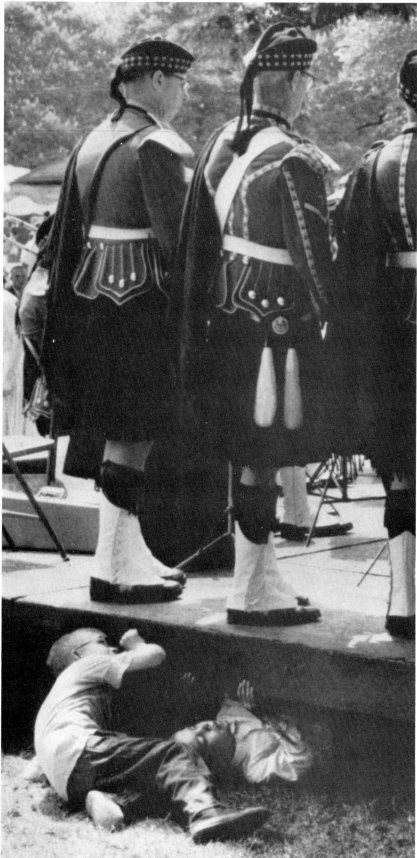

210

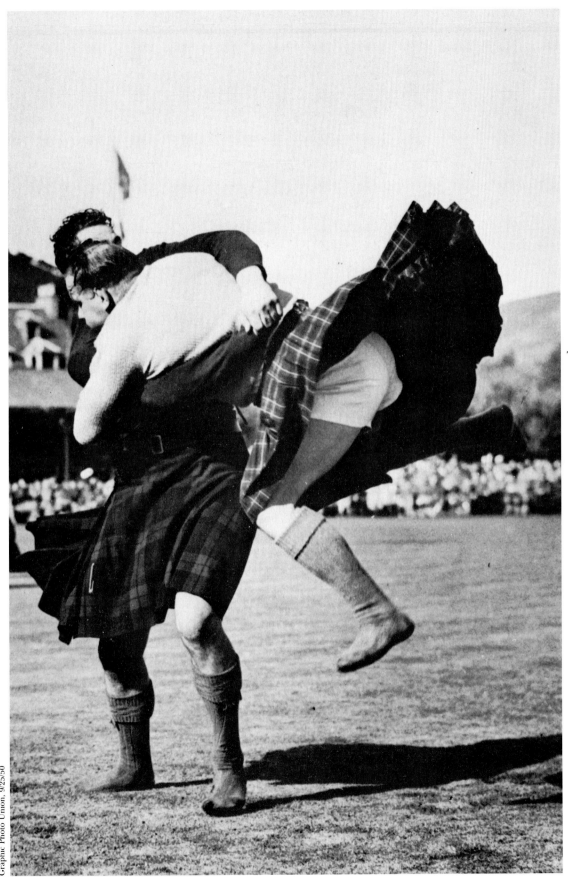

The answer.

Barney Sellers, *Memphis Commercial Appeal*, 4/15/57

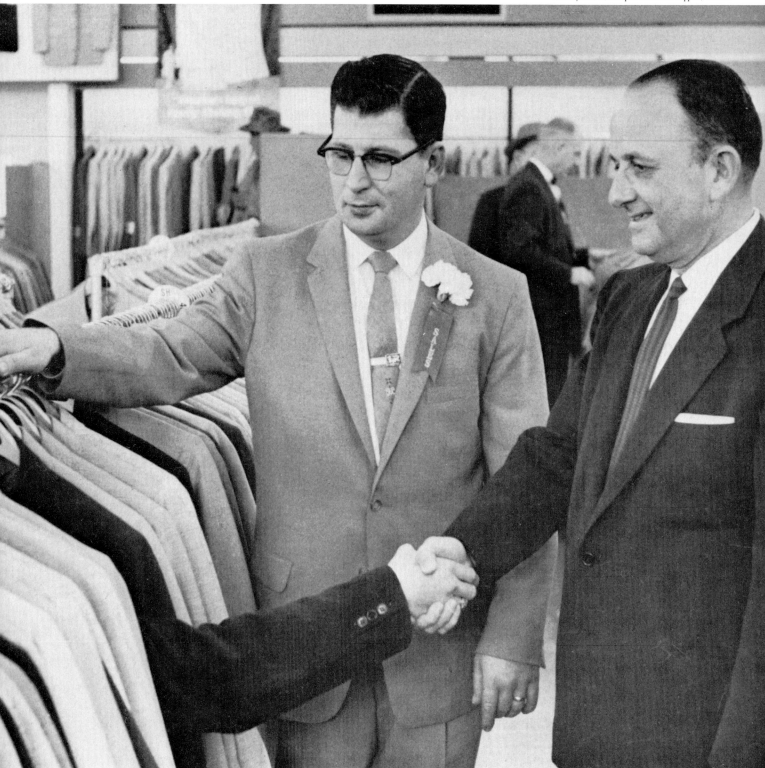

At the opening of a new Robert Hall store in Memphis, a size-39 suit helps sell itself.

Helping Hands

Charles Laffin, 1/20/61

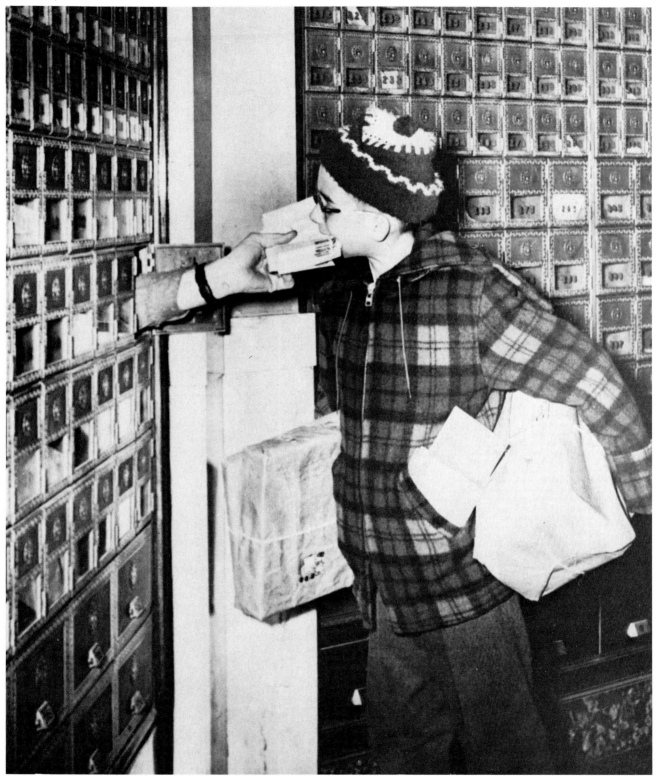

Already loaded down with packages, ten-year-old Philip Laffin of Ellsworth, Maine, gets oral free delivery for the letters.

Climbing the Walls

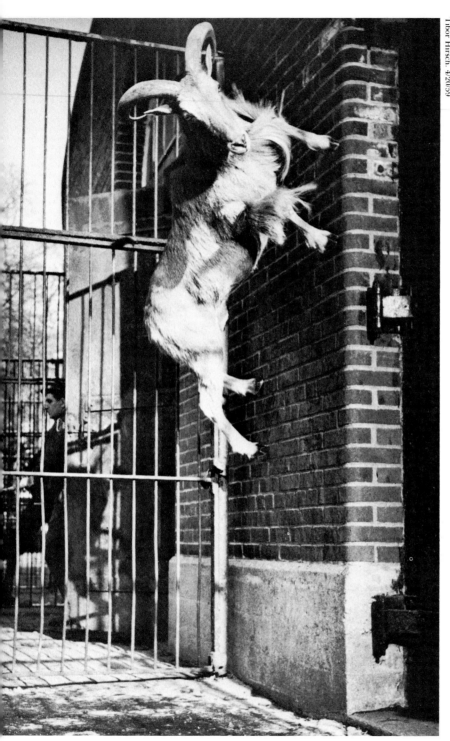

Tibor Hirsch, 4/20/59

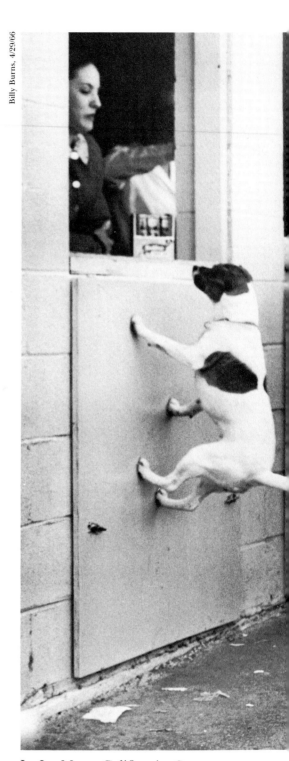

Billy Burns, 4/29/66

At Brooklyn's Prospect Park Zoo, a Barbary ram wishes he were climbing the high rocks of his African homeland.

In La Mesa, California, Spot wonders if his order is ready.

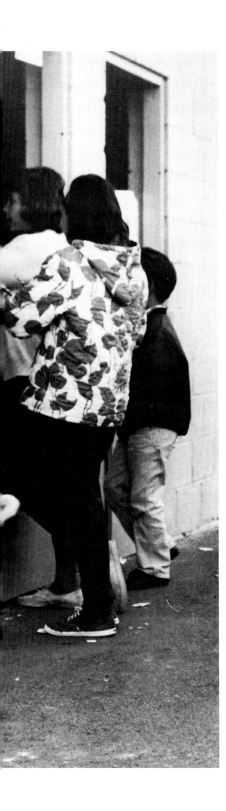

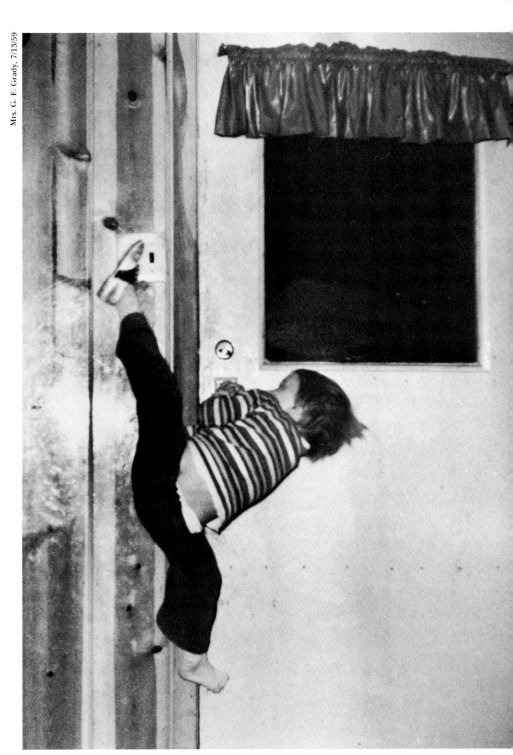

Mrs. G. F. Grady, 7/13/59

In Crescent, Oregon, four-year-old Susie Grady turns on the light.

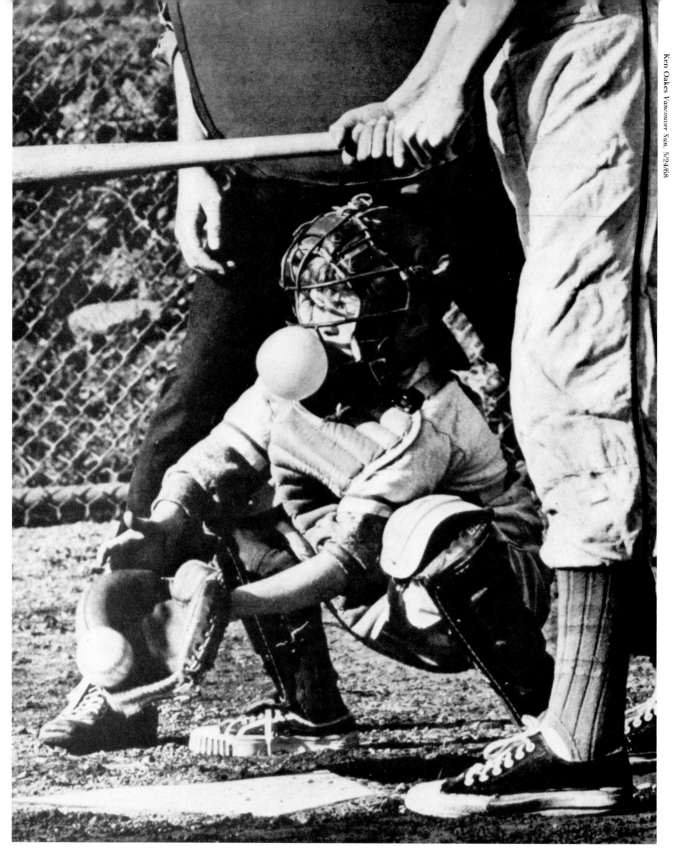

Ken Oakes *Vancouver Sun,* 5/24/68

A catcher blocks his own view but still makes the catch.

Unassisted Bubble Play

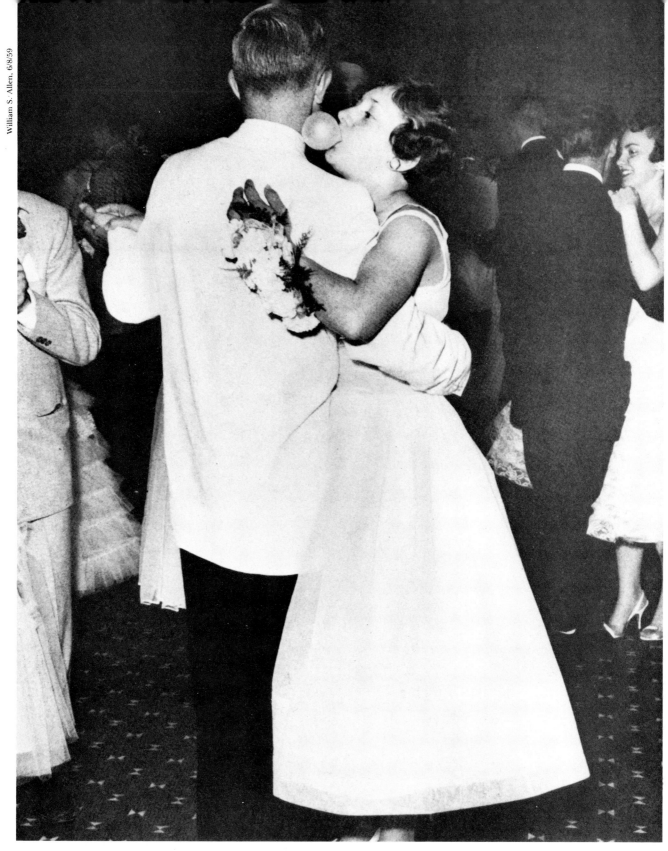

At her high school graduation prom, Suzie Spear of La Porte, Indiana, whispers sweet nothings in her partner's ear.

"Wipe Off That Grin, Girl"

At a training session of a Swedish militia group,
a volunteer finds something droll in target practice.

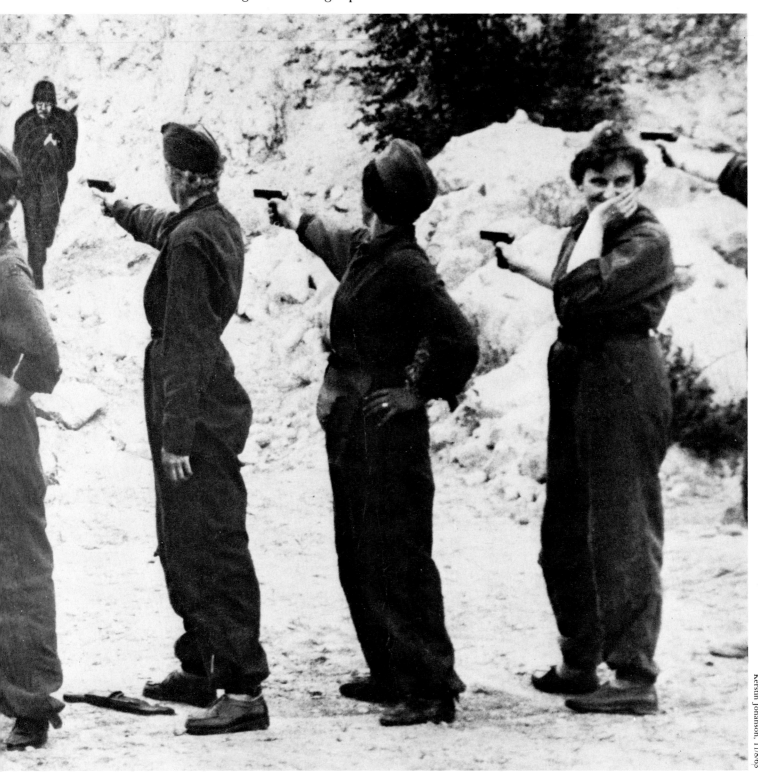

Kerstin Johanson, 11/8/63

218

Diane Sue Kennedy is some tough colonel
in the coed cadet corps at Ohio State.

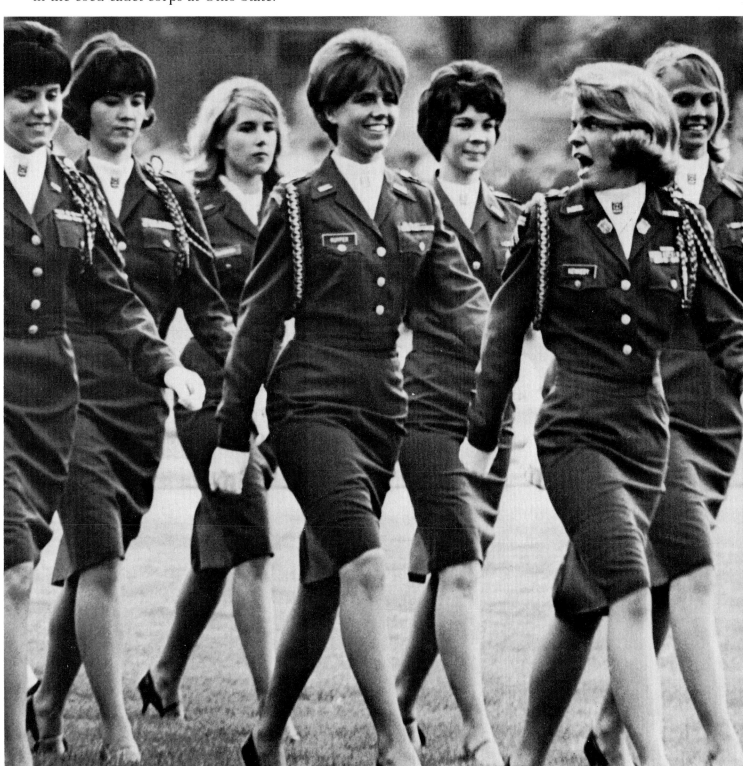

William Blackstone, *Columbus Dispatch*, 6/4/65

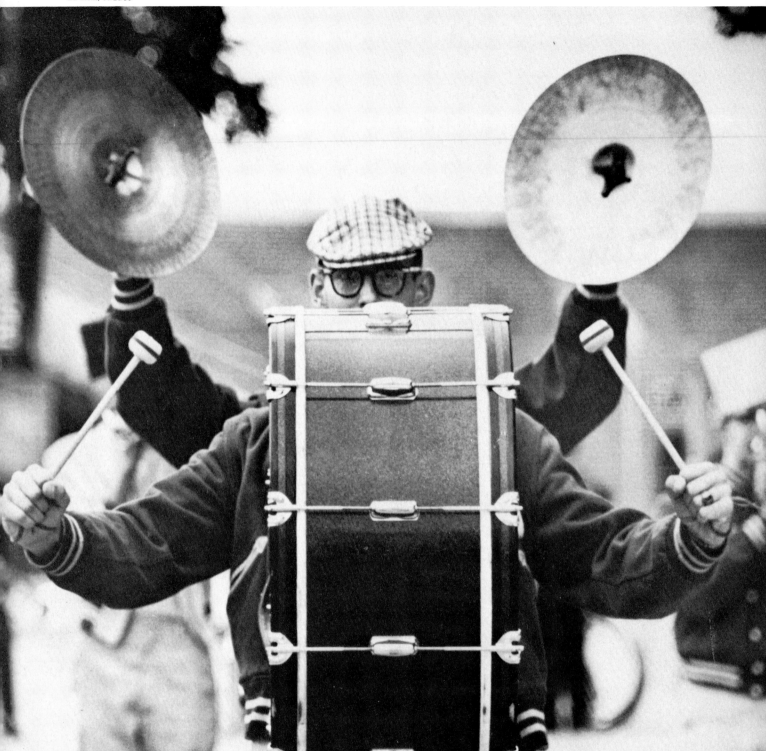

At a practice session of the University of Wisconsin band, what appears to be a one-man, four-armed percussion section is poised for the downbeat.

No Head for Music

Ken Oakes, *Vancouver Sun*, 4/9/65

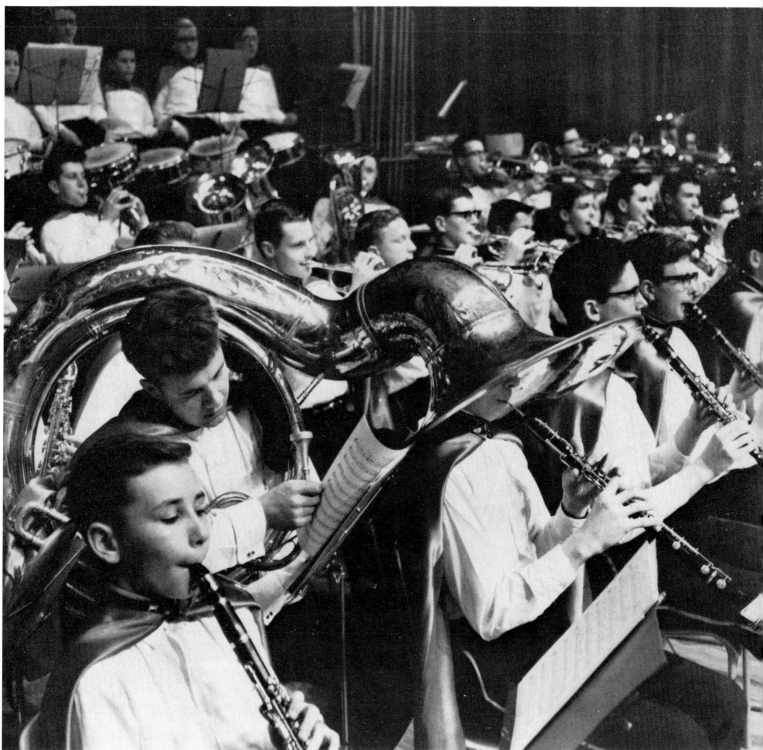

As the Kitsilano Boys Band of Vancouver bangs it out,
an oboe loses its head to a sousaphone.

Keystone, 6/26/64

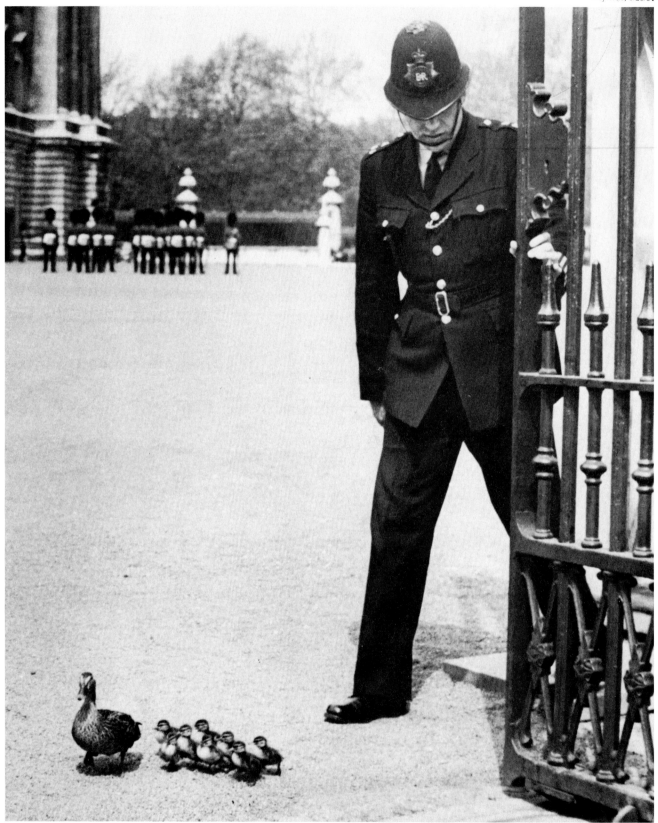

Youth Patrol

Her Majesty's constabulary makes sure a convoy of ducks has a safe waddle out the Buckingham Palace gate.

Bill Beale, *Washington Daily News*, 10/14/57

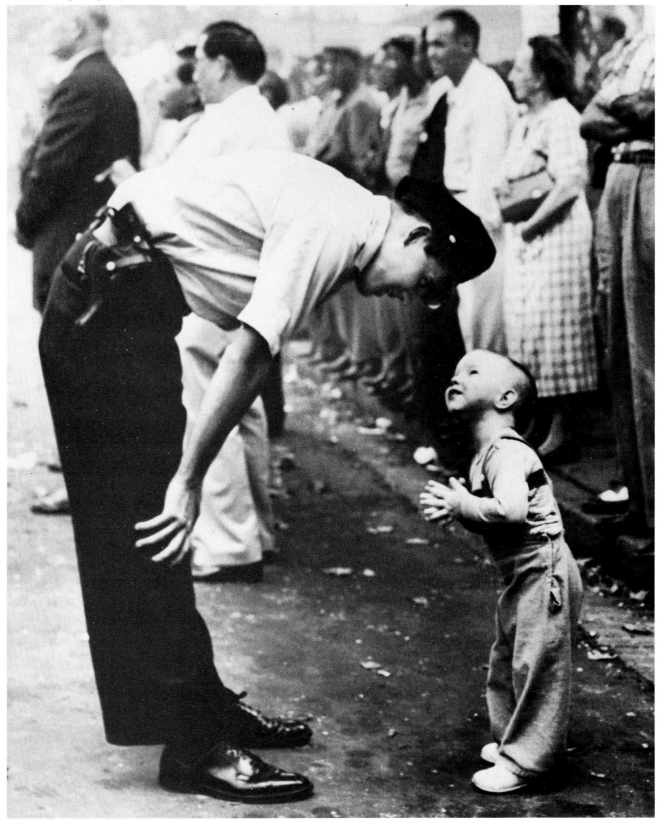

In Washington, D.C., policeman Maurice Cullinane gently coaxes two-year-old Allen Weaver back to the curb during a Chinatown parade.

Joe Scherschel, LIFE, 12/60

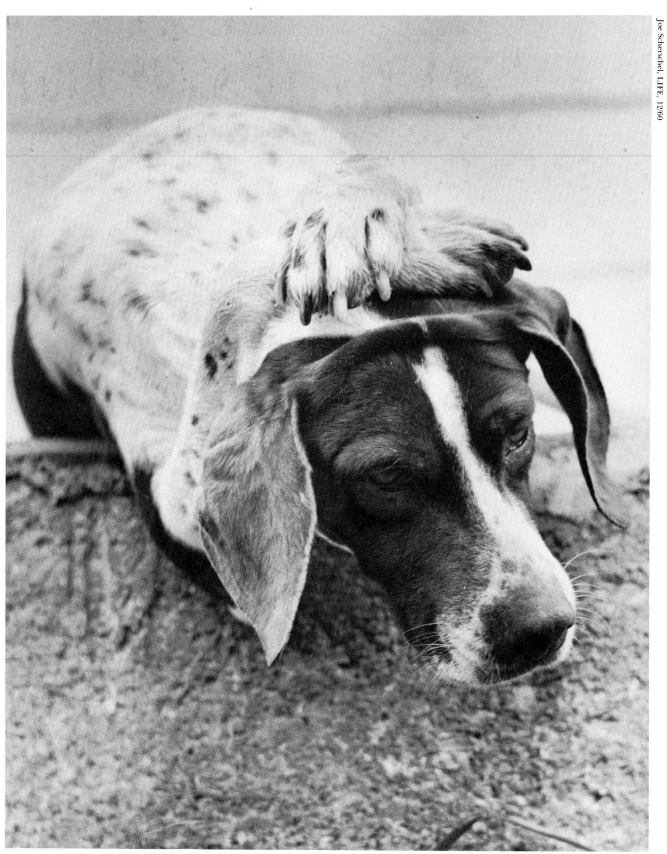

That's All, Folks